A Crash Course for
Panicked Parents

College
Admissions

SECOND EDITION

Sally Rubenstone & Sidonia Dalby
Smith College

MACMILLAN • USA

To Our Parents

Second Edition

Copyright © 1998, 1994 by Sally Rubenstone and Sidonia Dalby

Macmillan General Reference USA
A Simon & Schuster Macmillan Company
1633 Broadway
New York, NY 10019-6785

An Arco Book

Manufactured in the United States of America

00 99 98   4 3 2

Library of Congress Catalog Card Number: 97-071473

ISBN: 0-02-861931-5

CONTENTS

Acknowledgments   vii
Introduction   ix

1. All in the Family: Decisions and Dynamics   1
How Involved Should Parents Be in the
   College Selection Process?   1
Self-Assessment Surveys for
   Parents and Students   2
Pressure Points   15

2. Matchmaking, Matchmaking: Choosing the "Right" College   21
"What Kind of School Am I?"   22
List Value—The Long and Short of It   25
Identifying "Target" Colleges   26
Using Publications   34
Using Computers   37
Comparing and Contrasting   41
Getting Guidance: Public-School and
   Private-School Counselors   43
Who Are Independent Counselors...and
   How Do You Know if You Need One?   46

3. Testing, Testing   49
Just What Is the SAT, Anyway?   50
The ACT Assessment   68
Test of English as a Foreign Language
   (TOEFL)   72
What (if Anything) Should Be Done to Prepare?   73
Information Numbers   81

4. Finding Out More: Campus Visits, Interviews, College Fairs & Reps   83
Campus Visits   83
The Interview Itself   91
Second Opinions   100
When You Can't Get to Campus   101
Drawing Conclusions   104

5. Money Matters: Financial Planning and Financial Aid **107**
    Estimating College Costs 107
    Applying for Financial Aid 113
    Tips for Applying for Financial Aid 119
    Non-Aid Advice 129

6. Pushing Papers: The Application Itself **133**
    Different Decision Plans 134
    General Application Tips 136
    Tips for Tackling Specific Application Sections 142
    The Almighty Essay 147

7. How Admission Decisions Are Made **165**
    Transcripts 166
    Test Results 172
    Essays/Personal Statements 173
    Recommendations 173
    Extracurricular Activities 174
    Interviews 176
    "Hooks" 176
    Thumbs Up or Thumbs Down? 180

8. We're In—We're Out—What Now? (After Decision Letters Are Received) **183**
    Deposits 184
    Wait Lists 186
    Not Getting in Anywhere 188
    Not Wanting to Go Where Accepted 190
    Campus Security 192
    Planning to Transfer 193

9. Special Situations **195**
    Advanced Standing 195
    Deferring Admission to College 199
    Early Admission, Early Enrollment, Early Entrance 201
    International Students 203
    Attending a Post-Graduate (PG) Year at a Secondary School 205
    Students with Disabilities and Special Needs 207

10. **Words of Wisdom: Advice from
Educators and Once-Panicked Parents**   **211**

Appendix Checklist/Calendar for Parents   **216**

Index   **227**

Acknowledgments

Many thanks to everybody at ARCO, especially Linda Bernbach, for giving us the chance to put in writing the answers to so many questions that we are asked by parents of college-bound students.

Working with and meeting lots of great people is one of the "perks" that comes with a job in college admissions. A good number of them talked—and listened—to us while we researched and wrote. A great big thank-you to all the parents who completed questionnaires and were interviewed for this book. The admission offices at the University of Massachusetts at Amherst, Hampshire, Mount Holyoke, Smith, Amherst, and Saint Michael's colleges distributed some questionnaires, and we're grateful. We surveyed and called admission professionals, guidance counselors and other college administrators, and they were generous with their time and thoughtful in their responses.

Those who went above and beyond the call of duty include: Ed Wall, Patricia Wei, Jane Gutman, Joan Dorman Davis, Lee Stetson, Lee Coffin, John Polstein, Jon Hein, Bill Risley, Patricia Farrant, Sam Blair, Roger Eastlake, Chad Kleitsch, Elaine Kaplan, Bob Gilpin, and the folks at *The Vermont Connection,* especially Jenny Simmons. We also thank Jason Moynihan, Janet Adams-Wall, Gretchen Kellogg, Jim Levey, Sue Wallington Quinlan, Lisann Giordano, Ann Mecca, Andrea Wilson, Yahya Jeffries-El, Lisa Mayer, Jackie Murphy, Debbie Wright, Dick Steele, Bill Peck, Juliet Brigham, Mary Reutener, John Risley, Stacey Schmeidel, Kathleen Roos, Bonnie Cox, Susan Lewandowski, Tina Gorski-Strong, Emily Harrison Weir, Terran Whittingham, Tara Vaydya, M.J. Maccardini, Mary Williamson, Robert Mansueto, Mandaryn Gerry, and Elise Feeley and the Forbes Library reference staff. Colleagues at Smith were interested and supportive, and we are especially grateful to: B. Ann Wright, Nanci Tessier, Jennifer Desjarlais, Deb Shaver, John G. Eue, Claire Kmetz, Cathy Brooks, Marti Hobbes, Diane Cuneo, Chrissie Bell, Michelle LaPlante, Beatrice Kaminski, Nancy Subocz, Joyce Rauch, Myra Smith, Sharon Rust, Ann E. Shanahan, Hrayr Tamzarian, and Ann C. Playe.

Sally thanks Chris Petrides, Eddi and Al Simon, Liz Rubenstone, and Liria Petrides who supported her when she needed them and left her alone when she didn't *and* who sold countless copies of the book before page one was even written. She also thanks her son, Jack Christopher Petrides, for arriving unexpectedly after the initial edition of this book was published—so at age 45 she is finally a parent, and in 18 years she will need to be reminded to heed her own advice.

Sid especially thanks Betsy and Christina. While they *didn't* mind eating more take-out and watching extra videos, they *did* mind seeing less of her during the writing process. Fred, as always, was a peach and did more than his fair share of house and family work. Most importantly, though, he kept her calm (no small feat!) and made her laugh. She thanks her father, who is in heaven, and her mother, who is a saint on earth, for never panicking—ever.

We sincerely thank everybody for sharing stories, anecdotes, facts and figures, and pointing us in the direction of some revelations. It's not clear whether we *teach* more or *learn* more when we write. And since we're always on the lookout to learn new things, if you have an experience as a parent in the college admission process and you want us to know about it, don't hesitate to contact us, and we'll put your story in our files.

Introduction

You're sending a child to college, and you're bound to be concerned—or maybe more like anxious or, yes, even panicked. And, whether this is the first child to go, or the last, another child or an only child, you recognize that life as you know it will never be quite the same again.

In today's world, you don't have to be breathing into paper bags to qualify as a panicked parent. You realize that a higher education is a huge investment—of time and money, of emotion and energy. You worry that your child won't be accepted by a favorite school—or, worse yet, will get in, and go, and be miserable there. You wonder if you'll ever again be able to afford a new car, or *any* car, or eating at a restaurant without a drive-through window. You question if the teenager who can't decide what movie to see on a Saturday night will be able to move hundreds of miles from home and make choices that may influence his life decades to come.

As a parent, your part in the whole process is important, yet can—at times—be especially confusing. You've reached a turning point. Your child is going to college. You're not. You think that your voice should be heard, but you're not always sure what to say. There are myriad forms to fill out, tests to take, trips to make, and bills to pay. You want to provide support and assistance but you don't know what will help, and you're scared of what may hurt.

Can parents, indeed, contribute to prudent college selections and to favorable admission decisions? What can Mom or Dad do to realize (or ruin) a child's dream of attending a certain special school. Anything?

First, relax; you're in good company. There are nearly 15 million students in college. That means—with parents and step-parents, grandparents and godparents included—billions of people share your questions and concerns.

In the pages that follow, you will find practical tips on how to take the perplexity—and the complexity—out of the college admission process. You will learn what college officials really look for in a candidate, and what you and your child should look for in a college.

- Is there such a thing as a college match made in heaven? God only knows! See Chapter 2.

- Can a private college cost us less than a state school? Very possibly. Check out Chapter 5.

- Can preparation improve standardized test scores? Yes. See Chapter 3.

- Will a good interview get my child into a long-shot school? Maybe. See Chapter 4.

- Do some colleges give preference to certain groups or types of students? Often. See Chapter 7.

- Will we all still be speaking when this is over? We hope so. Quick...read Chapter 1.

CHAPTER 1

All in the Family: Decisions and Dynamics

I. How Involved Should Parents Be in the College Selection Process?

➤ **THE GOOD NEWS:** Even kids who have barricaded you from their bedrooms since seventh grade are likely to welcome—or, at least, *expect*—your input at college admission time.

➤ **THE BAD NEWS:** Somebody in the family needs to be the "organized one" and stay on top of piles of paperwork and deadlines. Ideally, this should be the student. Practically, it is usually the parent.

You may already have been terrified by tales of parents who seem to make their kid's college admission a full-time occupation. A college counselor at a private school in Texas remembers one such mother who "created a personal scrapbook for her son, had it professionally typeset and printed, hired a writer to compose the essays, and had a secretary fill out all the applications. After submitting the completed packages to her son for his signature, she FedExed the whole shebang to each college."

At the other end of the spectrum—but by no means alone—is the Brown alumna who recalls that her mother refused to take any part in the application process. "She sent me off on bus and train trips around the country to visit colleges by myself. In retrospect, I suppose it wasn't such a bad thing. It helped make me independent. But every time an admission interviewer asked me, 'Are you here today with someone who may have questions?' then it hurt."

1

As a parent, it is critically important that you don't become *too* involved in the selection and application process. After all, *you* are not the one who is going to college, and children should always feel that they have played a key part in this important decision about *their* lives. Since most will soon be living far enough away that you won't be there to constantly "remind" them about daily responsibilities, this is also a good time to make certain that they're ready to take the reins. Yet, don't err too much the other way and not give *enough* support—moral, financial, and even clerical—needed during this sometimes frustrating, always busy period. You should find the best balance between being overbearing and nagging and being apathetic and distant. Some choice, eh?

Colleges, by the way, don't give "extra credit" for parental involvement—nor for students who survive without it. Contrary to what the grapevine tells you, it doesn't matter who calls to request catalogues or directions, nor how many parents (or sets of parents) are downstairs in the waiting room during an interview. Admission officers only wince when it's clear that candidates are passing off Mom or Dad's efforts as their own, like the pre-packaged prospect described above or the applicant who can barely speak English but submits an essay that sounds suspiciously like *Self-Reliance*.

II. Self-Assessment Surveys for Parents and Students

Magazines these days seem to be full of "stress charts." They're designed to show you (as if sitting bolt upright in the middle of the night doesn't do it) how major life events can affect your arteries, your lungs, your heart, and your head. Even "good" stresses (births and marriages, moving to a bigger house or a better job) can propel you to the tip-top of the chart. Well, guess what…sending a kid to college gets you right up there, too, and if it's the first one to go—or the last—then, congratulations; you get extra points.

In only the past few decades, the college admission process—from the very first time the "C" word comes up at the dinner table until the last duffel bag is unloaded in a dorm room—has become a highly charged, often tense, and unduly disruptive experience for many families. Where does all this pressure come from?

- For starters, it comes from *colleges* themselves. Student recruiting is now a top priority. Schools print more publications and send them out sooner than ever before. They vie for hot prospects by offering free flights and campus weekends, complete with tickets to concerts and sports events. Exacting application requirements, endless forms, essays, and deadlines all add to the strain.

2

- Likewise, it comes from *society*. We live in a designer culture, where "name" cars and clothes and luggage—and *colleges*—assure us (and others) that we've "made it." The media, too, is relentless in reminding us of the importance of approaching college in the proper way and of the capriciousness of admission decisions even when we do everything right. Stores are brimming with books aimed to enlighten us about the most arcane aspects of the process (yes, like this one), and burgeoning businesses prey on fears of substandard test scores.

- *Students,* of course, put pressure on themselves. Where you live, where your child goes to school, and even the varying personalities that make one senior class different from the next will all determine how college admission affects your family.

- And finally, the really big-time pressure can come from *parents*. The current generation of upcoming college students is the first with a high percentage of parents who have attended college themselves. Those who went to renowned and prestigious places usually expect their children to "do as well." Those from less celebrated schools often demand that their children "do better."

Moreover, with college costs skyrocketing, parents have become savvy and careful consumers. They consider a college education an investment and expect immense returns. They scrutinize schools more critically than their own parents ever did and have more specific questions—and *demands*—which can also mean more stress on the home front.

Family life, as well, is not always as simple as it was when Ward and Wally Cleaver conferred in the study, while June baked brownies for the Beaver. Today, some students have one parent; some have more than four. Many have two who are scarcely speaking or who use the college application process as a weapon in their own power struggles.

➤ **THE GOOD AND THE BAD NEWS:** Both the strengths and weaknesses of parent/child relationships (and parent/parent relationships) will be amplified during the college search.

Below is a self-assessment survey that should help you and your child as you approach the college selection experience. There are no right or wrong answers, nor even any scores to tally at the end. The quiz has several purposes:

- To get the whole process up and running; to generate discussions; to foster awareness of some of the complex questions and issues that are part of college decision-making.

- To recognize potential hot spots where you and your child (or you and your spouse, or all of you) are likely to disagree, so that problems can be defused before they *really* heat up.

- To create pleasant surprises—those areas where you thought you'd disagree, but you don't.

- To pinpoint priorities that all of you will want to consider when you read Chapter 2 and start identifying "target schools." (So, don't throw your questionnaires away.)

The Rules

Actually, there aren't many. There are two separate but similar tests: one for parents, one for kids. First, make copies. That way, you can do your own; your child's other parent(s) or guardian(s) can have a shot, too. If your child is just starting high school, answer what you can, then retake the quiz in a year or so to see what's changed. Even parents of *seniors* who do the survey now and again in a few months may be amazed by differences. A sociologist-to-be in September could be considering medicine by March.

Don't hesitate to add comments, as needed, nor to make up your own responses if the multiple-choice options aren't multiple enough. When everyone has finished the quiz, call a powwow to talk about your answers, but respect the others' privacy. There may be some thoughts that each of you would rather keep confidential.

MOM AND POP QUIZ:
Self-Assessment Survey for Parents

I. Particular Preferences

- Name five things that your son or daughter is doing right now and you hope will CONTINUE TO DO in college (e.g., playing piano, flossing daily, learning Japanese, seeing a shrink, etc.):

    1. _____
    2. _____
    3. _____
    4. _____
    5. _____

- Name five things that he or she is NOT doing now, but you hope WILL DO in college (again, academic or otherwise):

    1. _____
    2. _____
    3. _____
    4. _____
    5. _____

- Name five things that your child IS doing right now that you hope WON'T CONTINUE in college (e.g., flunking English; taunting the dog; talking back to Grandma):

    1. _____
    2. _____
    3. _____
    4. _____
    5. _____

Pretend that there's a perfect college. We'll call it "Fantasy State." In your opinion, it's the ideal school for your child. Keep it in mind as you answer the questions below and, if you really have no preference in one area—or have several—be sure to say so. Put an asterisk (*) by those preferences you feel very strongly about:

II. Location

- How far is it from home? (Within an hour's drive or a day's? In a foreign country?) _____

- Do you prefer a big city? Suburb? Small town, etc.? _____

- Do you have other preferences or requirements (e.g., near a ski slope or far from one; close to grandparents or a major medical center)? _____

- Do you have a *specific* location in mind (e.g., Boston, California, NYC)? _____

- In what location do you think your child wants to go to school? _____

- How will your child react if your expectations conflict? _____

III. Enrollment

- Will your child be best off in a small college (under 2,500 students)? A medium-small one (2,500 to 5,000)? A medium one (5,000 to 10,000)? A large one (10,000 to 18,000)? A very large one (18,000+)? _____

- How good is your child at asking for help (anything from directions to tutoring) when needed? _____

- Do you prefer an institution that is primarily for undergraduates? _____ What advantages (if any) do you see in having grad students on campus, too?
  _____

- Would you consider a single-sex school? _____ Would you prefer one? _____ In a coed school, do you care if the male-to-female ratio is imbalanced? _____

- Do you prefer a school with a religious affiliation (and/or a strong majority of one religious group)? _____ If so, which one? _____

- Would a religious affiliation bother you? _____

- Do you prefer a school that draws its students from a wide range of states (and even foreign countries)? _____

- Racial/ethnic diversity? _____

- What preferences (and prejudices) do you think your child has regarding the size and student composition of the college he or she will attend? _____
  _____

IV. Academics

- Does your child have a major in mind? _____ If so, what? _____

- How certain about it do you think your child feels? _____ Does he or she have a career goal? If so, what? _____

- How do YOU feel about this choice of major and/or career? _____
  _____

- What other academic areas do you hope will be pursued in college? _____
  _____

- Are there subjects that your child is likely to avoid that you think should be studied? If so, what? _____

- Do you think your child works better when challenged by tough classes and bright classmates, or when near the top of a less competitive group? _____

- How hard do you think your child works in high school? See choices below:

  a. Very hard (maybe too hard, at times?) _____
  b. Hard (especially the night before tests and term papers)
  c. Somewhat hard
  d. What's work? Life's a beach!

- How hard do you think your child expects to work in college? (Use the same choices as above.) _____

- Do you think a college should have a "core curriculum" ("distribution require-ments")? _____

- What other special academic focus or programs appeal to you? (e.g., military, agricultural, or technical; study abroad opportunities, etc.) _____
  _____

- Is having your child attend a prestigious college important to you? _____

- Is it equally, more, or less important to your child? _____

V. Finances

- Will cost influence where your child attends college? _____ Are you planning to apply for financial aid? _____ How is your credit rating? _____

- How much money, if any, have you set aside for college expenses for this child?
  _____

- What amount do you expect your child to contribute from earnings and assets?
  _____

VI. Campus Life

- What extracurricular activities do you hope your child will pursue in college?
  _____

- How do you feel about fraternities and sororities? _____
  _____

- How do you expect weekends will be spent? See choices below. Check all that apply:

  a. Coming home (with the laundry)   e. Partying
  b. With the high-school honey   f. Working (as in making $$)
  c. Studying   g. Playing/watching college sports
  d. Some study; some socializing   h. Other _____

7

- Would you prefer a college with a reputation for being a conservative school? _____ Liberal? _____ A high-pressure school? _____ A party school? _____ Other? _____

VII. Living Situation

- Would you prefer your child to live at home? _____ In a single-sex dorm? ____ In a coed dorm? _____ In a coed room? _____ In a fraternity or sorority? _____

- How will your child do with a roommate? _____ How about more than one? _____

- Does dorm size matter? ____ Would you mind an off-campus apartment? ___

- Other living situation considerations? _____

- Where do you think your child prefers or expects to live? _____

VIII. Et Cetera

- Name five things not mentioned yet that you think your child can't live without at college (e.g., vegetarian food; wheelchair ramps; a French-speaking dorm; a maid; a French-speaking maid):
  1. _____
  2. _____
  3. _____
  4. _____
  5. _____

IX. Getting Personal

- What are your child's SAT I scores (or ACT or PSAT)? _____

- SAT II? __/__/__ GPA? _____ Rank in class? _____ On a 1-to-10 scale, how demanding were his or her high-school classes compared to the toughest ones the school offers? _____

- Using that same scale, rate the high school for competitiveness and difficulty compared to others nationwide: _____

- If "5" is "Most Selective" and "1" is "Not at All Selective," to which level of colleges do you expect you child to apply? _____ Which do you think are likely to say yes? _____

- Why do you want your child to go to college? _____
  _____

- Do you think she or he should go straight from high school? _____
  _____

- Do you have specific schools in mind now that you'd like your child to consider or attend? If so, which ones? _____

- What aspects of the college admission process and of having your child actually going to college are you most apprehensive about? _____
  _____

- Which are you most looking forward to? _____
  _____

- Which aspects of the college selection/admission process are likely to cause friction between you and your child?

  1. _____ 4. _____
  2. _____ 5. _____
  3. _____ 6. _____

- Do you think your child feels pressure from you to attend a specific school or type of school? Explain: _____
  _____

- Who do you think should decide which college your child should attend? See choices below:

  a. S/he should. Period.
  b. S/he should—with *strong* parental input
  c. S/he should—with *some* parental input
  d. Parent(s)—with some input from kids
  e. A guidance counselor
  f. The Psychic Friends Network

KIDZ QUIZ:
Self-Assessment Survey for Students

I. Particular Preferences

- Name five things that you ARE doing right now that you hope to CONTINUE TO DO in college: (These can be anything from studying science to shaving your head; playing polo to playing piano.)

    1. _____
    2. _____
    3. _____
    4. _____
    5. _____

- Name five things that you're NOT doing now, but HOPE TO DO in college (again, academic or otherwise):

    1. _____
    2. _____
    3. _____
    4. _____
    5. _____

- Name five things that you ARE doing right now that you DON'T WANT TO DO in college (e.g., sharing a bathroom with your baby brother; conjugating German verbs; singing alto):

    1. _____
    2. _____
    3. _____
    4. _____
    5. _____

- In general, how do you want your college to be most different from your high school? _____

- How do you want it to be similar? _____
_____

Pretend that there's a perfect college. We'll call it "Fantasy State." Keep it in mind as you answer the questions below and, if you really have no preference in one area—or have several—be sure to say so. Put an asterisk (*) by those preferences that you feel very strongly about:

10

II. Location

- How far is it from home? (Within an hour's drive or a day's? In a foreign country?)
  _____

- Do you prefer a big city? Suburb? Small town, etc.? _____

- Do you have other preferences or requirements (e.g., near a ski slope or major medical center; close to your boyfriend, girlfriend, grandparents, or an all-night deli)?
  _____

- Do you have a *specific* location in mind (e.g., Boston, California, NYC)? _____

- In what location do you think your parents want you to go to school? _____
  _____

- How will they react if your expectations conflict? _____

III. Enrollment

- Do you prefer a small college (under 2,500 students)? A medium-small one (2,500 to 5000)? A medium one (5,000 to 10,000)? A large one (10,000 to 18,000)? A very large one (18,000+)? _____

- How good are you at asking for help (anything from directions to tutoring) when you need it? _____

- Do you want an institution that is primarily for undergraduates? _____ What advantages (if any) do you see in having grad students on campus, too?
  _____

- Would you consider a single-sex school? _____ Would you prefer one? _____ In a coed school, do you care if the male-to-female ratio is imbalanced? _____

- Do you want a school with a religious affiliation (and/or a strong majority of one religious group)? _____ If so, which one? _____ Would a religious affiliation bother you? ____ Do you prefer a school that draws its students from a wide range of states (and even foreign countries)? _____ Racial/ethnic diversity? ____

- What preferences (and prejudices) do you think your parents have regarding the size and student composition of the college you will attend? _____
  _____

IV. Academics

- Do you have a major in mind? _____ If so, what? _____ How certain about it do you feel? _____ Do you have a career goal? If so, what? _____

11

- How do you think your parents feel about your choice of major and/or career?
  _____

- What other academic areas do you hope to pursue in college? _____
  _____

- Which subjects do you hope to avoid like the plague? _____
  _____

- Do you think you work better when you are challenged by tough classes and bright classmates, or do you do prefer to be near the top of a less competitive group? _____

- How hard do you work in high school? See choices below:

  a. Very hard (maybe too hard, at times?)
  b. Hard (especially the night before tests and term papers
  c. Somewhat hard
  d. What's work? Life's a beach!

- How hard do you expect to work in college? (Use the same choices as above.)
  _____

- Do you think a college should have a "core curriculum" ("distribution requirements")? _____

- What other special academic focus or programs appeal to you? (e.g., military, agricultural, or technical; study abroad opportunities, etc.) _____
  _____

- Is attending a prestigious college important to you? _____

- Is it equally, more, or less important to your parents? _____

V. Finances

- Do you think cost will influence where you attend college? _____ Are you planning to apply for financial aid? _____ Do you know how much money, if any, your parents have set aside for your college education? If so, how much? _____
  _____

- How much do you expect to contribute from your own earnings and assets?
  _____

- Do you plan to have a job during the school year while in college? _____
  A summer job? _____

12

VI. Campus Life

- What extracurricular activities do you plan to pursue in college? _____
  _____

- How do you feel about fraternities and sororities? _____

- How do you expect to spend your weekends? See choices below:

  a. Going home (with my laundry)   e. I'm strictly a party animal
  b. With my high-school honey   f. Working (as in making $$)
  c. Studying my buns off   g. Playing/watching college sports
  d. Some study; some socializing   h. Other _____

- Would you prefer a college with a reputation for being a conservative school? _____ Liberal? _____ A high-pressure school? _____ A party school? _____ Other? _____

VII. Living Situation

- Would you prefer to live at home? _____ In a single-sex dorm? _____ In a coed dorm? _____ In a coed room? _____ In a fraternity or sorority? ____ Do you want a roommate? _____ Could you handle more than one? _____

- Does dorm size matter? _____ Do you prefer an apartment off campus? ____

- Other living situation considerations? _____

- Where do you think your parents prefer or expect you to live? _____
  _____

VIII. Et Cetera

- Name five things you haven't mentioned yet that you "can't live without" at college (e.g., vegetarian food; wheelchair ramps; a French-speaking dorm; a gay students' association):

  1. _____
  2. _____
  3. _____
  4. _____
  5. _____

IX. Getting Personal

- What are your SAT I scores (or ACT or PSAT)? _____ SAT II? __ / __ / __ GPA?_____ Rank in class? _____ On a 1-to-10 scale, how demanding were your high-school classes compared to the toughest ones your school offers? _____ Using that same scale, rate your high school for competitiveness and difficulty compared to others nationwide: _____ If "5" is "Most Selective" and "1" is "Not at All Selective," to which level of colleges do you plan to apply? _____ Which do you think are likely to admit you? _____

- Why do you want to go to college? _____

- Do you want to go straight from high school? _____

- Do you have specific schools in mind now that you'd like to consider or attend? If so, which ones? _____

- What aspects of the college admission process and of actually going to college are you most apprehensive about? _____
_____

- Which are you most looking forward to? _____
_____

- While at college, will you worry about the situation at home (e.g., parents' relationship or welfare, problems with siblings, etc.)? _____

- Which aspects of the college selection/admission process are likely to cause friction between you and your parents?

    1. _____   4. _____
    2. _____   5. _____
    3. _____   6. _____

- Do you feel pressure from your parents to attend a specific school or type of school? _____

- Who do you think should decide which college you attend? See choices below:

    a. Me. It's my life.
    b. Me—with *strong* input from parent(s)
    c. Me—with *some* input from parent(s)
    d. Parent(s)—with some input from me
    e. My guidance counselor
    f. The Psychic Friends Network

III. Pressure Points

Since going to college is a Major Life Event (and there aren't that many for most of us), sitting down with your completed questionnaires should be a special occasion. Schedule a time in advance. Make sure that other pressing obligations (and younger siblings) are out of the way. Consider heading to a quiet restaurant or to a favorite secluded (and *neutral*) spot. This will underscore the importance of the meeting (and often make it possible to discuss conflicts clearly and calmly).

Emphasize the positive aspects of the process—your mutual hopes and dreams, the excitement of a wide range of opportunities and options. Remember that you are sharing an experience that is the culmination of many years of schooling and parenting, and that no decisions need be made overnight; no disagreements have to be resolved instantly; and "compromise" may be an important watchword along the way.

For example, Althea's parents envisioned her at a small, rural Catholic women's college. She was sold on Boston University—large, urban, and certainly coed. She agreed to investigate both and, in doing so, discovered Wellesley which became her first choice and pleased everyone.

Of course, not all stories have such happy endings. But there are some other points for parents to keep in mind that will ease tensions and help to precipitate a fruitful and (usually) peaceful college search:

Are you able to let go?

Ask yourself this question early on. Are you pushing Pomona because it's a great college or because it's around the corner? What fears do you have about how "family life" will change when this kid gets to college? (Will there be a "family" left at all?) Are you anxious about how to fill the time you once devoted to this child? *Letting Go: A Parents' Guide to Today's College Experience* by Karen Levin Coburn and Madge Lawrence Treeger (Adler & Adler) offers advice to parents dealing with the emotional side of sending a child to college.

Whose idea is this, anyway?

If you have always wanted to be a podiatrist or a psychologist, an accountant or a registered nurse, and are now pushing an unwilling child in that direction, consider going back to school *yourself*. (The federal government even gives a small financial-aid break to applicants with a parent in school.) Likewise, don't insist on a college that offers football or physics, Theta Chi or Sigma Xi, just because it was right for you. Try to keep your own goals or needs separate from what your child wants. It's tough. Eighteen-year-olds don't always *know* what's best for them. They may choose to study archaeology (or astronomy, French, or fashion design) only because that's what a friend (or TV character) is doing. Meanwhile, you worry that history majors end up waiting tables; that art-school grads sweep floors. (See "Major Dilemmas" in Chapter 2.)

Ask your child to explain choices; try to point out when plans seem to be from another planet ("I'll study acting at community college and become a movie star," or "With my marketing degree, I can build a theme park in the Grand Canyon"), but never deny a dream just because it's not *yours*. Some parents live vicariously through their children, just as some children live for their parents' approval. Each of you must learn to recognize whose voice you're really hearing.

Q&A

Q: Help! Our son has a list of college choices that don't sound at all like ours. He won't even consider the schools we're urging him to see. Who has the final say?

A: While parents are often considered the most influential people in students' choices of colleges, it's not always clear if that influence is positive or negative. Marc, for instance, felt that his mother had been ramming Harvard—where his dad had gone—down his throat since he was a toddler. As a result, he stubbornly refused to apply. Your son, too, may be rebelling against you and exerting his independence by bucking your authority. Or, your son may know better what he wants and what he needs in a post-secondary school. Talk with him. Ask him for specific reasons that he is choosing the schools he is. Are his reasons valid? Perhaps you'll learn something about him that you don't know. By the way, when parents refuse to pay (or complete aid forms) for schools they don't endorse, no one ends up happy.

Whose life is this, anyway?

While parents may anticipate arguments over college choices and career goals, and may also be on the ready to cajole and plead at deadline time, some are mystified when their children refuse to cooperate at all. The once-conscientious student now insists, "I'm not going to college, period," or, in essence, relays the same signal by ignoring the stack of catalogs and

16

applications that is multiplying on the kitchen counter. In order to best respond, you'll have to translate the message. Is this just your basic garden-variety procrastination? Is your child afraid of failing to meet high expectations or fearful of breaking away? Is college the right move now—or even at all? First, try a bit of nagging and dragging (i.e., a few ultimatums and college visits that *you*'ve arranged). Sometimes, this is enough to break the ice. If not, consider other options: a year off (see Chapter 9), or even another route altogether. Your child may be a talented carpenter, an inspired chef, or a compassionate nurse's aide. These professions all require training, but not necessarily college.

Is prestige at the top of your priority list?

Many parents put pressure on students to apply to those colleges that will increase their *own* status or self-esteem. Such parents may be unwittingly setting their kids up for rejection or—if accepted—for frustration. "Students tend to be more realistic than their parents when it comes to college choices," notes Roger McC. Eastlake, director of college guidance at Germantown Academy in Fort Washington, Pennsylvania. "Applying to college involves complex decisions that should be based on thorough research, not on what decal you want on the back of your car," agrees Doran Morford, director of college guidance at Greens Farms Academy in Westport, Connecticut.

Do encourage your child to seek a challenging college experience, but *don't* attach unrelenting—and *unrealistic*—importance to "name" schools. Above all, never confuse what kind of *student* your child is with what kind of *person* he or she is. There are hundreds of thousands of high schoolers out there who are clever and kind, reliable and even remarkable, who won't be heading to Harvard next fall—but who will still lead happy and productive lives that make their parents proud.

Is this a split decision?

Although we spend a lot of time here talking about "parents," as if they are a united front like Ozzie and Harriet or NATO, the truth is that you and your mate may not see eye-to-eye on this college business at all. (You may want to take the quiz on the preceding pages and compare notes *before* you share your thoughts with Junior.) Don't expect to always agree. Pick your battles (do you *really* care if Consuelo lives in the high-rise or the low-rise dorm?) and respect your child's role as a tie-breaker—or as a third force on the battlefield.

17

Q: What happens when parents are divorced?

A: Divorced or separated parents must be especially sensitive to the hurtful issues that college planning can stir up. Anna's dad insisted he could not afford to send her to a private college while she watched him splurge on luxuries for his second wife and "new" family. Sharon's father believed that his wife had abandoned him when she "found" feminism. He promised his daughter he'd pay her tuition as long as she didn't attend her first-choice school—a women's college. Don't let your kid become a pawn in your games.

As a divorced parent, you may be especially susceptible to the hard feelings that college selection can create. Perhaps you assumed that your son would want a close-by east-coast institution, but he's off to college near Dad in Des Moines. Try not to feel competitive when your child bypasses your alma mater for your ex's (or even for a step-parent's school).

College admission and financial aid offices do not function in the Dark Ages. There is room on most forms for all sorts of combinations and permutations of blended families. Officials are accustomed to parents who are AWOL or uncooperative and can usually offer advice. Your own situation may seem confusing, but you should never feel uncomfortable about explaining it nor about requesting special consideration where appropriate.

Finally, divorced or separated parents often both expect to take an active role in the college search. Sometimes a noncustodial mother or father will seem to spring out of the woodwork at admission time (though many disappear at tuition time). It is important that you, your ex, and your child communicate as clearly as possible and, especially, define your roles. Who will go on college visits? Who will oversee applications? Who will pay college costs? (Don't overlook application fees, either. At about $50 a pop, they can be a big-ticket item). Who gets to go to parents' weekend when all of this is behind you?

What's the sibling situation?

Beginning a college search means reminding yourself again (and again) that, if you have more than one child, they may be very different. Just as Brenda was a beautiful ballerina and Tammy couldn't get into the tutu, you are likely to find that the college (or *type* of college) which is a perfect match for your first child may not fit the second one at all. Commonly, younger siblings are

18

fearful of disappointing Mom and Dad after a superstar older brother or sister went to a big-name school. On the other hand, just because three kids have already trooped through the local state college, don't assume that it's the certain spot for number four as well. And parents of twins often find that college marks a turning point when a once-inseparable pair heads in diverging directions.

Likewise, even if *all* of your children are seeking similar schools, you can practically count on different approaches to the process. Danny, for example, may have dragged you on a dozen campus tours, insisted that you read every essay, and never met deadlines without nagging; now Audrey wants to do it all alone. She visited Vassar with her boyfriend, canceled *your* Greyhound ticket to Grinnell, and may ultimately end up at a college where you never even knew she *applied*. Shifting gears among different children is one of the signs of wisdom among parents.

And speaking of siblings, although you may have to tuck the little ones away during summit meetings with the college-bound, don't forget that this may be a confusing time for them, too. They recognize that change and anxiety are in the air. They know they will be losing an ally and mentor, tennis partner, math tutor (and occasional tormentor). Make sure you don't keep them in the dark—high school–age siblings, especially, can learn a lot as observers—and set aside time for special treats or attention.

Can't you just chill out?

You won't be able to forestall every fight or heal every hurt that the college admission process will engender. You can help, however, by heeding the suggestions above and in the pages that follow. You can also help by stepping back sometimes. Don't let college consume your lives. Make a dinner date with your spouse; take your son or daughter to a movie (if they'll be seen with you in public; if not, bring home a pizza). Make a list of off-limit words like "application," "acceptance," and "SAT," and see who can get through a day (or a meal or a minute) without saying them.

One top prep school offered students a workshop on dealing with their parents during the college search, and the room was packed. Sadly, several seniors confessed that they thought their parents would love them less if they didn't choose to apply to—or weren't accepted at—Mom or Dad's top-choice college.

Remember, *wherever* your child ends up, it's likely to be a place with thousands of books and hundreds of computers, with swimming pools and squash courts, and three squares a day on the table. So, above all, enjoy the adventure.

Chapter 2

Matchmaking, Matchmaking: Choosing the "Right" College

➤ **THE GOOD NEWS:** Picking a college is, in some ways, like picking a mate. Finding the right "match" is all-important. Research alone is not enough; chemistry plays a big part, and exploring your options ought to be exciting.

➤ **THE BAD NEWS:** One out of every two marriages ends in divorce. Far fewer college students drop out or transfer due to discontent. (This is only bad news if you're married. If your child is off to college, it's more *good* news. The odds favor a successful choice.)

By the spring of your child's junior year, it's time to start thinking seriously about college choices (or at least to *sound* serious when you're actually completely clueless). Making good matches is, indeed, the most critical part of the selection and application process. In some respects, it's also the hardest. There are no formulas to follow. A lot depends on circumstance and serendipity, on leg work and on luck.

If you're thinking of getting a tattoo in the near future, this is what it should say:

> "There is no such thing as the perfect college, just as there is no such thing as the perfect student or perfect parent."

Allow this thought to guide you throughout your search. There are over 3,000 colleges in the country, and more than one will be right for your child. Your goal, then, should not be to find THE college but to find **several** of the *many* places where your son or daughter can be happy and productive.

I. "What Kind of School Am I?"

Before deciding which colleges to choose, you and your child should give some thought to what *kind* of college you prefer. There are two-year schools and four-year schools, liberal-arts colleges and universities. Some are "public," which means that their fortunes are tied to the shirttails of state budgets. (Nearly 80 percent of all college students attend public institutions). Others are private, supported by tuition, endowment, and the generous gifts of friends and alumni (and alumni *parents*). Although many students mix and match and don't restrict their applications to only one type of institution, it's useful to have a hunch which way you're heading and to understand the differences you'll encounter.

Two-Year Colleges

Decades ago, almost all two-year schools were known as "junior colleges." Some were bastions of wealthy young women who bided time before marriage; others enabled far less well-heeled students to get a low-cost education close to home.

Today, two-year schools are known as either junior, community, or technical colleges. Of the nation's nearly 1,500 two-year institutions, about three-fourths are public, and their tuition is ordinarily far lower than that of four-year schools. Most offer programs that can lead to transfer, as well as occupational programs designed to prepare students for careers—such as secretarial studies, automotive technology, or computer programming—which demand specific training beyond high school, but not necessarily a bachelor's degree. The "associate's degree" is awarded at such institutions, and it is the "terminal" or highest degree required in certain job fields.

Some (primarily private) two-year colleges have a selective admission process and require standardized test scores. Many others offer "open" (or "noncompetitive") admission to all applicants with a high-school diploma or its equivalent. Be aware, however, that even noncompetitive schools may have academic prerequisites for certain departments. Technical majors or nursing programs, for example, usually require preparation in math or science.

Four-year colleges frequently flaunt their "diversity" as a selling point, but it is the two-year school that truly attracts students from wide-ranging backgrounds and of varying ages and ability. Two-year schools are ideal for students who are eager to get out in the working world quickly and for those who are reentering academia after time away. Flexible scheduling, convenient locations, and low costs can make them wise choices for those who must live at home, who have families of their own, or who hold full-time jobs.

They can also be a way for students who struggled (or "vacationed") through high school to test the waters of college or to prove themselves before "trading up." In fact, although two-year colleges aren't for status seekers, and you'll rarely find students wavering between Brown University and Bunker Hill CC, they are often a first step to a more selective school. Some of the top private institutions in the country (e.g., Amherst and Williams) take the bulk of their transfers from community colleges and provide ample financial aid to applicants who would have never made it in as freshmen or who were scared off by the private-school price tag.

Conversely, there are also stories like Peggy's. She attended an elite private high school, earned a B.A. at Stanford but, years later, returned to a nearby CC to learn real-world skills in film production. As parents, don't limit your sights to *only* the local community college, but, on the other hand, don't be too quick to dismiss it—or any two-year school—as an inappropriate choice for your child. For more information on two-year schools and programs contact:

> The American Association of Community Colleges
> One Dupont Circle NW
> Suite 410
> Washington, DC 20036
> 202/728-0200

Liberal Arts Colleges

Although the liberal arts have been around at least since the days when Socrates held court at the old agora, parents and students are still often confused by the term. Some envision left-wing enclaves of aspiring sculptors, actors, or musicians and tie-dye clad teachers. In fact, liberal arts colleges can be far from liberal and may provide only minimal instruction in the arts. They do, however, enable their students to sample from a broad range of disciplines, with the aim of preparing them to reason and to communicate, based on the lessons of history and literature, philosophy and physics, and dozens of other disciplines. While not career-oriented in the strictest sense (e.g., no certificate programs in dental hygiene or criminal justice), liberal-arts schools insist that today's changing high-tech world demands not narrowly trained specialists but thinkers and problem-solvers who have learned how to *learn.*

Whether you buy into this is up to you. You may still be sold on Arnold's accounting college or Selma's speech-pathology studies. Even some liberal-arts schools now hedge their bets by offering programs like engineering and journalism with a vocational ring to them. Yet, Latin majors go to law school, music majors work on Wall Street, and many of the nation's greatest leaders (as well as wealthiest business tycoons) have been products of a liberal arts education. Liberal arts colleges are generally geared toward undergraduates, although some may offer graduate study, too. (See "Major Dilemmas" later in this chapter.)

Universities

A university usually includes a "school of liberal arts" but also offers other "colleges" with a more professional orientation (e.g., "The College of Engineering," "The School of Allied Health Sciences," or of "Hotel Management"), as well as programs of graduate study. On the plus side, universities often provide a range and sophistication of facilities that liberal-arts colleges can't equal, along with the opportunity to take advanced-level grad courses. On the down side, undergrads sometimes complain that they are an afterthought at universities where faculty research and graduate students take a front seat.

Q&A

Q: There are schools we've never heard of that cost as much as Harvard. Is a private college a better investment than a public one?

A: Some parents assume that private schools are bound to be better than public because they cost more; others wonder why anyone would pay exorbitant tuitions when state colleges abound. While most folks agree that big-name colleges can be worth the big-time bucks that they must shell out to send their kids there, what about the lesser-known spots that still carry sky-high stickers? Are they, too, worth the price of admission? What about state schools that up their fees for nonresidents?

"There are no simple solutions," says college counselor Roger Eastlake. "Each student and family situation is different. The not-so-famous colleges don't usually have the same ability to offer the kind of financial aid that the well-known, well-endowed schools do. Still, are they worth scrimping and sacrificing for? One really has to look at intangibles, to ask 'Can this college provide a quality of life, a more personalized experience than its public equivalent? What will work best for *this* child?' Too commonly parents say, 'Well, how's my kid going to get a job after graduating from thus-and-so college that nobody's heard of?' And I remind them that even the 'old-boy network' isn't what it used to be. I try to guide students to select the most broadening experience possible, to

24

find the greatest opportunity for growth, which in some cases may be at a private school and, in others, at a state college or university."

Claire and Joe spent more than $150,000 to send three children to college. Their oldest daughter thrived at Hartwick College, a competitive but hardly prominent private school in upstate New York, and then earned a master's degree in a prestigious graduate program. Number two, a son, was thrilled with his choice of Springfield College in Massachusetts, enjoying small classes and individual attention. The youngest child, however, did not like the costly college she attended and felt that her parents' money would go farther at a state school. "She transferred to the University of Massachusetts and loved it," Claire recounts. "Each child is different. What's right for one isn't always right for the other. Sometimes we asked ourselves, 'Are we crazy to be spending this kind of money?' but looking back on the positive experiences our kids have had—and at the ten years of loan payments still ahead—neither of us has any regrets."

II. List Value—The Long and Short of It

How many colleges should your child plan to apply to? "Is three enough? Is six too many?" It really depends. Some students have their sights set on only one school. If it seems like a sure thing and offers "rolling" or "early" decision (see Chapter 6) so that if the news is bad you'll have time to turn elsewhere, then there may be little need to file more than one application. On the other hand, students shooting for highly competitive schools may have to sow many seeds with the hope that at least one will blossom.

Your child should aim to apply to five or six colleges which include the following:

- one or two "long-shot" or "reach" colleges

- two or three "likelies" (at least a 50-percent chance of acceptance)

- one "sure thing" or "safety" school (if this choice guarantees admission but not necessarily affordability, your child should apply to an additional "financial-aid sure thing")

Admission guru Ed Wall, director of college counseling at Cushing Academy in Ashburnham, Massachusetts, who has seen the process from every angle (former dean of admission at Amherst College, Lawrence University, and The University of Southern California, guidance counselor, independent consultant, author, and parent), wisely advises his charges that safety schools should always be those where they are "satisfied to go, if not deliriously happy."

In order to end up with a "short list" that looks something like the one above, your child should begin with a "long list" of 20 or so "target" colleges that you will then explore via publications, computer, visits, videos, etc. The long list should include both familiar schools as well as those that are discovered during the search.

Begin by brainstorming. Buy a notebook. We'll call it your "College Bible." Start a page for every school you want to consider. Make it a family affair. When it comes to creating a long list, there's no reason to go to war. If Junior's thinking "Pepperdine," and Dad's saying "Panhandle State," put them both on the roster. (Maybe only one will make the short list later on; maybe neither will.) Don't try to fill up all the pages; save some for schools still unknown. This is not the time to be narrow-minded, either. No matter how long Sam has been set on Santa Cruz or Mom has been touting Michigan, it's important to explore a range of options, even if it's just to see how the first-choice spot will stack up against its competition.

III. Identifying "Target" Colleges

Just what, exactly, are you looking for? How do colleges land on your list? If you haven't yet completed the questionnaire in Chapter 1, do so before continuing. Your child should fill it out as well. Examine the priorities that emerge from your answers. Consider inconsistencies. Perhaps your son wants a large school but admits to being shy about asking for help. That's a sign that a small college may be a better match. If prestige is important but your daughter has only average grades, then status schools are going to be far reaches. In other words, be practical. "Fantasy State" may offer year-round golf on one edge of its campus and year-round skiing on the other. Your child's college won't.

Location, Location, Location

One of the questions that demands your closest scrutiny is the "where" issue. It can be the most emotional of all college-related decisions. Parents are often torn between wanting their children to take advantage of exciting but far-away opportunities and hoping that Sunday family dinners won't be out of reach. Teenagers, too, may be angry if parents seem too clingy, but disappointed if they don't.

The key in deciding where a child should attend school lies in thinking about the reality of a choice. While it is a great learning experience to study in another part of the country, travel costs can be quite high, and it may be very lonely not to be home for Thanksgiving or spring break. Likewise, a week of camping out west was Stacy's favorite summer vacation, but at the University of Montana, where only a quarter of the student body comes from elsewhere, Stacy, a Connecticut native, felt like she was in a foreign country. On the other hand, Scott, another New Englander and an avid outdoorsman, fit in right from the start. Before romanticizing distant schools, see how many out-of-staters attend, and consider how your child would adapt to being in the minority.

Other location points to contemplate: Is your child an urban animal or a country mouse? Even those who are "psyched" to try something new should anticipate a big adjustment. Ask, too, "Where is this college *really* situated?" Alexis, from Illinois, applied to a Massachusetts school that looked close to Boston on the map. In fact, it was nearly 50 highway miles away, with little public transportation—not exactly what she had in mind for an afternoon cappuccino in Kenmore Square.

And how far is not far enough? Joo-Hee chose a college less than two hours from her family. Every Friday, her parents would arrive in their station wagon, bring her home for the weekend, and return her to the dorm on Sunday night. "They just assumed that that was what I wanted," she reflects, "and I never questioned it. If I had it to do over, though, I'd pick a school farther away and make myself have a campus social life. When I talk to friends now, I realize that I missed out on one of the most important parts of college."

Amy, on the other hand, went to school in her hometown in order to take advantage of a special scholarship for local students. She lived in a dorm, met classmates from all over the world, and usually even did her own laundry. "I saw my parents about once a month," she notes, "and I saw my hometown from a completely different point of view." Likewise, Lucy's parents couldn't afford to let her live on campus, but she took an active role in several clubs and practically camped out in the commuter lounge. After four years, she, too, felt she'd had an authentic college experience.

Again, be realistic. Will your child be able to establish his or her own identity by attending college nearby? Is going far away too much of a challenge for this child at this time?

Sizable Differences

A large university can be exciting—or impersonal. A small school can be supportive—or stifling. Among the most common reasons for transferring, size is near the top of the list, with "too big" and "too small" getting pretty even play. Small colleges commonly translate into smaller classes and more faculty contact. They can, however, be too homogeneous or lacking in specific curricular offerings. Large schools may offer opportunities, such as editing a daily newspaper or studying Swahili, that a smaller school can't equal. Extroverts and self-starters may thrive on a big campus. Students who are shy or who lack the self-discipline to work when there are endless temptations to do otherwise will probably be better served by a small college where they won't be as likely to fall through the cracks.

Reach or Realistic?

A list of target colleges shouldn't be top-heavy with places that aren't likely to admit your child. When you start to consider a school, look carefully at its "freshman profile." These profiles offer a range of statistics about an institution's entering class and are typically found in viewbooks and general guidebooks (see "Using Publications," later in this chapter).

Pay attention to grade point averages, class ranks, and test results. Compare the numbers with your child's grades and scores. Is this college a long shot or a likely? If accepted, will your child be at the top of the heap or burning the midnight oil to keep up? Selectivity ratings, found in most general guidebooks, are also an aid in evaluating schools you've never heard a thing about. Some of the most competitive (and excellent) colleges in the country, like Cooper Union, Rice, and Harvey Mudd, attract the same super students as the Ivy League but only a fraction of the fanfare. However, be aware that selectivity statistics can also be misleading. The U.S. Coast Guard Academy, for example, accepts only about 9 percent of its applicants. Stanford takes twice as many at 19 percent, yet boasts average combined SAT scores that are nearly 150 points higher.

When comparing SAT scores, be aware that the tests were "recentered" in 1995, adding about 100 points to combined verbal and mathematical tallies. (See Chapter 3.) Using out-of-date freshman profiles can make what is really a long-shot school seem like a likely one. For example, a college that routinely welcomed students with verbal SAT scores of 580 prior to 1995 may expect scores of 650 on today's test. Some highly competitive colleges no longer require standardized test scores, but most still do—and they weigh them more heavily than many admission officials are willing to admit.

When compiling target colleges, it's important to be wary not only of colleges that are too competitive, but also of those that may not be competitive enough. A student whose grades and test scores far surpass those on the freshman profile may end up unchallenged and bored. On the other hand, some students do best in less stressful environments.

Q&A

Q: My nephew, Jeffrey, was second in his high-school class, president of the literary club, and first violinist in the school orchestra. His SAT scores were over 1500, yet he was still denied admission to every Ivy League college on his list. What went wrong? Should I discourage my son from applying to such places?

A: There are a handful of colleges in this country—the Ivy League schools among them—that are so hyperselective that their offices of admission ought to be renamed offices of rejection. Parents who, for years, have puffed up with pride at a child's academic and extracurricular achievements are shocked and dismayed when first-choice colleges say "we're sorry..." in April.

It's easy, indeed, to underestimate just how difficult it is to be admitted to these top schools. Dartmouth takes about one applicant in every five; Harvard, one in eight. While the statistics alone don't seem too daunting, consider the fact that nearly every student who applies to such schools is pretty well qualified to attend. Harvard, in fact, receives more applications from valedictorians alone than there are places in the freshman class.

Your nephew may be what we call the "average outstanding kid." Yes, it may sound like an oxymoron, but the Ivy League colleges and a few others (e.g., Stanford) have their pick of the most accomplished 18-year-olds in the nation. Jeffrey was competing not only with other lit. club presidents but with virtually thousands of student-government presidents—and with young musicians who may have been selected for orchestras on the state or even national level. Sure, his grades and scores were excellent, but at top colleges, that's simply expected—not special.

Sadly, many high schoolers have their hearts set on only the Ivy League (or equivalent) institutions, and they believe that, if they do everything right, they'll get there. At this rarefied level, however, the outcome can be unpredictable. Jen and Jan, for example, were good pals and friendly competitors since grammar school. Jen was admitted to Brown, but not Wesleyan; Jan got into Wesleyan, but not Brown. Go figure.

If your son is an outstanding student and has other strengths and successes on his record, he should certainly be encouraged to apply to the most selective schools, if he wants to. He should, however, also be encouraged to seek out those other colleges that may be a tad less competitive but might meet his needs as well as the Ivies will—if not even better.

Major Dilemmas

Of course, in choosing a college, academic offerings should be a key consideration. Yet, one common misconception (particularly among parents) is that a student must have a major in mind before applying. Too often, high-school seniors are pushed into picking a direction before they are ready. Many simply have no idea of what they want to do, and even those with minds made up should have the freedom to change them. Ideally, college is a time when teenagers are exposed to new ideas and career options, and it's not surprising that the number of transfer students climbs every year, as would-be doctors become museum curators or physicists turn to film studies.

➤ **THE GOOD NEWS:** Many successful graduate-school applicants and Ph.D. recipients selected their major fields after nearly two (or even three) years of experimentation.

➤ **THE BAD NEWS:** Universities (and some colleges) may insist that students apply to specific "schools," departments, or programs. Admission to some areas is quite competitive, while others are scarcely selective at all. Years ago, canny candidates figured out that at many institutions it was wise to apply to undersubscribed departments and then to switch to the popular ones, once admitted. Nowadays, however, that little maneuver can backfire. Such an "internal transfer" may be difficult. Always ask admission officials what a change of intended major will entail; don't expect to pull the wool over their eyes with the old "bait-and-switch" trick. Counting on an internal transfer is a dangerous game; hoping for one may make sense.

Another typical parental problem is the belief that if Junior does have a field in mind, it's the "wrong" one—that philosophy majors or classics majors aren't employable; that only areas like physical therapy, architecture, or computer science will evolve into jobs. In Arthur's family, though, the shoe was on the other foot. He hoped his son Joshua would follow in his footsteps to a small, prestigious liberal-arts college, but Josh would only consider business schools. "My generation doesn't have the luxury of experimentation that yours did," he told his disappointed dad. Fear not. Many studies show that college majors have only limited ties to career selection and success. Law schools love liberal-arts grads; advertising execs may have biology backgrounds.

Moreover, at most colleges, a major takes up only a third—or fewer—of the total number of courses that students elect over four years. Astronomers have time to take theater and dance; pharmacists study Shakespeare; social workers may learn Swedish. "I have been in both liberal-arts environments and in large state universities that offer programs like business, engineering, and agriculture," explains Bill Wright-Swadel, Director of Career Services at Harvard University, "and I've seen some students choose a major because it fits with a life goal that they pursue following graduation, while others choose a wide range of careers that their major does not predict at all. Commonly, *other* experiences like studying abroad, internships, and extracurricular activities may be more likely than the major to influence the first job choice after college."

As you identify target schools, you should certainly aim for those with academic offerings in fields that your child enjoys—or wants to try. Even students who haven't made major decisions are bound to know of *something* that intrigues them and which warrants a closer look (and, if not, it may be time to consider postponing college altogether). If you and your child have differing opinions, state your case and then back off. It's fine to remind an aspiring engineer that she hated math and physics or to tell a diplomat-to-be that he dropped both French and German. But, as you read in Chapter 1, you must listen to your child's voice and honor your child's choices.

Asking Around

Don't underrate the rumor mill when it comes to getting suggestions for target schools. Ask not only guidance counselors and teachers, but also your boss or your baby-sitter, your daughter's tennis coach or your son's scout leader. Anyone who's been to college or has sent a child to one, whose interests you share or whose opinions you respect, is fair game. "Why did Molly pick Barnard over Bennington?" "What does Don like about DePaul?" "How are the dorms at Denison?" "…the food at Fairfield?" "…the chemistry classes at Colby?" Other parents, especially, love to share war stories about the admission process (and what they'd do differently if they got to do it again), so take advantage of an insider's experience.

And listen to the scuttlebutt. Your hairdresser's niece is doing an internship at Ithaca; your neighbor's nephew at St. Lawrence just spent a semester in Nairobi; your aerobics instructor got a scholarship to Bard. It's an excellent way to familiarize yourself with lesser-known colleges and unusual opportunities, and if a school sounds good, put it on the long list.

Something Old, Something New

The majority of all applicants eventually end up at colleges that they had already heard of *before* beginning the search process—through siblings or schoolmates, through reputation or location or, perhaps, by virtue of a stellar sports team. Of course, choosing an institution simply because last year's class president or next year's NBA first-round draft choice goes there can be a mistake if the school has little to offer *your* child. Yet such subjective factors do play a part in decision-making and aren't necessarily bad. Having a "good feel" about a place to start out with is an important initial step, as long as it's not the *only* step. The best matches are made when students (and parents) spend time snooping beneath the surface of a school; so put the "feel good" places on the list and then look further.

The Love Connection

In Megan's mind, choosing a college was easy. She just waited to see where her boyfriend planned to go and followed suit. Her parents were perturbed. Meg was a far better student than her boyfriend and would be limiting herself to less selective schools. They actually liked Meg's beau but questioned the wisdom of getting tied down at 18.

As parents, you may have to expect that some schools will land on a target list only because they're where a heartthrob is heading. Our advice? Stay cool, for starters. Once your child has taken a closer look, these colleges may end up on the cutting-room floor. If not, and you see your child courting disaster, then you must say so. If the beloved is bad news, if the relationship means abandoning long-held goals, then you have to point this out carefully but insistently. Sometimes, it's what children actually hope to hear. They realize themselves that it's time to go separate ways. But breaking up, as we all know, is hard to do. A push from Mom or Dad is sometimes what's needed to help a child make the choice that he or she really *wants* to make.

Yet, be assured that a surprising number of love connections do work out—one way or another. Meg (and her beloved) went to a college where she was at the top of her class, doing research with a professor as a freshman. The boyfriend, however, was history by mid-terms, and Megan—armed with a 4.0 average—had no trouble transferring to a more competitive college the following fall. But she still won't let Mom and Dad say, "We told you so." "It was a good learning experience for me," is the most Meg will concede. "In the future I won't be so quick to let someone else dictate my plans," she explains, "and the confidence I developed from being a star student stayed with me even after I transferred."

Religious Differences

Since many colleges and universities have a religious affiliation, it's important to evaluate where this fits into college plans. For a student with strong religious beliefs, a school where many others share these views may be a wise choice.

Conflicts may erupt when parents insist that an unwilling child must choose a sectarian school, yet, sometimes the opposite is true. Patti, a member of the Church of Jesus Christ of Latter-day Saints, wanted to attend Brigham Young University with a majority of students from similar backgrounds. Her family, however, prevailed upon her to experience a more diverse community.

When considering an affiliated institution, it is important to be aware of special requirements (e.g., religion classes or mandatory chapel) and rules or restrictions. Don't summarily dismiss a school because its religious orientation is different from your own. Ask admission officials what percentage of students on campus practice the prevalent faith. How well are "outsiders" accepted? What activities and attitudes are affected by the affiliation? Moreover, a college may label itself "nonsectarian" and still have a population of predominantly one faith, so many of the same issues will apply there, too. Reading student newspapers can be an especially useful way to put your finger on the pulse of a campus climate.

Q: What special considerations are there—if any—for students of color (or their parents)?

A: Be aware that some colleges do more to recruit "minority" candidates than they do to retain them, and it's important for prospective students to get a sense of what campus life will be like *after* they enroll.

Deborah Wright, former dean of admission at Simmons College in Boston, cautions students of color to get beyond the statistical answers and to probe into the attitude and "feel" of the campus. She counsels students to ask, "How involved are students of color in campus life? Are they running for office? Are they resident advisors? Are they active in a variety of student activities (and not just the Black Student Association, etc.)? Are they contributing to the community as a whole? Is it an inclusive or an exclusive community?"

Admission offices can give you the names of students of color to contact, if you need them. While these individuals are likely to be "ringers" who speak well of their school, they also tend to be those who are articulate and knowledgeable about the institution. In addition, admission offices commonly have publications and other information that is directed at minority students. If you're interested, just ask.

Continues

Continued

Of course, the questions and needs of students of color are wide-ranging and are often influenced by differences in socioeconomic and educational background, by gender and by rural or urban upbringing, among other distinctions. You should feel free to inquire about *your* specific concerns, such as the graduation rate of students of color, special scholarship opportunities, campus organizations, multicultural courses or programs, whether there have been racially motivated incidents (and how they have been handled), etc. Most admission counselors can answer your questions. You may, however, be referred to a staff member in charge of minority admission or to someone else on campus. You might want to also ask college officials and high-school guidance personnel about additional publications and events that are sponsored by organizations like the New England Consortium of Black Admissions Counselors (actually a misnomer—it serves other students of color, as well).

African-American families may also want to explore one of the more than 100 historically black U.S. colleges. An important advantage of attending such a school is the opportunity to emulate successful role models. For example, writer Toni Morrison and former Supreme Court Justice Thurgood Marshall are both Howard University alums. Similarly, tribal colleges have been established on or near Indian reservations and offer undergraduate and graduate degree programs that help preserve Native American culture.

Even if an entire college career at such an institution doesn't seem like the right choice, your child may want to consider an exchange program (or even a transfer).

IV. Using Publications

➤ **THE GOOD NEWS:** Publications provide an excellent way to further investigate target colleges and to add new schools to a list.

➤ **THE BAD NEWS**: The amount of propaganda that besieges the college-bound today is mind boggling, and it's important to have a handle on how to use it and when to take it with a *block* of salt. It's also helpful to understand the different types of publications you'll encounter.

- *Search Pieces* are short brochures that admission folks call "throwaways" among themselves. And for good reason. Gazillions of these teasers are sent out to high schoolers as a result of the "Student Search," which identifies prospective applicants from information provided on standardized admission test registration forms. (More on this in Chapter 3.) Colleges tell "Search" what qualities they're seeking (e.g., women from Wyoming; Native American applicants; anyone with scores above 1,300; anyone who's breathing…) and Search responds with a list (names and addresses; not specific test scores). Soon your mailbox is swollen with pithy pamphlets from all sorts of institutions. "At first I was flattered," recalls Gina, a recent Oberlin grad. "I thought that these colleges especially wanted *me*. Then I found out that everyone was getting the same stuff, or similar."

Search pieces are invitations to investigate or apply; not guarantees of acceptance. They *are* worth a second look and can, indeed, introduce you to colleges you hadn't previously heard of or considered. (Make sure to return reply cards if you want more information.) Keep in mind, however, that many are created by marketing mavens who know more about advertising than they do about education. The slick results are designed to entice teenagers and tend to make all schools—from Hiram to Hamilton; from Florida State to Bismarck State—seem strikingly alike. All boast of "caring, sharing faculty," "fine facilities," and "a place to learn and grow." Sound familiar? So, let the teasers whet your appetite, then turn to a guidebook (see below) or a guidance counselor, a current student or a recent alum, to get another angle.

- *Viewbooks,* commonly confused with *catalogs,* are glossy magazine-style publications, like search pieces, only longer. They're usually full of color pictures and often offer upbeat anecdotal information about grateful students who have been piloted to prosperity by the institution in question, along with profiles of those caring, sharing teachers who have sacrificed lucrative high-tech careers to lovingly mold young minds. Viewbooks can also be valuable exploration tools for readers who are sufficiently astute and cynical to corroborate their lavish claims through other sources.

- *Catalogs* are book-like bulletins that list and briefly describe course offerings, academic programs, admission and graduation requirements, tuition and fees, etc. More functional than folksy, catalogs are aimed at a school's students and staff, not specifically at applicants, but are indispensable to your decision-making.

Typically, after first contacting a college to request information, your child will receive a search piece or viewbook. You may find that other materials (e.g., catalog, application) will follow automatically.

If not, should the school seem promising, then phone (or write) and ask to have them sent. (If your child is aiming for a particular department within a university—e.g., nursing, agriculture—be sure to say so. Some such "schools" publish separate literature.) High-school guidance offices and public libraries are often a good place to find catalogs, too, though some may be a bit out of date.

As colleges today compete for candidates, literature seems to be among their growing arsenals. Many schools now produce myriad specialized brochures on topics ranging from science departments to campus security; from the career counseling office to the crew team. If a search piece or viewbook doesn't list additional brochure options, ask the admission office what's available. While you may feel that you'll drown in the deluge that follows, it could end up being the biochemistry booklet or the baseball brochure that really gets your child fired up about a college.

- *General Guidebooks* are sold in most bookstores and list facts and figures on nearly every institution in the country. Academic offerings, admission deadlines, acceptance rates, test-score ranges, student activities, and so on can be seen at a glance. No home should be without one. Look for titles like *Lovejoy's College Guide;* or The College Board's *The College Handbook. Barron's Compact Guide to Colleges* fits right in a purse or pocket (well, a *large* purse or pocket) and is easier to schlep from campus to campus than the megatomes. General guidebooks are updated regularly, but never take them as gospel, especially where admission requirements and deadlines are concerned.

  There are also some fun-to-read guidebooks around that are perfect for the bathroom bookrack. These tend to fall short on hard-core facts but offer entertaining tips about hot profs and campus hangouts, popular courses, parties, and student stereotypes. *The College Finder* by Steven R. Antonoff (Ballantine Books) and *The Ultimate College Shopper's Guide* by Heather Evans and Deidre Sullivan (Addison Wesley) are similar manuals that provide list after list of colleges in diverse and often amusing categories, from "schools that graduate at least 90 percent of entering freshmen" to "campuses where movies were filmed" to schools with Pizza Huts on campus, with racquetball scholarships, windsurfing programs, or top-rated marching bands. (Remember that quiz question on what your child can't live without?)

And speaking of lists, magazines everywhere are coming out with their college hit parades, from *U.S. News and World Report*'s best *colleges* to *Kiplinger*'s best *buys*. Admission officials and guidance counselors are, for the most part, up in arms over such insistence on comparing colleges as if they were cars or clock radios and fanning the flames of competition among parents and student status seekers. "The reason that high-school counselors and college people are so upset is because these rankings interfere with the counseling process that is so important in making the right match between a student and an institution," maintains Smith College administrator B. Ann Wright. In lambasting a *Money Magazine* rating where Smith was erroneously footnoted as a predominantly black institution, Wright noted, "They throw all the data in and they crunch the numbers, and whatever comes out they print without regard to the intuitive understanding of what really should be involved at all." Magazine lists should be kept in perspective. After all, the *Motor Trend* "Car of the Year," may not be the one you want or need, and you may not even fit comfortably in its driver's seat.

V. Using Computers

In some families, Mom or Dad is the computer whiz. In some, only the kids know where the "on" switch is, and, in others, there is little or no computer access at all.

➤ **THE GOOD NEWS:** Thanks to modern technology, those with even rudimentary computer skills can "visit" target colleges, correspond with admission offices, students, and instructors, check out library holdings and syllabi, and access multimegabytes of data and details in minutes. Families without computers in their homes can often get online at public libraries or in high-school guidance offices or computer centers.

➤ **THE BAD NEWS:** There is now so much information readily available via computer that an already formidable process can become even more overwhelming. How much time do busy high-school seniors (or their parents) really have to e-mail prospective profs at target colleges, digest menus at a dozen dining halls, or take part in online chat sessions with dorm advisors and debate-club presidents? And a student who gets lost in cyberspace may not earn the grades that first-choice colleges expect.

It would take an entire book to discuss all of the ways to use computers to help your child choose and apply to colleges (and if you want such a book, check out The College Board's *Internet Guide for College-Bound Students* by Kenneth E. Hartman). Below, however, are some suggestions to follow and places to start. Keep in mind that e-mail and World Wide Web addresses can change. Those listed here were accurate when this book went to press.

Home Pages and Web Sites

Many colleges and universities now have their own World Wide Web sites that can be helpful when choosing and exploring target colleges. From an institution's home page, you are sure to be able to "link" to information that might otherwise take weeks to arrive in the mail: admission requirements, course descriptions, enrollment statistics, etc. Most Web sites provide a "tour" of campus, access to student (and often faculty and staff) publications, information about alumni, etc. Many college Web sites also include lists of student organizations and, sometimes, links to the organization's home page. It's not uncommon for Web sites to list e-mail addresses for the office of admission, academic departments, student organization leaders, etc.

One private school college counselor tells the story of a student from Saudi Arabia who was at odds with his father about his first-choice college. The son wanted the University of Rochester. Dad was pushing for Boston University, which he felt would offer more opportunities to be with other Arab undergraduates and to practice the Islamic faith. The son, however, had no trouble convincing Dad to come around once he accessed the U. of R.'s home page. From there he found links to information for Muslim students that even included menu offerings and prayer schedules.

While a college's home page usually features a pretty campus picture and some of the same statistics found in general guidebooks, once you go beyond it, you'll be getting closer to the institution's real flavor. Student-newspaper headlines, sports-team highlights, fraternity and sorority happenings, local weather reports, and so on all reveal a bit about a place's personality. In addition, you may find links to departmental and faculty home pages that include news about specific courses and even syllabi. Student home pages are often accessible, too. These are likely to be entertaining—albeit rarely objective—looks at a college and its community.

Home-page addresses can be found in viewbooks (and other admission-office propaganda), in many general guidebooks, by doing a "search" on the Web using the college or university name, by calling admission offices, or by accessing one of the numerous sites that provide lists of thousands of institutions and direct links to their home pages.

Try these:

- Christina DeMello Search (www.mit.edu:8001/people/cdemello/univ.html)

  or

- Yahoo Search (www.yahoo.com/Regional/Countries/United_States/Education/Colleges_and_Universities/)

Matches Made in Cyberspace

There are also a number of Web sites that students can use to help find colleges with particular traits (e.g., a Slavic studies department; an enrollment under 1,000; a location in the Southwest, etc.). Your child enters specific interests and aims, and the computer spits back target schools. This is a good way to add new possibilities to the list, but, like computer dating, don't trust a machine to decide what really turns a person on. Moreover, computer-generated lists are rarely complete. Never eliminate a college just because it didn't show up in a cybersearch.

The Web sites listed below are among those that provide search services. Most offer other features, too, such as bulletin boards and chat lines, career and major data, and even off-to-college packing tips for when all of this is over (and, yes, the day *will* come).

- College Board Online (www.collegeboard.org). Click on "Students and Parents" when you reach the home page to avoid being mired in details designed for admission officials and guidance counselors. From this site, students can register for SATs, tackle the SAT "Question of the Day," find appropriate scholarships, etc.

- CollegeEdge (www.collegeedge.com). Site highlights include a forum where college-bound students can chat with their peers. (See "Talk is Cheap," below.)

- College View (www.collegeview.com). Numerous features include the opportunity to e-mail admission questions directly to "experts."

- Peterson's Education and Career Center (www.petersons.com). There's a keyword search (e.g., "golf"), as well as application essay tips and more.

- The Princeton Review (www.review.com). The "Counselor-O-Matic" helps students determine where they'll get in. (No guarantees, of course, but it's fun.)

Q&A

Q: Won't all these online searches and other services cost us as much as a college education?

A: Don't worry, most of these services offer free advice—although sometimes you get what you pay for. Typically, it's the subscribing colleges and universities that assume the costs of having their names and descriptions (and, sometimes, applications) included at Web sites. Often, site sponsors (e.g., The Princeton Review and Kaplan) hope that students will be enticed to sign up for their courses, software, books, and other products after checking out the freebies on the Web. Your child will have to have a credit card handy when registering for tests online or for applying to some colleges electronically.

If, however, you are paying for Internet access by the hour, your kid could run up quite a tab. Consider, instead, electing flat-rate charges (usually about $10 to $20 per month) while the college heat is on. If you're already using one of the major Internet service providers, you can get your money's worth by checking out their offerings for the college-bound. America Online subscribers, for instance, can click on keyword "College Board" or get testing tips at keyword "Kaplan."

The biggest cost to college applicants is likely to be their time. There's a lot of college-related information on the Internet that's more entertaining than it is essential.

Talk Is Cheap

If your child is a regular Internet user, chances are, he or she has already found ways to "talk" with peers via chat rooms and bulletin boards. Some of these are designed specifically for college-related topics. At the CollegeEdge Web site, for example, recent "forums" raised questions that included: "What are good schools for drama?" "Should I pick Rhodes College or Wake Forest?" and "Who knows about life at Simmons?"

At www.dejanews.com you or your child can search for news groups where your questions can be posted. (Just type in "college admission" and the computer will seek out appropriate discussions.)

Keep in mind, of course, that encouraging such behavior is tantamount to giving a teenager license to spend even *more* time than usual on the telephone. Remember, too, that many of the heard-it-through-the-grapevine responses espoused via Internet will be subjective ("My sister's boyfriend loves Bowdoin") or, in some cases, downright inaccurate.

E-mail is another way to communicate with college officials and students. If addresses (for administrators, faculty, student-organization leaders, etc.) aren't available at a school's Web site, try calling the office of admission and asking. ("Could you please give me the e-mail address of a student majoring in art history" or "…a freshman living in Parker Hall," "…a faculty member in the chemistry department," etc.) When you can't get to campus, some of the questions listed in Chapter 4 may also be asked electronically. Again, the danger here is that students (or parents) can spend a lot of time gathering information that is very subjective and not always representative of the real scoop at target schools.

Et Cetera

As you continue to read this book, you'll learn other ways computers can be part of the college search. For example, in Chapter 3 you'll find out how to register for standardized tests and answer practice questions online. In Chapter 4, you'll make "virtual visits" to campus. In Chapter 5, you can learn how to determine your financial-aid eligibility and locate scholarship sources, and in Chapter 6, you'll see that there are a number of ways to apply to colleges online. Some school home pages even have direct links to electronic applications.

How much use is made of these options will depend largely on your child's computer access and interest level. And, for those of you—like us— who were born when Howdy Doody was considered a technological marvel, rest assured that it's still perfectly possible to complete the entire college admission process without ever touching a keyboard.

VI. Comparing and Contrasting

So what do you do when your pile of propaganda starts to resemble the Sears Tower? First, put it all in one place. If you haven't done so already, designate a specific and out-of-the-way spot for all of the books and forms that will be multiplying over the months to come. (You haven't known true desperation until your child loses an application on the eve of its due date!)

Next, get more. Yes, for every college on your growing target list, a letter (or e-mail) should be sent or a phone call made to the office of admission requesting viewbooks, catalogs, and special interest publications. It can take several weeks for literature to arrive, and it's helpful to have it in hand before interview appointments are scheduled—so get going.

As you and your child sort through your publications pyramid, save those (whether solicited or not) from colleges that seem appealing— recycle the rest. (Super-organized applicants start a file for each college they're considering. It's a handy spot for catalogs, viewbooks, correspondence, etc.)

Now, turn to a general guidebook for some cold, hard facts that may confirm—or refute—the pretty pictures and flowery prose. Do you want a diverse community? "Politically correct" brochure photos (often staged for recruitment reasons) can be misleading. Guidebooks will give enrollment breakdowns such as minority populations and in-state residents. Does your child expect to live on campus? Get housing options and availability from the guides.

Check also for special features such as study-abroad opportunities, cross-registration with nearby colleges, pass/fail plans (great for those who are timid when trying new turf), and ROTC. "Honors programs" are a good way for outstanding students to find each other at a large university. Accelerated programs, like the one offered by Coe College in Iowa, enable students to earn a bachelor's degree in just three years (a good money-saver for Mom and Dad). Programs like Syracuse University's 3-2 engineering and M.B.A. options allow participants to whiz through undergrad *and* grad school in five years. "Student Life" sections of guidebooks include social ambiance, extracurricular activities and, often, telling statistics (e.g., how many students join sororities or participate in organized athletics).

Better yet, if you have the time and opportunity, go beyond the guidebooks and ask students at target schools how things *really* work. Whether you're visiting on campus or chatting in person, by telephone, or e-mail, the "Questions for Students" in Chapter 4 may give you some ideas of what to ask. (But beware—no single individual can speak for the experiences of an entire student body.)

While you've got your noses in the general guidebook—or your fingers on the computer keys—try to pick out new places to add to the target list. For instance, if Junior is keen on California, what unfamiliar entries sound like possibilities? Check out Claremont McKenna or Occidental. Guidebooks are usually cross-referenced by state and size and selectivity—sometimes by academic offerings. Look for priority categories and see what clicks. The World Wide Web can help you to conduct searches by major, location, etc., despite the limitations discussed above in "Using Computers."

Take out the questionnaires you completed in Chapter 1. What about those things your child can't live without? At which target colleges will you find them? In what other ways do target schools live up to the dreams of "Fantasy State?" Above all, look carefully at selectivity ratings and freshman profiles to gauge your child's chance of admission. (See "Reach or Realistic?" earlier in this chapter.)

Sooner or later, some schools are going to call out to your son or daughter (and/or to you), while others will start to pale. Go back to the "College Bible," that notebook where the target list was born. Encourage your child to use its pages to make an "Exploration Sheet" for every school that is still in the running. Make sure that one page is labeled (at the top) for all schools still being considered. Now, add each mailing address and phone number (and e-mail address, if appropriate), followed by "Dates to Remember" (deadlines, interview appointments). Below that, make two columns: one for "pros" (e.g., marine biology department; internship program; near Aunt Elaine) and one for cons (e.g., too big or expensive; foreign language requirement; near Aunt Elaine). Save the rest of the page (and the reverse side, if needed) for contact records and notes (e.g., "Oct. 15: spoke to Ms. Muldoon, asst. dean of admission. She said okay to take SAT II in Jan."). This format, of course, isn't carved in stone (and high-tech types may prefer to store information in a computer) but you will find that life is simpler and more pleasant when all your data and doodles are kept together.

VII. Getting Guidance: Public-School and Private-School Counselors

Typical public-school counselors handle hundreds of students with wide-ranging needs. Counselors must be equally informed about the Armed Forces and the Big Ten, music conservatories and hair-styling academies. They deal with scholarship opportunities and unplanned pregnancies, suicide prevention, and drug dependency—all on any given morning.

➤ **THE GOOD NEWS:** Many are superheroes. They do all of it well.

➤ **THE BAD NEWS:** Unfortunately, due to budget cuts, some high schools have no guidance counselors at all, and some have too few who carry unrealistic loads (and a handful are just downright inept).

Even in private schools, where loads are lighter and may be limited to admission advising alone, the situation can be far from ideal. Here, college counselors range from among the very best in the business to inexperienced, untrained "generalists" who may be teaching eighth-grade English and sophomore Spanish at the same time. Some private-school counselors face pressure from administrators who insist that a list of acceptances to prestige colleges is the most important "report card" by which their institution will be judged, and from parents who insinuate that a thumbs-up from a big-name school is the reward they deserve for years of tuition bills.

No matter where your child goes to school, it is up to *you* to evaluate the strengths and weaknesses of the available guidance counseling and to participate in the admission process.

Q&A

Q: What can parents do to get the most from school counselors?

A: Have realistic expectations about what is available to you and your child through the guidance counselor. If the counselor is not willing or able to go further than shepherding students through standardized-test registration and distributing federal financial-aid forms, you will have to take an aggressive role in the college search. If, on the other hand, the guidance counselor...

- offers thorough suggestions about college selection, application completion, and deadlines;

- is well-informed about a range of institutions, and urges students (and parents) to explore those they may not have heard of or considered;

- gives a realistic assessment of acceptance but doesn't discourage application to "dream" schools; and

- provides thorough financial-aid information, and doesn't insist that expensive colleges are only for rich folks; then

you can relax and take a back seat. "Travis had planned to apply to several state colleges," says his mother, Joanne. "His father and I knew little about other options ourselves, but the school counselor pointed out two quite selective colleges that had academic-merit aid programs. She called both to see if Travis' grades and test scores would make him a contender, and the answer was yes. She also helped him to do the required paperwork. I'd been told in advance by other parents that we'd lucked out and gotten the best counselor at the high school, and she certainly lived up to those expectations."

John, the father of another high-school graduate, realizes now that he assumed his daughter's counselor would be taking a more active role than she did. "Perhaps because Kate was in a private school," he reflects, "I expected her counselor to make suggestions about where Kate should attend college and then monitor the process to be sure that deadlines were being met. With hindsight, I'd sit down with the counselor at the start and outline the responsibilities each of us would have. For example, someone has to play the 'heavy' to make sure that the 17-year-old is getting everything completed on schedule. Someone should be reading the essays to see if they say what they should, and in an interesting way. Someone has to be deciding which schools should stay on the list and which shouldn't. I think the whole thing would have worked better for us if each of our roles and duties had been clearer from the outset."

Because guidance counselors' abilities and availability vary so widely, it's up to you, the parents, to determine how much support and useful information you will be getting.

- **Don't play hooky on Parents' Night.** Sure, the coffee is lousy and you'll have to endure endless questions from other parents who are far more panicked than you are, but, even in the fanciest high schools, counselors simply do not have the time to repeat general information to everyone who stayed home to watch "Seinfeld."

- **Schedule a conference** if you feel you need one. While this is pro-tocol at most private schools, at public schools it's often only for those who take the initiative. "I welcome parent appointments," notes Sam Blair, chairman of the guidance department at Little Rock Central High School in Arkansas, "but even good schools like mine rarely have the staff to routinely contact every parent. It makes us awfully nervous not to have direct parent contact, but with six counselors handling over 300 10th- through 12th-graders each, we serve too many masters. The parents we see are the ones who call us." Even if you don't arrange a conference, visit the guidance office to find out what resources are available: catalogs, guide books, computer software, etc.

- **Ask for a school profile.** When sending transcripts to college admission offices, guidance staff members enclose a brief "school profile" that details the curriculum available and explains the grading system at your child's high school. Profiles also commonly include information about the community in which the high school is located, the percentage of students who go on to college, where they go, etc. By reading through your child's school profile, you will learn what information admission offices will receive—and what they won't. For example, if "British Literature" is an Advanced Placement course at your child's school, is that clearly stated on the profile?

Continues

45

Continued

- **Ask your counselor to alert colleges to situations that may not be obvious from a transcript.** If a simple-sounding course ("The Alphabet from A to Z") is really one of the toughest on the roster, admission offices won't figure it out for themselves. If Mr. Snurd, the chemistry teacher, is convinced that "C" is a to-die-for grade, the counselor should be certain to put Brian's "B-" in perspective for Princeton.

- **Alert your counselor to situations that he or she might not be aware of that affect your child's school performance.** The more candid you can be with your counselor about a messy divorce, substance-abuse issues, and other home-grown problems that your child may be struggling with, the better the counselor can present your child's transcripts to target colleges.

- **Don't be a pain in the you-know-what.** Use good judgment to decide how often to contact guidance counselors. Although it is up to you to call counselors with questions or concerns (and don't wait by the phone for them to call you), do be sensitive to their unwieldy work loads. If you think you require a symbiotic relationship with a counselor, consider hiring an independent consultant. (See below.)

The other fine line that parents must tread is in recognizing that good guidance counselors really do know their stuff. Don't expect them to spin straw into gold. One of the worst things you can do to sabotage the entire process and to undermine your child's esteem is to insist on an unrealistic list of target schools. Be open to suggestions from the counselor, even if Harvard and Yale aren't on the list.

VIII. Who Are Independent Counselors...and How Do You Know if You Need One?

Also called "Independent Educational Consultants" (or various permutations of the same), these individuals offer private, in-depth, college admission advice to students and their families...for a fee.

➤ **THE GOOD NEWS:** "Parents want unlimited and instantaneous access to information, and we provide that," maintains Jane Gutman, a Los Angeles independent educational consultant. "Even private-school counselors have other duties and can't always be available. Our clients can pick up the phone any time."

46

➤ **THE BAD NEWS:** "Independents" are pricey. Top-of-the-liners charge about $3000 for conducting a college search. Even on the "low" end, expect to shell out close to $800. Many do offer pro bono work, but often only to those in dire straits. "The students who most need outside help—those in public schools where counseling budgets have been severely cut back or curtailed—are usually the ones who can't afford us," admits Gutman. The bulk of her clients attend private schools.

Independent counselors offer advice, not inside tracks to highly selective schools. Joan Dorman Davis, who served the Seattle area as an independent counselor for nearly two decades, spoke for many of her colleagues when she explained her role several years ago. "Sure, many of my clients apply—and are admitted—to the handful of colleges that are the toughest to get into," said Davis, who charged about $1000, "but my job is broader than that. I help protect kids from heartbreak, from operating under the assumption that top grades, test scores, and extracurriculars mean certain admission everywhere. I'm like a big, red stop sign, constantly saying, 'Yes, you're good, but what if you don't make it? Let's see what else is out there.' Some of my most satisfied clients have gone to colleges I introduced them to."

Q: How does one pick a qualified consultant?

A: "Choose your independent consultant the way you would pick a physician or a lawyer," suggests Bill Risley, a Connecticut-based private educational consultant with a coast-to-coast clientele. "Ask around; get referrals from other parents." If you're stuck for leads, the **Independent Educational Consultants Association** (4085 Chain Bridge Road, Suite 401, Fairfax, VA 22030; phone: 703/591-4850; fax: 703/591-4860) is a good place to start. They will send you a free directory of member counselors nationwide.

"But," cautions Risley, "there are an awful lot of tinkerers and moonlighters out there. Even professional association membership doesn't assure quality. Ask for references and check them out thoroughly. Talk to prospective consultants before signing on to make certain that the chemistry is right." Following are other suggestions from Risley for picking a pro:

Continues

47

Continued

- **What related job experience have they had?** The best independent consultants have often done time as college admission officers and high-school guidance counselors. Others claim qualifications as questionable as "I got both my kids into Brown."

- **How often and extensively do they visit campuses?** Risley claims to troop through 40 to 60 schools each year, not only seeing admission offices and facilities, but haunting student hangouts to get the real scoop from insiders.

- **How else do they stay current?** Does the counselor attend meetings of the National Association of College Admission Counselors (NACAC) or other professional groups? What else does he or she do to keep up with changing trends in the business?

- **What is their specialty?** Educational consultants often offer wide-ranging services. If you ask them for their area of expertise, they'll ask you what you're after. Testing for a dyslexic third grader? Vocational training for a mentally handicapped teen? You want it? They've got it. Some consultants, especially in urban areas, focus on private elementary school or high-school placement. Make sure the expert you hire claims to be a *college* specialist.

- **What promises do they make?** Good counselors give guidance, not guarantees; they make matches, not miracles, and they won't fill out your child's application form or write his essay, because they're smart enough to realize that colleges will be onto them if they do.

CHAPTER 3

Testing, Testing

"We survived sleep-away summer camps and cheerleading try-outs, glasses, braces, drivers' ed, and the purple-haired prom-date-from-hell. But nothing upset the family equilibrium more than the day that Daria received her SAT scores."

"Miles agreed to take the tests because the guidance counselor says he's supposed to, but he insists he's not even going to try to do well and won't apply to any schools that require them. I think he's limiting his options, but he refuses to listen. I also think that he's terrified, and he is immunizing himself—and us—against disappointment."

"We had been warned to play the SAT thing real cool. I figured that if I didn't make a big deal about it, then Kevin wouldn't get all tied up in knots either. Wrong! He was putting all sorts of pressure on himself, and when I tried to tell him to relax, that it was only a test, he said, 'Get a life, Mom.'"

Every year, about two million high schoolers take SAT exams and almost as many take ACTs. Some take both. By the time a student arrives at an authorized test site, clutching sharpened number-2 pencils in sweaty palms, most families have already experienced the tension and apprehension, the myths and misgivings that the notorious process produces.

Decades ago, when standardized entrance testing was conceived, one goal was to create a more democratic system so that candidates from little-known public high schools could compete with those from the celebrated academies where a headmaster's handshake or the proper pedigree was a passport to a big-name college career. Ironically, however, what was once intended to *open* doors is now capable of *shutting* them—on many bright, ambitious applicants whose numbers alone aren't up to snuff.

Through all of the hopes and heartaches you have shared with your child—basketball playoffs or ballet recitals, student-council elections or state orchestra selections—you have undoubtedly learned that parenthood hardly grants you the power to shield those you love from humankind's incessant reminders of inequalities and insufficiencies. So, too, may the SAT or ACT tests separate your son from his favorite cousin, your daughter from her closest friend.

There are, however, measures you can take to assure that the testing process is approached in a positive frame of mind. The pages that follow address what parents most want to know about college entrance exams. So, learn what you can about test scores and how they are used, what you can do to affect them, and what you can't. Separate rumor from reality and then…relax. After all, *you're* not the one who has to take the darn things.

I. Just What Is the SAT, Anyway?

Testing terminology can be confounding—perhaps especially so for those with older offspring who took college entrance exams before 1994. Since then—and certainly since *your* day—test names, formats, and even the scoring system have been revised.

In the "old," prerevision days, many high-school students took the PSAT/NMSQT (Preliminary Scholastic Aptitude Test/National Merit Scholarship Qualifying Test) in October of their junior year. (You may recall that before 1971 the National Merit folks had their own separate exam.) Although some format changes have been implemented, the PSAT/NMSQT is still alive and well and will be discussed, at length, below.

Next, in the spring of junior year (or the following fall) came the SAT (which once stood for "Scholastic Aptitude Test")—with separately scored verbal and mathematical components—and then, several "Achievement Tests." All of these exams were sponsored by the infamous "College Board" and created and administered by the Educational Testing Service (ETS), an enterprise based in Princeton, NJ—and with more secrets to keep than the Pentagon.

The SAT and Achievement Tests *used to* fall under the umbrella name of the "ATP" (Admissions Testing Program) which has now been relabeled "The SAT Program." This program includes:

- The SAT I: Reasoning Tests (formerly the SAT)

- The SAT II: Subject Tests (formerly Achievement Tests)

Moreover, the "A" in SAT now stands for "Assessment," not "Aptitude," a change designed to reflect increased emphasis on skills learned in school, rather than on innate abilities. But College Board bigwigs claim that, while the entire battery is *collectively* labeled the "Scholastic Assessment Tests," the "SAT" label on each *individual* exam is merely a trademark, and—like the "S" in Harry S. Truman—doesn't stand for anything at all. Confused yet? We're just getting started.

As in the past, the SAT I focuses on verbal and mathematical skills. Students receive separate scores for each of these two areas. The SAT II offers one-hour exams in subjects which include English and math as well as foreign languages, history and natural sciences.

The aim of the testing program is to assist college admission officials in comparing applicants from different educational backgrounds and to predict the applicants' academic performance in the first term of college. How well these tests fulfill these aims is a subject of ongoing and often heated debate.

Both the College Board and ETS maintain World Wide Web sites that offer a wealth of information and links to countless other sites—and even more information. Students can now sign up for tests online, tackle sample questions, request score reports, access school and college codes, etc. You'll find the Web addresses at the end of this chapter. But if you came of age when the hula hoop was king, fear not. The information available electronically is also covered in several free College Board publications. These can be easily ordered by telephone. Details are at the end of the chapter.

The PSAT/NMSQT

This is a test that is routinely administered to students in October of their junior year and is frequently a family's first brush with college admission examinations. *

The PSAT/NMSQT has several purposes:

- to serve as a practice or warm-up for subsequent SAT testing

- to give students, parents, and counselors some indication of future SAT performance

- to determine qualification for several scholarship programs discussed below

- to allow students and colleges to find each other through the Student Search Service, also discussed below

---

* *In some parts of the country, the ACT Assessment (and its preliminary test, PLAN) are administered in most schools in lieu of the SAT program. These tests will also be discussed in this chapter.*

  A growing number of schools give the PSAT (or PLAN) as early as junior high as a method of evaluating their own effectiveness—not as a college admission tool. Similarly, some programs (e.g. the Johns Hopkins Talent Search) use SAT scores to select participants. If your child has results from such tests, do your best to ignore them when you begin the college search process.

Early in your child's junior year, PSAT/NMSQT registration information (the *Student Bulletin*) should be distributed in school. The test will ordinarily be given right in your child's school, usually during a school day sometimes on a Saturday.

PSAT/NMSQT Scores

In December, scores will be mailed directly to your child's high school and distributed to students along with an explanatory booklet.

Students will receive separate scores for verbal and mathematical test components. The scores range from 20 to 80, designed to correspond to the SAT score scale of 200 to 800. Thus, by adding a zero to the PSAT scores, you will get a rough approximation of future SAT results. In 1992, average PSAT/NMSQT scores for college-bound high-school juniors were: verbal—about 41; math—about 44. In 1996, those averages were: verbal—47.5; math—48.4.

No, high-school juniors didn't simply get smarter in those four years. Instead, starting in the fall of 1994, the scoring of PSAT tests was "recentered," adding roughly 10 points to a typical student's combined math and verbal tally. SAT scores were recentered in spring 1995. Recentering is explained more thoroughly in the SAT section in this chapter.

➤ **THE GOOD NEWS:** *Colleges rarely see PSAT results and do not use them as admission criteria.* Good scores can help to take the trauma out of upcoming SAT tests. Poor scores may help identify weaknesses in time to remedy them or, at least, to take some of the sting out of sad SATs. (You will read more about SAT preparation at the end of this chapter.) PSAT scores usually improve due to what is known as "maturation." In other words, by the time the SAT I is taken, the student is more aware of what to expect, has completed more schooling, and (dearest to parental hearts) is even a tad more grown-up.

➤ **THE BAD NEWS:** When an honors student with high aspirations scores below 50 on a PSAT section (a not-so-uncommon occurrence), it is a rude awakening to parents and their progeny. While "maturation" will probably lead to a stronger SAT I performance, score improvement is unlikely to be significant enough to allow admission to the *most* competitive colleges and universities (without a huge "hook"). (See Chapter 7.)

Scholarships

Several scholarship services determine award recipients on the basis of PSAT/NMSQT junior-year results. Most well-known of these is the **National Merit Scholarship Program** (which awards prestigious recognition to top test performers and $2,000 scholarships to an elite coterie of NMS winners).

Other programs which use PSAT/NMSQT results include: the **National Achievement Scholarship Program for Outstanding Negro Students** (offering merit grants to qualified winners); the **National Hispanic Scholar Recognition Program** (which assists colleges in identifying and recruiting academically talented Hispanic students); the **National Scholarship Service and Fund for Negro Students** (which provides free college advising) and the **Telluride Association Program** (offering scholarships for summer study in the humanities and social sciences).

The Student Search Service

Students who check the appropriate box on the test registration form become fair game for colleges participating in this service. These schools—which range from renowned to obscure—ask the service to give them names of appropriate candidates who may fall into one or more of a range of categories: e.g., science majors; students from the South; Native Americans, etc. The College Board does not send scores to "Search" colleges. Some scholarship programs, in addition to those described above, also use "Search." If your child is eligible, these services will automatically notify you. ("Search" also locates students through information provided on SAT and Advanced Placement Test registration.)

PSATs and Parents

The first thing you will probably wonder is if your child should be doing something special to prepare for the PSAT/NMSQT. While there are commercial prep courses available which will be discussed at length at the end of the chapter, we recommend that students get ready for this test simply by using the sample materials and instructions that are provided in the *Student Bulletin*. Try not to make a big production about the PSAT, but if your child is interested in obtaining a test-preparation guidebook (or computer software), it's a worthy investment. Because the PSAT/NMSQT is essentially an abbreviated version of the SAT, don't feel you need to purchase material specifically designed for the shorter test.

You may need to intercede in the PSAT process if your child *wishes to try this test in grade 10.* Though most schools don't typically test sophomores, many will do so if parents prod. (The test can still be retaken the next fall. Only junior-year scores are used by the National Merit Scholarship Program.) *There is really no down side to taking a trial PSAT/NMSQT in the sophomore year.* Like the 11th-grade test, it serves as a good warm-up and an indicator of academic weaknesses—with more time left to work on those shaky spots. Frankly, we recommend it, as long as it's presented to your child as a laid-back, non-threatening option—and if Junior balks anyway, don't push.

SAT I: What Parents Really Want (and Need) to Know

Q: When and where should the SAT I be taken?

A: The SAT I: Reasoning Test is offered on Saturday mornings in October, November, December, January, March, May, and June. Arrangements can be made for those who require special accommodations due to religious beliefs or physical disabilities. See your counselor or call the all-purpose number at the end of the chapter.

The SAT I (formerly just the "SAT") and SAT II (formerly "Achievement Tests") are generally administered concurrently, so students *cannot* plan to take both on the same day.

Ideally, a student will take the SAT I test for the *first time* in May of 11th grade. This allows near maximum course work to be completed, but also leaves the June date open for the SAT II: Subject Tests. Because the summer following junior year is an excellent time to explore colleges, don't postpone testing until grade 12; scores serve as an important guide in selecting target schools. Junior-year testing also facilitates "early-decision" or "early-action" application options, which will be explained in Chapter 6.

Another important consideration in picking an initial test date is *where* the test will be administered. If possible, your child should take the test at a familiar place—his or her own high school—with its own friendly feel and smell (in many schools that means sweat socks; in others, it's chicken à la king). Some schools serve as authorized test centers for every test administration; some for selected dates only; some not at all. Your child may have to register to take tests at a nearby school. The *Registration Bulletin*, available from guidance offices or by calling the College Board, lists all tests sites and dates. Plan ahead. The *Registration Bulletin* also explains procedures, for those who live more than 75 miles from a test center, on how to change test sites or dates and on what to do if your child is ill and misses a test.

Q: How often should tests be retaken?

A: If junior-year scores are satisfactory, there is no reason to retake the test, but nearly half of all college-bound students will go for it at least once more, in the fall of their senior year. (October or November test dates are best; December will work for colleges with deadlines in January or beyond. Later test dates may mean that scores don't reach colleges in time or that parents may need to pay for pricey "Rush Reporting.") The College Board maintains that the majority of students who take the test in 11th and 12th grades will improve on the second testing, without any special coaching, showing an average growth of 15 to 20 points on both the verbal and mathematical sections. **We do not recommend taking the test more than two times, because rarely is there anything to be gained.**

➤ **THE GOOD NEWS:** If your child has taken the SAT I more than once, many colleges will consider only the best two scores (verbal and math), even if they come from different test dates. Some will use the highest total score from a single testing.

➤ **THE BAD NEWS:** Some schools use only the *most recent* scores, even if previous ones are better.

➤ **THE GOOD and/or BAD NEWS:** SAT score reports always include both new and old test scores. So, even if a 440 verbal is the one that "counts," admission officials will probably see last spring's 340. Conversely, they'll also see that a 530 math score was once a 600 and, maybe, chalk it up to an off day.

Q: How do "we" register?

A: There is hardly a more thorough reference work around than the official SAT *Registration Bulletin*. (Most guidance departments always have them; the College Board information number provides an order service, too.) A registration form and envelope will accompany it. The *Bulletin* is

Continues

55

Continued

clearly written, covers most imaginable contingencies, and will guide you or your child through filling out an otherwise intimidating form. (Make sure you also get the free companion publication called *Taking the SAT I*).

You or your child can also sign up for the SAT tests electronically by accessing either the College Board Web site (www.collegeboard.org) or the Educational Testing Service site (www.ets.org). You'll need to have a major credit card handy. Special circumstances (e.g., services for students with disabilities) cannot be accommodated online.

Following are some points to keep in mind when you begin the registration process:

- The SAT I requires a $22.50 fee paid at the time of registration.[*] Special service charges, where applicable, must be added. Guidance counselors can obtain "fee waivers" for low-income students, but only two are granted per applicant, regardless of how often the SAT I is taken. (Two SAT II waivers are also granted per applicant.)

- A Social Security number, while not required, will make score reporting and record retrieval easier and more error-proof.

- Urge your child to say "yes" to the Student Search Service (described in the PSAT section above). Again, it's an option on the registration form.

- Take advantage of Score Reports to Colleges and Scholarship Programs. The SAT fee entitles you to four "free" reports. Use them. Don't wait to see if scores are good enough, because later score reports will include all previous scores, anyway. (Exception: a child who is considering a college with no testing requirement may want to see scores before sending them to that school. Likewise, the SAT II offers a "score-choice" option, described later in this chapter. Your child may *not* want to use the free score reports for these tests.)

- Treat registration deadlines with reverence. Deadlines for "regular registration" are about five weeks before each test date. There is a "late-registration" option which buys nearly two weeks more for a $15 surcharge. Of course, the sooner you sign up, the greater your chances of getting your first-choice test site. Stragglers may be

[*] *All fees are for 1997–98. Fees may be slightly higher for New York residents.*

56

assigned to locations in unfamiliar communities or neighborhoods, and getting there alone can be enough of a "test" for one day. "Standbys" will also be admitted to tests on a space-available basis (for a $30 stand-by surcharge). For those with registration forms already on file, telephone sign-up is available for another small additional fee (plus test costs). Deadlines are the same as those for mail registration.

Prior to the test date, an "Admission Packet," which includes an "Admission Ticket," will arrive in the mail. Your child will not be admitted to the test site without this ticket and one of the forms of identification outlined in the *Registration Bulletin.* If the packet hasn't appeared at least a week before test time (or if the dog eats the admission ticket), call the College Board information number.

Q: **What is the test format?**

A: There are three scored verbal sections and three scored math sections. Two of the verbal sections are 30 minutes long, and one is a 15-minute section. Likewise, two scored math sections are 30-minute sections and one is a 15-minute section. A seventh, unscored section may be either a 30-minute verbal section or a 30-minute math section. Questions in the unscored section are being tested for use on future exams. The unscored section will not necessarily appear as the seventh section on Susie's exam and will not be identified or identifiable. At testing time, your student must treat every section as if it counts.

The verbal component of the SAT I is entirely "multiple choice" and includes sentence completion questions, analogies, and critical reading passages.

The "new" math component (as of 1994) includes not only multiple-choice and quantitative comparisons but also some questions (about 10 out of 60) for which students will produce their own answers, with no choices provided. With increased emphasis on "applied mathematics," **calculator use is permitted and encouraged.**

Questions within each section go from "easiest" to "hardest." Because all carry equal point value, students should concentrate on those they are most sure of. Those who answer only 50 to 60 percent correctly will still receive "average" (or slightly above-average) scores.

Continues

Continued

Scores are computed by totaling correct answers and then subtracting a fraction of a point for each incorrect answer. There is no gain or loss for omitted answers. Thus, **students should make "educated guesses" but never random ones.**

Including registration and break time, the entire test will take about three hours.

Q: Who knows the score...and when?

A: Approximately five weeks after the test date, scores will be mailed to your home. Your high-school guidance department and all colleges or scholarship services specified on the test registration form will also receive them. Scores are never given over the telephone.

The opening of the score envelope is an excellent time for you to practice that time-honored parental posturing known as "keeping your cool." After all, if Junior pulled down some big numbers, dancing around the dining room is still premature—he hasn't actually been accepted anywhere yet. On the other hand, if the scores are really low, then you must summon all of your Academy Award-winning abilities. Chances are, the test will be retaken, and you don't want to turn up the heat in the pressure cooker any more than it already is. Cursing or complaining on your part is only going to jeopardize your child's performance on the next test. (And not to bring up a sore point but...scores are addressed to your child, not to you. Occasionally, the Educational Testing Service receives calls from parents who can't pry test results from their kids. ETS won't tell *you* either, but a guidance counselor will probably squeal. If not, then you'll just have to work it out with Junior—or, suggests one ETS employee, off the record, "Beat 'em to the mailbox!")

In addition to the four "free" score reports (to colleges or scholarship services) that are included in each test fee, the registration form allows space for four additional reports (with a nominal charge for each, of course). If you paid properly, these reports will all be in the appropriate hands even before scores arrive at home. Extra reports can be ordered at any time. Your child will have received (and perhaps already lost!) an "Additional Report Request Form" that is mailed out with test admission tickets. Requests for extra reports are also taken by telephone (it's that same magic number at the end of the chapter). Again, there is a small charge for the phone service.

Allow five weeks after your request for these scores to reach their destinations, although, yes, for yet another extra charge, "Rush Reporting" can get *new* test scores in the mail about three weeks after tests are taken or can launch *old* scores in two working days after a telephone request is made.

Q&A

Q: What do the score reports mean?

A: Your child will receive separate scores for the verbal and math components of the SAT I test, each ranging from 200 to 800.

Each score report also includes: percentiles that compare your child's scores to those of college-bound seniors, both nationwide and in your state; a record of up to six previously taken SAT I and SAT II tests; a regurgitation of information reported on the Student Descriptive Questionnaire section of the registration form; and some rather superficial admission data provided by those colleges to which score reports were sent.

High schools and colleges receive similar report forms. College admission officials cannot tell from score reports where *other* reports have been sent.

Q&A

Q: My son is gloating that he outscored his sister on the SAT I, but we've heard that the scores were adjusted since our oldest daughter took the test eight years ago. What does that mean?

A: In June 1994, the College Board announced that the SAT I and II scoring scale would be "recentered" to increase national test score averages. Students who took the SATs in or after Spring 1995 were scored

Continues

Continued

on this new scale, which typically added about 80 points to verbal scores and about 20 to math. In other words, the same performance that once generated a verbal score of 520 will now net about a 600; the "old" math score of 530 has jumped to roughly 550.

National averages for high schoolers who took the SAT I in 1992 were: verbal—423; math—476. The 1996 averages, scored on the recentered scale, were: verbal—505; math—508. According to the College Board, the goal of the new system was to bring average scores back to the 500 mark, where they began. The insiders insist that—despite claims of critics that the whole business is a cover-up designed to compensate for downward-spiraling high schools—falling averages reflected a larger and more diverse pool of test-takers...not dumber kids.

But what's confusing for parents—many of whom took the SATs themselves and feel like it was just yesterday—is that scores that once opened doors to top-tier colleges (e.g., anything over 600) are now no longer so impressive. For instance, before recentering, fewer than 250 students per year achieved 800s on the verbal section of the test. Now 4,000-plus hit the perfect mark.

What's also confusing is that, while recentering has added points to *most* test scores, the number of points is not consistent (e.g., what was once a 270 math score is now a 290, but the old 370 has become a 420) and—here's where you'll really go nuts—many of the math scores at the high end of the scale (e.g., above 650) actually go *down* when recentered.

Test results for students who have taken the recentered SATs include the letter "R" next to numerical scores. As you and your son explore college options, make certain that you are not comparing his recentered scores with outdated figures. Some general guidebooks offer both original and recentered averages, which is especially helpful to us older folks.

Q: How do colleges use test scores?

A: Almost every college that requires standardized tests will be quick to insist that scores are *not* the most important factor in an admission decision and that the secondary school record is far more significant. While this is true in theory, it is also crucial to keep in mind that many applicants to colleges (at all levels of selectivity) have very similar high-school records and so test scores can—for better or worse—become the tie-breakers. At the most selective institutions, SAT scores are usually *far* more critical than many admission officials want to admit.

➤ **THE GOOD NEWS:** Once you have received test scores, it becomes easier to identify colleges where your child will be accepted.

➤ **THE BAD NEWS:** If your kid's scores are not at least in the ballpark at your top-choice colleges, and the youngster offers no unique talents or special circumstances (see Chapter 7), then it's time to turn your interests and efforts elsewhere. Remember that "average" SAT scores reported by colleges may be skewed by alumni children, athletes, economically disadvantaged applicants, and other "hook" cases. More representative are "middle-50-percent ranges" that lop off the top quarter and the bottom quarter of an accepted class.

Here are samples of some approximate middle-50-percent SAT I scores.[*] Pre-1995 figures are followed by recentered ones. When comparing your own child's numbers to such charts, be sure to look at recentered ranges.

SAMPLE MIDDLE-RANGE SAT SCORES

College	Verbal	Math	(R) Verbal	(R) Math
Princeton	610–710	660–750	680–760	670–770
Swarthmore	600–700	660–740	670–760	650–740
Columbia (NY)	570–690	630–730	640–750	630–730
Carleton	570–670	630–720	640–730	630–720
Duke	570–670	660–740	640–730	650–740
Notre Dame (IN)	530–630	630–720	600–690	630–720
Georgetown	550–650	590–690	620–710	600–680
U. of Virginia	520–630	610–710	600–690	610–700
Colorado Col.	520–620	570–670	600–680	580–660
U. of Michigan (Ann Arbor)	490–610	600–700	570–670	600–690
Syracuse	450–570	520–650	530–640	540–650

Continues

[*] *Sources: The Right College (6th edition, ARCO) and The College Handbook (College Board, 1997).*

SAMPLE MIDDLE-RANGE SAT SCORES *CONTINUED*

College	Verbal	Math	(R) Verbal	(R) Math
U. of Vermont	430–530	480–610	510–600	510–610
Seton Hall (NJ)	400–480	440–550	480–560	480–560
Slippery Rock U. (PA)	350–450	390–500	430–530	430–520
WV Wesleyan	370–500	410–570	450–580	450–580

As you can see, many of these ranges are broad, and an applicant may be at the low end of the verbal scale and the high end of the math—or vice versa. Just as you will use such ranges to roughly determine how your child stacks up against other applicants, so, too, will colleges use standardized test scores in several manners to see if one candidate is comparable to others. Here are some of the ways that admission offices use standardized test scores:

- **To choose among students from seemingly similar backgrounds with seemingly similar records.** The most selective schools get loads of amazing applicants, but test scores show some to be just a bit more amazing than others. Likewise, there are lots of nice "B" (and "C") students around. Standardized scores are one factor that admission officers use to make distinctions.

- **To see how top-performing students from weak or disadvantaged high schools may fare when placed with those with stronger academic backgrounds.** A valedictorian with 350 SATs could get eaten alive at a highly competitive college; a salutatorian with 500s will probably hold her own.

- **To give the benefit of the doubt to students in first-string high schools.** Admission officers recognize that there are some schools out there where Albert Einstein himself would be lucky to land a B in physics or to fall in the top decile of his senior class. SAT scores can help put such "super schools" in perspective.

- **To see how hard a student is working.** An "A" student with mediocre SATs may be viewed as a go-getter or a poor tester, but high test scores combined with middling grades suggest that the candidate is an underachiever. Most schools will favor the former.

- **To make cut-and-dried decisions.** The majority of colleges and universities are not beholden to rigid score cut-offs, but some do screen out prospects whose tests don't meet minimum requirements. Even within an institution, cut-offs may vary from "school" to "school" or from major to major. However, most institutions or departments with minimums usually check applications for special circumstances and unusual talents or offer an appeals process for those with inadequate test results.

- **To award scholarships or merit aid.** Increasingly, colleges are trying to lure top prospects with financial incentives that are based on academic ability, not need. Usually, contenders for these awards—which range from full scholarships to token grants—are identified on the basis of both school record *and* test performance. For instance, Smith's "STRIDE" program offers paid research assistantships to outstanding applicants. Only those with excellent high-school records and test scores are selected.

- **To determine athletic eligibility.** NCAA eligibility depends on test results. (See Chapter 7.)

Q: What if "our" scores are awful?

A: One of the pluses of PSATs is that they serve as a warning of SAT scores to follow. If SATs are significantly *lower* than PSAT results, then you should be concerned. Was your child ill, upset, or preoccupied on the test day? Was the score on one section of the SAT consistent with the PSAT, while the other section was not?

The College Board Question-and-Answer Service is available to all students who took the SAT I on several—but not all—of the national test dates. It can be ordered via the registration form, or for up to five months after the test, using a form that comes with the score report. The Q & A Service provides a copy of the actual test, a copy of your child's answer sheet, the correct answers, and scoring instructions. It is an excellent way to see where the screw-ups lie, to help identify recurring errors for future tests, or to ascertain if the test was scored correctly.

Continues

Continued

If the Q & A Service is not available for your child's test date, and you believe that a scoring error was made, you can request a "Hand Scoring" service for $25. There is also a "Student Answer Service" for $5. This report lists which questions your child answered correctly and incorrectly (or omitted). But, because it does not include the questions themselves nor your child's answer sheet, few test-takers find it helpful.

Of course, most unwelcome scores are *not* (unfortunately) the result of administrative slip-ups. So then what?

- **If this is the first time your child took the SAT I, he or she should plan to retake it.** Remember, the best first testing is in the spring of 11th grade; the retest should wait until the fall of 12th.

- **Consider one of the preparation options discussed in section IV of this chapter.**

- **Does your child have a diagnosed learning or physical disability?** If so, did you already take advantage of untimed tests or other special accommodations? If a disability is suspected, consider a professional evaluation before the tests are retaken.

- **Reset your sights.** To a great degree, "good" and "bad" test scores are relative. For example, a combined score of 1,200 is certainly very respectable. Yet, while in one household, it is cause for celebration; in another, it could sabotage hopes for a long-shot college. "An applicant with below 1,250 and no special connections, 'hooks,' or unusual talents is *unlikely* to get into Yale," admits Associate Director of Admission Patricia Wei. "There are simply too many applicants with similar qualifications and better tests."

If your child's test scores fall below middle range at target schools, you may be barking up the wrong ivy. The most competitive colleges will admit some applicants who don't hit 1,250, but usually these are kids with special clout. Without it, you'll need bigger numbers. There are just too many kids around who are as wonderful as yours (well, almost) and who have stronger test scores, too.

"High-reach" applications are fine, but make sure that you use SAT results to make *realistic* choices, as well. There are lots of excellent institutions that don't expect astronomical numbers.

There are also excellent institutions that don't expect any numbers at all. SATs or ACTs are optional at some well-respected schools, including those below. Good scores will work in your favor, but if you don't send them in, the colleges don't automatically assume they were horrendous (even if they were!).

Antioch (OH) (Tests are "recommended" but optional.)

Bard College (NY)

Bates College (ME)

Bowdoin College (ME)

College of the Atlantic (ME)

Franklin & Marshall (PA) (Tests are optional only for those in the top 10 percent of their high-school class.)

Hampshire College (MA)

Ohio State U. (Tests are recommended. Those without them will be given ACT upon entering, for placement purposes.)

St. John's College (MD and NM)

Union College (NY) (ACT or three SAT II Subject tests are required. SAT I is optional.)

Wheaton College (MA)

Hint: If one (or more) of these colleges is on your short list, don't have scores sent until *you* have seen them first. If your scores are not so hot, tuck them under the mattress. If the scores are good, then order reports. Colleges that don't require test scores *will* probably use them for those candidates who submit them anyway.

Q&A

Q: Are tests biased against females and minorities?

A: Some "experts" say yes; some say "no." Others say "they were, but they aren't anymore." Arguably, even if the tests themselves are perfect (ha!), there are still societal problems that penalize many girls and minorities when it comes to standardized tests. Some females are brought up to believe that math and science are male domains. By the time they get to high school, they may have fallen behind in these areas. Many of the most problem-plagued high schools in the nation are those that serve primarily people of color. These students, too, may approach standardized admission tests with poorer preparation and expectations.

Continues

Continued

Most colleges will, to some degree, give extra "slack" to minority students from disadvantaged communities and put emphasis on class rank, not test scores. Young women, however, don't get much leeway, except at single-sex schools. The outstanding women's colleges (e.g., Smith, Mount Holyoke, Bryn Mawr) have somewhat lower SAT averages than their coed counterparts, but they attract bright, serious students and can be a smart college choice for those whose test scores lag behind their proven abilities.

SAT II: SUBJECT TESTS

Still commonly called by their erstwhile name, "Achievement Tests," these hour-long College Board exams are not as widely required as the SAT I, but many highly competitive colleges do demand them. (Often, however, the ACT can be substituted for both the SAT I and SAT II.)

It's nearly impossible to stay on top of which colleges want what, but typically, most (who expect subject tests at all) require three, though some ask for fewer. Because many stipulate that Writing and/or Math[*] be among those selected, a safe bet is to elect both of these, plus one more from the other subjects listed below:

Writing (includes multiple choice questions on language usage and an essay)

Literature

English Language Proficiency (for nonnative speakers)

Math Level IC

Math Level IIC

American History & Social Studies

World History

Biology

Biology-E

Biology-M

Chemistry

Physics

[*] *A few specialized institutions (e.g., Cal Tech) expect or prefer Math Level II and one science test.*

66

Chinese with Listening

French (reading only or with Listening)

German (reading only or with Listening)

Modern Hebrew

Italian

Japanese with Listening

Korean with Listening

Latin

Spanish (reading only or with Listening)

Subject Test Hints

- **Plan ahead.** There are six SAT II dates annually. Registration information is in the same *Bulletin* that is used for SAT I. (Make sure to pick up a separate free publication called *Taking the SAT II.*) **Remember, the SAT I and II cannot be taken on the same day.** Some SAT II tests are not offered on every test date. Up to three tests can be taken on one day. The 1998 cost: $13 registration; $5 per test ($10 for Writing; $7 for Language with Listening).

- **Schedule tests as close as possible to course completion.** For instance, if your daughter takes biology in 10th grade and does well, she might want to take the Subject Test that spring, not a year or more later when she wouldn't know a stamen from a pistil if it turned up in her corn flakes.

- **Foreign language tests are designed for those with two to four years of study. (European language tests are often tough for those with only two years of prep.)** Colleges, however, tend to take bad language scores less seriously than those in other areas because so many districts have weak language programs. Comprenez?

- **Science and history test questions are designed for students who have taken a one-year introductory course (at the college-prep level),** not just for AP aces.

- **English Literature DOES NOT require knowledge of specific authors or their works.** It presents reading passages and questions on them (and is, perhaps, the easiest test to do well on for those who are reasonably bright but haven't learned much in school).

- **Math IC and IIC require a calculator ("scientific" or "graphing"; a "four-function" is not adequate for this test). Students with solid backgrounds (and grades) in trigonometry and/or pre-calculus should probably take the Math II test.** (Consult your high-school math department, and read "Comparisons Among Tests" in *Taking the SAT II*). Some students who qualify for Math II decide to take the "easier" Math I instead, believing that they are certain to score well, and are surprised when classmates taking the harder test get better results. Why? One theory is that the Math II test covers material that is more current to advanced students.

- **Most students take no more than three subject tests and do not re-take them.** However, those who are strong in one area (e.g., sciences, foreign language) may find it advantageous to take additional tests. Good SAT II scores can help to counteract weak SAT I results.

- **Unlike the SAT I, the SAT II offers an optional score report called "Score Choice."** Students can elect to withhold some SAT II scores from colleges and report others. The catch? Once a score report is okayed, it goes on the cumulative record and can't be eliminated. But if you wait to see scores before reporting them, you forfeit the free score reports included in test fees.

- **A number of colleges, even fussy, fancy ones, are in the process of evaluating their SAT II requirements**. Why? Students from disadvantaged backgrounds sometimes attend secondary schools where they are not properly advised to take SAT II tests. Many admission boards believe that if they waive the tests for these applicants, they must waive them for all. Ask target colleges about policy changes, but remember…just because a test is not *required,* doesn't mean it's not advisable, especially if your child shines in an area like foreign language, social studies, or science.

II. The ACT Assessment

The ACT Assessment is best known to families living in the Southeast, Southwest, and Midwest U.S., but it is administered practically worldwide. Even elite Eastern colleges, former SAT strongholds, will now accept ACT scores instead. In fact, many colleges that require SAT I and II permit the ACT to be substituted for both.

In the majority of cases, the decision to take the ACT versus the SAT is left to the hands of fate. If you live in a state—or your child attends a school—where one test is more prevalent, then that is the choice that is probably your best bet. However, some reasons to buck the trend will be listed later on.

In ACT regions, many high schools administer the PLAN assessment test (formerly the "P-ACT+") to 10th graders. Like the PSAT, this test also serves as a warm-up for the ACT, but its primary purpose is to provide families and, especially, schools with a way to evaluate their curriculum and instruction so that appropriate changes can be made. As a result, the PLAN test is usually not a high-pressure experience for sophomores.

The ACT test itself, like the SAT, is best taken in the spring of 11th grade, and again in the fall of 12th, if desired. (Only about one-third of all students take the test more than once; few do so more than twice, although studies indicate that scores do improve as students complete increased course work.) The registration and testing processes are also very much like those for the SAT Program, so make sure you have read the SAT I section above, even if your child will not take that test. Also, like those who take the SAT, ACT students can opt for a "search" service (the ACT version is called the Educational Opportunity Service) and can order copies of completed tests and answer sheets. Two free booklets (*Registering for the ACT Assessment* and *Preparing for the ACT Assessment*) will tell you everything you need to know. The ACT has a World Wide Web site (www.act.org) that lists test dates and centers, provides test-content details, sample test items, testing hints, online registration, etc. ACT service charges are less (but only slightly) than most SAT fees. Here, however, are some other differences that you might want to note:

- There are six ACT administration dates, but in some states where the SAT reigns supreme, you may have to travel to reach an ACT test site.

- Ordinarily ACT score reports are mailed to schools, not home, but students can choose where they prefer them to be sent. (All June-test-date scores go to the home address automatically.) ACT score reports are not cumulative. This means that students can decide which scores colleges see…or *don't* see. There are three forms of mail-order additional score reports: "Regular" will arrive within a month, "Priority" will arrive within four days, and "Mailgram" will arrive within 36 hours. (There are small fees for each, and telephone requests are honored for an additional service charge.)

ACT FORMAT

The ACT includes four main parts, each divided into sub-sections:

English

- Usage/Mechanics
- Rhetorical Skills

Mathematics

- Pre-Algebra
- Elementary Algebra
- Intermediate Algebra
- Coordinate Geometry
- Plane Geometry
- Trigonometry

Reading

- Social Studies
- Natural Science
- Prose Fiction
- Humanities

Science Reasoning

- Data Representation
- Research Summaries
- Conflicting Viewpoints

ACT questions do not progress from easiest to hardest, as SAT questions do. The entire test lasts three hours, plus about 45 minutes for breaks and registration. Calculators are permitted but are not imperative.

ACT SCORING

The ACT is scored on a 1–36 scale. Each sub-section (e.g., "Usage/Mechanics") is scored on a 1–18 scale. Each section (e.g., "English"), on the 1–36 scale. **There is no penalty for wrong answers, so guessing is encouraged.**

Colleges are most concerned with the **Composite Score** which is an average of the English, Mathematics, Reading, and Science Reasoning tallies. **The national average composite score is 20.8.**

Students who grow up in ACT-land often have a sense of what these scores mean. They know, for example, that a 31 Composite is something to brag about. (It's the average at Stanford and Brown, among others). A 28 is nothing to sneeze at either (and is an approximate midpoint at places like Carnegie Mellon and Oberlin); while a 22 or 23 is the going rate at many state universities. But if your brain only functions in terms of 100s, then try this highly unofficial formula to compare ACT scores to SATs:

Multiply the ACT composite by 40, then add 210. The result will be a crude equivalent of an SAT I Verbal & Math total (on the recentered scale).

Example: 28 (ACT Composite) × 40 = 1120 + 210 = 1330

A student who scores 28 on the ACT would be likely to score about 1330 on the SAT.

Q&A

Q: Which test should "we" take?

A: Only a handful of colleges insist on one test and not the other, and the list is dwindling rapidly. (Most of these, in fact, are schools which draw largely from one geographic region and require the test that is most popular in that region).

Even colleges that claim to "prefer" one test above the other will never discriminate against applicants who took the "wrong" one; most will scarcely notice. Thus, it's fine to go with the flow and sign up for the test that prevails in your area. Why, then, would anyone want to swim against the testing tide?

Reasons to go out of your way to take the SAT

- Actually, it's the PSAT that is a qualifier for the National Merit Scholarship Program (and several other scholarships) which ACT (or PLAN) students aren't eligible for. Most other scholarship services accept scores from either, and the registration booklets include lists of scholarship services to which score reports can be sent directly.

Continues

Continued

Reasons to go out of your way to take the ACT

- Students who are unduly anxious about taking SATs may feel less pressure attached to a lesser-known test.

- In many colleges, the ACT replaces both SAT I and II. Of course, students with strength in foreign language, science, and/or history, won't get to strut their stuff with the ACT.

Students who take *both* tests (and use the formula above to compare them) commonly find that there isn't a significant difference in their scores. Indeed, recent changes have brought the two exams closer together. Still, there are some score-watchers who insist that the SAT puts more focus on aptitude (smart kids with fair grades will shine here), while the ACT emphasizes achievement. "I have observed that when conscientious (but perhaps not brilliant) students do poorly on the SAT I, their scores are better if they then try the ACT," claims independent college counselor Jane Gutman. "The ACT is primarily a reading test where questions follow passages. Even the 'science' section really requires only minimal science background (although some avowed non-scientists will still freak out at the first sign of saline solutions or biomasses). There is no out-of-context vocabulary on this test, an area that trips up many SAT I-takers."

Some students will insist on taking both tests, but only rarely is this a necessity. If admission literature does not state that either exam is acceptable, check directly with an admission counselor.

III. Test of English as a Foreign Language

Known as the TOEFL (pronounced "toe-full") test, this exam is required or recommended for students whose native language is not English. It is most commonly taken by those living outside of the United States or who have only been in the U.S. a short while. In some cases, colleges will accept TOEFL in place of required SAT or ACT tests. However, the reverse is also true—if a student has spent more than two or three years in a school where English is the primary language of instruction, then some colleges will not count TOEFL results at all and, thus, taking the test is a waste of time and money. If your child's situation is not clear-cut, check with individual colleges to see what they expect.

The TOEFL has three components: Listening Comprehension, Structure & Written Expression, and Reading Comprehension. It is scored on a 200–677 scale. The more competitive institutions usually expect scores above 600. Many schools indicate that students scoring below 550 are not prepared to follow a college curriculum in English; however, there are some colleges that will accept students with far lower scores. Some even offer special English programs for nonnative speakers.

Unlike SAT scores which are archived until the end of time, TOEFL test results are kept on file for only two years.

There are over 1,200 TOEFL test sites worldwide. To receive an information booklet and registration form, contact:

TOEFL Registration
PO Box 6154
Princeton, NJ 08541-6154
609/771-7100 (questions); 771-7243 (to order materials)
TOEFL information is also available online at www.toefl.org

There are a few other tests that some colleges will accept in lieu of TOEFL, such as the English Language Proficiency Test (ELPT), an SAT II exam. Check with admission officials before registering.

IV. What (if Anything) Should Be Done to Prepare?

Admit it. You probably skimmed through most of the chapter to get to this section. The only thing you *really* want to know about admission testing is whether you should fork over the big bucks for a commercial prep course. Perhaps you're also wondering what other ways there are to prepare or if preparation is even possible at all.

Both College Board and ACT officials maintain that the *best* way to get ready for standardized tests is through following a challenging high-school curriculum and staying abreast of assignments. It is no secret, either, that bookworms significantly outscore less avid readers—often even on mathematical tests (those questions have to be read, too).

In olden times (like, when *you* were in high school), prep classes were almost nonexistent, but so was cable television. If this isn't already the 11th hour, then by all means get Jason and Jennifer away from the TV set, the Nintendo games, or the telephone and put a book in their hands. (Good luck!) It's really the best preparation you can provide.

Okay, so that didn't work. The tests are two months away. The PSAT scores were, well, disappointing. What now?

The market is flooded with books, software, videos, courses, and even flash cards (remember them?) that all promise to improve standardized test scores, and, to some degree, they do "work." The catch, of course, is that your kid has to work, too, to get anything out of them.

Take the quiz below to see how (or if) you should invest your time and money:

1. How eager is your child to prepare for college entrance tests? She or he...

    a. is the one who insists on doing something.

    b. is willing to do what we suggest.

    c. thinks it's probably a waste of time.

    d. makes barfing noises when we bring it up.

2. How much time do you think s/he can devote to taking a class?

    a. Three hours a week or more

    b. Two hours a week

    c. One hour a week

    d. Every second is already scheduled.

3. How much time will s/he spend preparing at home?

    a. About eight hours per week

    b. About four hours per week

    c. About two hours per week

    d. About ten minutes per week

4. Does s/he tend to see projects through to completion?

    a. Yes, sometimes compulsively

    b. Most of the time

    c. Only if they are interesting

    d. If we threaten

5. Does s/he get anxious at test times?

    a. Extremely—the whole family is off the wall.

    b. Usually—these college tests seem to do it.

    c. No, test scores are often above class achievement.

    d. No, as long as the mall will still be open when the test is over.

6. What is his or her approximate junior- or senior-year average?

    a. A

    b. B

    c. C

    d. Don't ask

7. What were his/her combined PSAT scores? (Or use "PLAN" or "ACT" scores and conversion formula or SAT scores with a 0 added to choices below.)

    a. Between 80 and 110

    b. Between 110 and 140

    c. Over 140

    d. Below 80 or didn't take them yet

8. Which statement comes closest to your child's reaction to the PSAT (or other entrance tests already taken)?

    a. It took a while to get in the swing of it.

    b. I kind of went blank.

    c. It was easy.

    d. It was too hard.

9. What's the likelihood that you (or another adult) could prepare with your child on a regular schedule of two to four hours per week, over 10 weeks?

    a. We could probably pull that off.

    b. If we really made an effort and organized in advance.

    c. Sounds like a long shot.

    d. We haven't finished that soapbox racer we began in 1987.

10. How big a bite would $700 take out of your budget?

    a. It's small change compared to what college will cost.

    b. It's a big chunk of change, but we've spent more money for worse reasons.

    c. It would mean some really creative financing.

    d. Are you crazy? We had to *borrow* to buy this book!

11. Your child seems to absorb information best when:

    a. in a classroom situation.

    b. reading independently.

    c. working one on one.

    d. watching the Home Shopping Channel.

The best time to get serious about SAT or ACT preparation is in the spring of junior year, before the "real" test is taken for the first time. (For practical purposes, the summer of that year works best for test-prep, and tests can be retaken in the fall).

If you answered "a" or "b" to questions 1 through 8 above, then your child is probably a good candidate for some sort of preparation program. Despite raging debate over the effectiveness of such programs and the validity of claims of titanic score surges, common sense can tell you that preparation means practice, and practice makes…well, if not perfect, then at least improvement.

Especially helpful is the administration of an entire timed test. This can be done at home, but it's one area where coaching *classes* clearly have the edge because they can best simulate genuine testing conditions (complete with sneezing, belching, groaning, and furious scribbling).

Any form of preparation will enhance your child's familiarity with the testing process and that, in turn, is bound to boost confidence. The pros and cons of several preparation methods are listed below. Use your quiz results to determine which is best for you and your child.

Freebies

➤ **THE GOOD NEWS:** Excellent booklets (*Taking the SAT I, Taking the SAT II,* and *Preparing for the ACT Assessment*) are available at no cost at most high-school guidance departments or by contacting the appropriate offices listed at the end of the chapter. These booklets are not the same as registration bulletins but usually accompany them. They provide test-taking tips, preparation strategies, and practice questions. **At the very least, your child should be thoroughly acquainted with this material before taking an exam.**

If you answered "c" or "d" to questions 1, 2, and 3, and "c" to questions 7 and 8, then this may be the way to go.

➤ **THE BAD NEWS:** While brevity makes these booklets manageable, it also means that they lack information that might be helpful. For instance, the SAT I version offers "explained answers" for a few sample questions only; the ACT gives no explanations at all. The longer manuals described below also provide study aids such as vocabulary lists and mini math lessons.

Test Preparation Manuals

➤ **THE GOOD NEWS:** Most bookstores offer a broad selection of preparation books and tomes for every existing major test at around $20 each.

Look for volumes that:

- are written in a user-friendly style that seems fun to read (well, sort of, anyway)

- include several complete practice tests that mimic the real McCoy

- provide not only practice-test answers but also *explanations* of answers

- explain test structure and test-taking strategies

- offer comforting advice about quelling anxiety

- were published after SAT changes in 1994. They should *not* include antonyms; and *should* include "double" passages (with differing viewpoints) and calculator math problems. (Library copies are not always current. Brother's or sis's old test books may be out of date, too.)

➤ **THE BAD NEWS:** *Buying* the book is not enough. If your child is not likely to systematically read the material and do the lessons and practice exercises provided, then this prep method will flop. Likewise, while last-minute cramming can help students understand test-taking strategies, that same information can be had for free from the College Board or ACT booklets.

Computer Software

➤ **THE GOOD NEWS:** Prep programs are available for both Macintosh and PC use. Expect to pay about $30 to $50. For computer buffs, these interactive exercises can be entertaining.

➤ **THE BAD NEWS:** Like books, this method won't work if the software is harboring six species of spiders on the shelf. It also necessitates a computer and a quiet spot in which to use it.

Online Assistance

➤ **THE GOOD NEWS:** The number of ways to prepare for tests online is burgeoning. These range from entire test-prep courses and practice tests to helpful hints and sample questions. For example, Kaplan's Online SAT course (www.kaplan.com) combines the benefits of self-paced study with those of a structured program. The cost is about $60. From The Princeton Review's home page (www.review.com), students can access at least four different complete SATs at no charge, while The College Board Web site (www.collegeboard.org) offers an "SAT Question of the Day," along with correct answers and explanations.

➤ **THE BAD NEWS:** The full-length tests and study programs require the discipline to use them. The less time-consuming practice questions and testing tips provide good warm-up opportunities but probably won't help students make significant gains in verbal and math skills.

Try any of the following methods if quiz answers included 1 a, 4 a or b, 7 b or c, or 11 b:

School-Based Coaching Courses

➤ **THE GOOD NEWS:** Unlike most commercial courses (they're next; we're working up to them), classes offered in school (either as part of the curriculum or as an after-school option) are either inexpensive or cost-free. (Similar classes may also be available through local adult-ed programs or community colleges.) To some extent, these programs will force students to be aware of test formats and strategies, although good results require effort (and homework).

Even College Board literature concedes that short-duration familiarization courses (20 hours or so) seem to increase scores an average of 10 points on the verbal section and about 15 points on the math. Longer courses (c. 40 hours), which stress skill development, can bring average verbal gains to 15 to 20 points and math to 20 to 30. The literature also points out, however, that these averages are drawn not only from those who make dramatic score improvements but also from those whose new numbers rise little or (gasp!) decline.

➤ **THE BAD NEWS:** Quality of instruction and course content in such homegrown classes can vary tremendously. Some are taught by moonlighters with little experience. If the class is boring or disorganized, it will be of limited use. If your child is not especially motivated in regular school classes, you can bet that he or she will *really* snooze through this one. (Commercial courses can be better prepared to deal with reluctant pupils. See below.) The time would be far better spent participating in a club or sports or other more meaningful activity.

"There is a proliferation of coaching courses all over the country," notes ACT official Patricia Farrant. "We don't endorse or participate in any one of them. It's really a 'buyer beware' situation. Some are fine. Some are less than fine."

Look for quiz answers 2 a or b, 10 c or d, 11 a.

Commercial Coaching Courses

➤ **THE GOOD NEWS:** Some private companies devote much of their efforts to college test preparation, and as a result they know their business, and they understand their market. They stay on top of test changes, and they've learned how to keep teenagers alert and engaged, even on Saturday mornings. Of course, all of this expertise doesn't come cheap.

If you decide to go with a pricey prep class, then it's your turn to do the homework. Investigate which firms have the best reputation in your area. Some commercial programs are regionally based; some are national. *The Princeton Review* (TPR) and *Kaplan Educational Centers* are the "Coke" and "Pepsi" of coaching courses. Both hold classes from coast to coast and each claims to outdo the other. Kaplan insists that only three independent studies have compared test-score gains, and that Kaplan has nipped TPR every time. The Princeton Review counters that they have a $10,000 bet on the board that challenges Kaplan to agree to a national score increase study. (The proceeds would go to charity.) Kaplan, they maintain, won't touch it. Kaplan claims that TPR emphasizes "test-cracking" at the expense of teaching important underlying skills. Princeton says that's hogwash, that they do both and must do it best because they see more students. (So there!)

On paper, the differences between them are actually few. Both offer preparation courses for the PSAT, SAT I & II, and the ACT. The SAT I class is the best-seller, and its cost varies regionally. Expect to pay between $600 and $800 for about 27 to 40 classroom hours. Both programs include several complete SAT tests taken under "authentic" conditions. Both also give discounts to students who take more than one of their courses and offer financial aid to high-need students.

The Princeton Review "guarantees" a 100-point score increase (verbal and math combined), but claims that the average gain is 110 to 160 points, with the top 25 percent jumping 190 points or more. Kaplan cites an average increase of 120, with the top 28 percent gaining at least 170 points.

➤ **THE BAD NEWS:** Kaplan and Princeton Review courses both require home study, and students are clearly told that score increases are linked to output. "Most will get better scores by osmosis from simply sitting in our classroom," maintains one Kaplan official, "but each extra hour of work means more dramatic improvement." As parents, you've surely learned by now that buying the top-of-the-line baseball bat doesn't mean your kid is Willie Mays; music lessons don't often make Mozarts.

Kaplan will refund fees to those who make no score gains at all, and both firms allow their courses to be retaken for no additional charge. However, TPR limits this option to those whose scores have increased under 100 points and who have fulfilled homework and attendance obligations. They offer enrollees "free" diagnostic computer software for home or school use to strengthen weak areas. Kaplan also provides home-study aids and unlimited use of "learning libraries" at their centers.

And the winner is...Whether you pick Kaplan or the Princeton Review should hinge largely on convenience and schedule and, especially, local reputation. (For class locations or other information, call TPR at 800/2-REVIEW or Kaplan at 800/KAP-TEST.) Although both firms keep close watch over materials, teacher training, and evaluation, with so many classes and instructors, quality will inevitably depend on where you are. Ask around and—while you're at it—check into lesser-known companies that may be successful in your area.

Look for 2 a, 3 a or b, 7 a or b, 10 a or b (a must), and 11a.

Et Cetera

- If you've already earmarked the family fortune for a coaching course, you might consider a private tutor instead. A guidance counselor or independent educational consultant can probably tell you if there is an individual nearby who has had appropriate experience. Look for someone who plans to administer an actual test to your child and then zero in on weak spots. Tutoring won't be as much fun as a commercial course, but for kids who work best in one-on-one situations, this could be the way to go. You can also call Kaplan (the test-prep company discussed above) and engage their private tutoring service, available in 15- or 30-hour packages at about $100 an hour. (Did you choose 10 a and 11 c?)

- For a few (and far-between) families, the private tutor can be *you*. If you answered "a" or "b" on question 9, but "c" or "d" on 10, then you may be candidates for "home schooling." A preparation manual (or software) is the real teacher; you are primarily "the enforcer."

- Read, Read, Read. Many studies have proven the benefits of regular reading to young children—and of insisting that they read to themselves as they grow older. Even if this has never been a habit in *your* household, some experts argue that the months that might be devoted to test-prep programs can be equally well spent curled up in the corner with a good book. Even reluctant readers who fought through *War and Peace* or drowned in *Moby-Dick* can find a friend in Tom Clancy or Robert Ludlum, Alice Walker or Amy Tan. It doesn't have to be Shakespeare or Steinbeck—it just has to be every day. (Did you answer "c" on question 4?)

A Word to Wise Parents

No matter which preparation methods you elect, never lose sight of the importance of keeping test anxiety to a minimum. Be an ally, not an antagonist. Instead of nagging about completion of registration forms or score order reports, stay on top of deadlines yourself and help your child complete tasks on schedule. Leave test weeks free of other obligations, and try to put controversial family issues on the back burner during those times, too.

Above all, don't make your child feel that his or her value as a person is in any way linked to scores—or that *your* status at the country club or coffee klatsch is on the line. Try to implant in your own mind the seemingly disparate beliefs that, yes, test results may affect where a child goes to college; but, no, that really won't determine future happiness or success.

V. Information Numbers

The SAT and ACT registration bulletins contain all sorts of useful information that you may want to refer to repeatedly, even months after the last test has been taken. Put them in a safe place (with the passports and car titles, not the dog-food coupons and garbage-disposal warranty). But for handy reference, detach the page that follows and hang it where it won't be missed (the refrigerator door, the bathroom mirror, or the TV screen).

SAT I & II Information: 609/771-7600

Touch-tone phone service available 24 hours, daily; Customer Service Reps available Mon.–Fri., 8:30 A.M. to 9:30 P.M. (Eastern Time)

- to request publications • to reregister • to order score reports or "rush" scores
- to change test choice, date, or site • for other questions call during customer-service hours

Call toll-free (800/728-7267) to reregister, to order score reports, or rush scores. (Major credit card and touch-tone phone required.)

or write: THE SAT PROGRAM; PO BOX 6200; Princeton, NJ 08541-6200

(For students with disabilities: write to SAT Special Needs Services; BOX 6226; Princeton, NJ 08541-6226 or telephone 609/771-7137 or TTY service: 609/882-4118.)

PSAT Information: 609/771-7070 (PO BOX 6671; Princeton, NJ 08541-6671)

World Wide Web sites:

> **College Board: www.collegeboard.org**
> **Educational Testing Services: www.ets.org**
> **TOEFL tests: www.toefl.org**

ACT Information Numbers:

Mon.–Fri. 8:30 A.M. to 4:30 P.M. (Central Time)

Registration Information: **319/337-1270** (or write to ACT Registration; PO BOX 414; Iowa City, IA 52243-0414)

Reregistration (touch-tone phone and credit card): **800/525-6926**

ID Requirements: **319/337-1510** (ACT Test Administration; PO BOX 168; Iowa City, IA 52243-0168)

Score Reports: **319/337-1313** (ACT Records; PO Box 451; Iowa City, IA 52243-0451)

Universal Testing (Special Needs): **319/337-1332** (ACT Universal Testing; PO BOX 4028; Iowa City, IA 52243-4028) or TDD: 319/337-1524

World Wide Web site: www.act.org

ANTICIPATED TEST SCHEDULE

Test/Date*	Registration Due Date	Form & Fee Mailed?	Packet Received?
1.			
2.			
3.			
4.			

* Make sure to obtain proper ID: *official photo ID (e.g., driver's license, passport, school or work ID card); published photo with name in caption (e.g., in newspaper or yearbook); ID letter (with physical description) on school letterhead, signed by student and school official; notarized statement with photo.*

4

Finding Out More: Campus Visits, Interviews, College Fairs & Reps

Every spring, counselor Ed Wall loads his 11th-grade advisees into a bus and takes them on a college tour. They visit one nearby private college, one smallish public school, and then a huge state university. Never mind that few of his traveling companions will actually end up at the stops on this itinerary. "I simply want them to get an idea what a college campus looks like," Wall explains, "and of some of the differences among various types of schools. Many 16- and 17-year-olds have never really seen a college up close." Parents, too, notes Wall, should organize outings to area schools early in the search, even before target colleges are identified. By summer, he suggests, students ought to be planning visits, tours, interviews or information sessions at target schools and, finally, by fall of 12th grade, should arrange to spend the night, if possible, on top-choice campuses.

I. Campus Visits

Without a doubt, a visit to campus is the best way to make college matches. Sure, there are bound to be those random and red-herring moments that may make or break a school unfairly. One young woman determined her favorite college before even getting out of the car. "I saw this guy who looked just like Tom Cruise; you know, the movie star," she told her admissions interviewer later, "and I knew right way that this was the place for me." Conversely, eager applicants have been turned *off* by bad weather, campus construction, or the crabby graduate student who gave bad directions at the front gate. Nonetheless, if a picture is worth a thousand words, then a morning or afternoon on campus surpasses a million catalogs, viewbooks, and World Wide Web sites. Sometimes it doesn't take much more than a snack in the student lounge to determine if a fit seems right.

Where to Visit

Take a look at the "long list." Has your child read the appropriate publications for every target college? There's no point in getting all the way to William and Mary before discovering that there's no journalism major, nor in trekking to Temple if you want a rural campus. Eliminate the colleges that only sound so-so, then try to see the others. When cost and distance permit, schedule trips to each front-runner school.

➤ **THE GOOD NEWS:** The more colleges you visit, the easier it will become to discern differences and to pinpoint priorities. "It wasn't until I had seen seven schools," Leah recounts, "that I realized that some libraries had 'open stacks,' where I could look among the shelves myself for books I needed, while others had 'closed stacks,' which meant that titles had to be first picked from a card catalog or computer, then ordered at a main desk. I didn't want to do research that way. I like to browse."

➤ **THE BAD NEWS:** "If it's Tuesday, this must be Brandeis." And two dozen colleges later, you can't remember where you've been at all. Pragmatism may dictate that you see too many schools in too short a time. If you live in Oklahoma, you're simply unlikely to get to Ohio more than once. Try to limit stops to only two schools per day, and no more than 10 colleges on a single trip. In fact, 10 colleges in an entire year is plenty for any applicant (or an applicant's parents) to digest. (And be sure that notes get written down during—or right after—every visit to avoid confusion later. Some far-sighted families even tote camcorders for the express purpose of campus-ID films.)

When to Visit

Again, the ideal world and the real world don't always coincide. Aim to see schools with students on campus. For many, that means September through mid-May. Even some colleges with year-round sessions are not in full swing during the summer, but for many families, summer is still the best time to hit the highways. You'll just have to use your imagination if a campus (or an entire town) seems "dead" (and perhaps visit again at "crunch time"). Commonly, high-school and college spring vacations do *not* overlap, so if you are well organized, March or April of your child's junior year can be a good time to see campuses in action. Before finalizing any visit, check with the admission office to see if you'll be arriving in the midst of "autumn recess," "reading period," or "semester break." World Wide Web sites often include these schedules too.

The timing of your visit to campus will also depend on what you plan to do once you get there. Many colleges offer group information sessions which usually include a Q & A period and often a video. These may augment or replace an on-campus interview, depending on policy and availability at your target schools. Some colleges schedule interviews six (or even seven) days a week; some have none at all. The University of Pennsylvania, for example, encourages interviews by alumni in applicants' communities but does not hold them on campus.

In addition, you should ask admission offices about other special programs, like the University of Iowa's "Hawkeye Visit Days" or "Miami Mondays" at the University of Miami, which offer tours, presentations, class visits, and campus cafeteria meals to prospective students and their parents. Some colleges may invite you to attend open houses sponsored by specific programs or departments.

Q&A

Q: My daughter, a high-school junior, hasn't done a thing about planning campus interviews, and it's almost April. When should these be scheduled? Is she missing the boat?

A: Few families are ready to march off to target colleges prior to spring of 11th grade, and many colleges refuse to interview applicants before then, anyway. (Of course, there are always extenuating circumstances. If you're heading from Hawaii to New Hampshire for Uncle Albert's wedding in your child's sophomore year, a sympathetic admission officer may agree to an interview—even after the receptionist has *insisted* that only juniors and seniors are granted personal sessions. Be sure to insist yourself—but nicely.) Most students begin the interview circuit in earnest in the summer between 11th and 12th grades and then continue in the fall. Colleges are generally willing to interview students until it's time to make admission decisions in the winter of the senior year.

While you may luck into a last-minute vacancy (or even get seen as a "walk-in"), interview appointments are best made at least two weeks in advance. Most are held during business hours, Mondays through Fridays and sometimes on Saturdays. Gone is the era when students were

Continues

Continued

instructed to write a polite note to the director of admission in their best handwriting to request a meeting. While interviews can still be scheduled by mail, far more expedient are phone calls to admission receptionists who can tell you immediately if your desired dates and times are open. Again, although Junior may learn from the experience of making the calls, it is usually Mom or Dad who has a better grasp of what will best fit in the travel plans, and colleges certainly don't care one way or another (nor will you do damage to admission chances if you have to cancel and reschedule). Some colleges will schedule appointments by e-mail, too, which is cheaper—but usually not easier—than a phone call.

While an interview can be an important aspect of the college selection process and a key feature of a campus visit, it can also be worthwhile to see a school without an interview appointment and, if the place passes muster, return later for a more official visit. "We did a 'reconnaissance mission' in the summer after Kerry's junior year," says Frank. "We drove up to New England and looked at about a dozen colleges. We took tours at some places and just walked around on our own at others. In October, Kerry had interviews at two of the schools we'd seen, stayed overnight at two more, and claimed that she wouldn't be caught dead at the others."

Other Visitors' Tips

The Princeton Review's *Visiting College Campuses* includes lots of useful information on more than 250 institutions, ranging from Auburn to Wellesley. You'll find tour schedules, on-campus overnight opportunities and interview options, as well as driving directions, airport and accommodations information, and area tourist attractions. If you're planning trips to unfamiliar territory, this book may leave the AAA in the dust.

It is usually not necessary to submit an application before having an interview, and a campus visit can be an excellent time to decide if a student even wants to apply at all. Guided tours are not only a good way to see a school but also an opportunity to grill a real student. If your child will be living on campus, don't miss a stop at the dorms. (Be sure to check out those bathrooms, too—especially in coed residences.) In fact, it's wise to pay particular attention to *every* place in which your child is likely to spend lots of time. Such hot spots could include the weight room or the music practice room, the language lab or the chemistry lab.

Check out the bulletin boards along the way. They often say a lot about an institution's opportunities, ambiance, and attitude. Likewise, pick up student publications—especially the college newspaper—to get more of an inside scoop than admission-office propaganda is likely to give. (Look for free copies piled near doorways of major buildings.)

Most tours are available without advance notice, but some colleges require appointments even for group tours, so call ahead to check schedules and make reservations, as needed.

Overnight Stays

Colleges often welcome overnight visits from applicants, or even from those in the earliest stages of exploring, and this is an excellent way to get an inside glimpse at any school. The Bucknell University "Host and Hostess" program—typical of many—offers overnight accommodations on Sundays through Thursdays, when classes are in session. Guests, who must bring a sleeping bag or bed roll and pay for their own meals, are matched with Bucknell students who share similar academic interests. Appointments should be made two weeks in advance. At Antioch College in Ohio, special guest rooms in the dorms are available to candidates, and each dorm has a host in residence. Meal tickets are provided, and weekend stays are possible, if necessary. Ask each admission office about options and availability when you call.

"Networking" is another good way to find a campus host. Most college students enjoy showing off their school to visitors, so don't be shy about calling your dentist's daughter at Duquesne or last year's Pep Club president at Pomona. Similarly, coaches are often eager to pair prospective players with current ones (where NCAA regulations permit), or a call to the debate-society chairman or literary-magazine editor can likewise lead to an overnight invitation.

Q: We've heard that there are college visits conducted by private "escort services." Is this a good way to see schools?

A: Group touring of college campuses is a burgeoning business, and there are pros and cons to this approach—that is to say, some programs

Continues

COLLEGE ADMISSIONS: A CRASH COURSE FOR PANICKED PARENTS

Continued

are, indeed, run by pros, folks with years of experience in admission and guidance—while others may be spawned by those with more mercenary motives.

Typically, tours are held in the summer (or during school vacations) and high school students spend a week or so visiting a range of campuses, spending overnights on several. The best of such outfits not only help participants get the most out of these visits, but also offer tips on self-assessment, interviews, and applications along the way.

At $1,000 or more, this option isn't for everyone, but compared to the price of a comparable college trip for your family (be sure to factor in hotels, meals, and Rover's kennel costs), it may be worth a closer look. Be sure to check out tour organizers by getting references from previous participants. *College Impressions* (PO Box 665; Canton, MA 02021; 617/828-6227) is one such service that comes well recommended. It offers eight different itineraries with 12 colleges and universities on each. Inevitably, your child is bound to see some schools that he or she has no interest in, but, on the plus side, may also be introduced to new target colleges.

"Crunch-Time" Visits

Increasingly, applicants find that they like to see schools *after* they've received admission decisions, during that perplexing period when they have only a few weeks to decide which college they'll actually attend. While campus visits early on do assist in determining where students ultimately apply, it also makes sense to avoid financing cross-country junkets to colleges where your child won't even be accepted. "We told Jeffrey that he could look at U.C. Berkeley *if* he got in," Jeff's mother, Sandy, recounts. "The rest of his choices were all near us in the East. We certainly weren't thrilled when Berkeley rejected him, but we were glad that we hadn't paid for a plane ticket to San Francisco." Likewise, says Dylan, "I was desperate to go to Brown. I knew I couldn't be objective about another school. I applied to four colleges but didn't visit any other campuses in the fall. When Brown denied me, I collected myself and went to the three places that had said yes. As it turned out, I was really impressed with two of them, and I think it was helpful to visit with a mind-set that said 'This isn't window shopping. These places all want me, and in five months I will live at one of them.'"

Colleges, too, can be eager to entertain on-the-fence accepted applicants. Most will offer overnight accommodations; some issue invitations to special "open-campus" events. (See Chapter 8.)

In an ideal world, candidates would visit colleges before applying in the fall and, again, before making final decisions in the spring. Of course, if this were an ideal world, Ed McMahon would come to your house and give you a check for 10 million dollars which should just about cover four years of tuition and late-night snack attacks. In *this* world, however, you may have to decide between pre-acceptance and post-acceptance visits—or, perhaps, make no visits at all.

Q&A

Q: How much time should we expect to spend on every campus we visit?

A: If you're planning on an interview and tour, you'll need a minimum of about two-and-a-half hours. Most tours last an hour or so; interviews range from 30 to 60 or so minutes. Colleges are pretty good about coordinating the two so that you don't spend all morning in the waiting room reading yesterday's *USA Today*, but there is usually some lag time in between. Be sure to arrive 10 or 15 minutes before an interview appointment. There will probably be a short form to fill out. Colleges can't normally cater to latecomers, and you might find your child's interview time shortened or juggled if you're not prompt. (If you get lost or stuck in traffic, try to call ahead.)

It's always wise to check on estimated tour, interview, and overall timing when you call for an interview appointment. If you have specific questions about financial aid, you might need to see a financial-aid officer (often separate from admission staff). Call ahead for an appointment, when possible, and add extra time. You may also wish to inquire about sitting in on a class or eating a meal on campus. (If campus meals aren't available, the next best thing is the student snack bar or a nearby student hangout.)

You might also want to plan time with a coach. For top athletes, NCAA rules will govern meetings, but for most aficionados at the Division III level, a call from you or your child will make a coach's day. Don't be shy. (It's also effective if you get your child's coach to call ahead and chat with his or her collegiate equivalent in coachly vernacular.) For some families,

Continues

89

Continued

the infirmary, counseling services, or special-needs coordinator should be on the schedule, too. A few seek out music teachers or—if a child has a strong interest and specific questions in a particular academic area— a professor. Just for the record, typical applicants *don't* run around meeting half of the campus personnel. Most stick with the standard interview-and-tour routine. If you do wish to see someone special, the admission office can give you names and phone numbers, but it's usually up to you to schedule the meetings.

➤ **THE GOOD NEWS:** Faculty and, especially, coaches are generally happy to meet prospective students and their families. Don't feel as if you're harassing them; they're glad to encourage a promising candidate to attend their school and may even put in a good word with the admission office.

➤ **THE BAD NEWS:** Planning college visits can be more complicated than taking a family of five to Disney World, especially if you expect to see several schools on the same trip. Don't be timid about changing arrangements if one key person (e.g., the oboe instructor or tennis coach) isn't available.

Q: What happens at a campus interview. Do parents get interviewed, too?

A: An interview is usually a one-on-one session that involves an applicant and a member of the admission office staff. In section II below ("The Interview Itself"), you will find more information on what goes on behind that closed door and how you can help your child to prepare.

Parents are never *required* at admission offices but commonly choose to accompany their children. They are rarely invited to sit in on interviews but are almost always given a chance to ask questions afterwards. Often this Q & A period is brief and may be in the admission-office waiting room where there is little privacy. Occasionally, parents may wish to speak to admission counselors alone (e.g., you may want to discuss your child's health problem or physical disability). In such cases, notify the admission office at the start of the session so that there will be time left in the schedule for your talk. (Remember, specific financial-aid questions may need to be directed to a different department.)

➤ **THE GOOD NEWS:** Some parents, especially those who did not attend college themselves, may feel intimidated or overwhelmed in an admission office. Relax. We couldn't find one admission counselor who could think of a single thing that a parent *ever* did at an interview that botched their child's shot at acceptance. Neither Mom's vinyl go-go boots nor Dad's John Wayne impersonation will fluster admission pros (though your child may want to vanish through the ceiling tiles), and no question should ever be considered too stupid to be asked.

➤ **MORE GOOD NEWS:** Just like your offspring, you may find yourself tongue-tied in the lobby and remember what you really wanted to know only when you're halfway back to Dubuque. Don't hesitate to telephone admission officers any time you have questions or concerns. (Make sure you get each interviewer's card or name before leaving.)

II. The Interview Itself

While colleges don't often insist on personal interviews, many strongly recommend them and may look askance at candidates who live within two or three hundred miles and don't take the time to come to campus. Many colleges also offer "official" interviews with their alumni in an applicant's home city or state (and even in foreign countries).

An interview is a no-lose proposition. Well, almost, anyway—especially if you read the tips that follow. Yes, it's a remote possibility that your child will mess up so badly that he blows his (otherwise decent) chance of admittance, but, insists a dean at Swarthmore College in Pennsylvania (one of the most competitive colleges in the country), "that doesn't happen very often." "It's highly, highly unlikely," concurs an official at Hobart and William Smith Colleges in Geneva, New York.

Parents often want to know how much an interview "counts"—as if its value can be specified in percentage points. Most admission officers agree that the process is far too subjective to be so weighted. They'll tell you that the high-school transcript is far more important—and, indeed, it is. However, the interview can be especially helpful for borderline candidates. It gives them a chance to explain irregularities in their transcripts and to present themselves in a positive way that may not come across in the application itself. (In other words, your child's got about 27 minutes to make that D in geometry look like a valuable learning experience and not a disaster.)

Moreover, admission counselors consider an interview to be "an exchange of information," not the Spanish Inquisition. Their questions are not likely to put your child on the spot, nor will they have "right" or "wrong" answers.

In admission circles, interviews are said to have three main functions: first, to gather information about a student; next, to evaluate the student and the student/school match; and, finally, to *recruit* the student by showing off the school's best side.

Q: Who will conduct the interview?

A: Your child may talk to a dean, an associate, an assistant, a part-time counselor, or even to a faculty member or a student. The assignment rarely reflects the "importance" of a candidate. What *is* important is the skill of the interviewer and how well he or she relates to your child.

Alumni interviews may replace or supplement the campus interview. Sometimes they are longer or more informal than their campus counter-parts, but not always, and quality varies markedly. Keep in mind that when it comes to getting questions answered, alumni may not be as up-to-date as admission officials or students, and no viewbook or video can replace a visit to campus.

Q&A

Q: Do we need to bring anything with us to the interview?

A: You should ask before arriving, but the answer is likely to be no. However, unofficial transcripts and résumés are helpful to some inter-viewers—while others won't so much as glance at them. It's also helpful for your child to review this information before the interview. You'd be surprised by how many students freeze when asked what courses they took last term. It's useful, too, if your child knows his standardized test scores, GPA, and, if available, class rank.

Art aspirants often appear with bulky portfolios, but most inter-viewers are hardly critics, and, unless your child is applying to an art school or art program where a portfolio has been specifically requested, don't expect more than a fast flip-through. Consider bringing only one or two "masterpieces" instead. The only thing your child shouldn't leave home without is the "College Bible," a good place to record questions, answers, and impressions. (But while you've got the packing list out, don't forget rain gear—especially an umbrella—and comfortable walking shoes, if you're planning to take a tour.)

What to Expect and How to Prepare

One young woman recalls getting stuck with an interviewer who had recently spent some quality time in South America. "What do you think of Chile?" was the first question he asked her. "I'm a vegetarian," she replied, confused. "I won't eat it if it's made with meat."

Fortunately, interviewers rarely ask such questions, nor any that resemble science or social-studies quizzes. They won't expect your child to know who's chief of state in Mauritania nor what the Third Amendment says. Nonetheless, an interviewer may want to see if your child is aware of the world beyond the high school. Boning up ahead of time via newspapers (both local and national) and news magazines is a sound preinterview strategy.

Interview formats will vary. Some are quite open-ended. The interviewer may begin by saying, "Tell me about yourself," and then expect the student to take it from there. Others might have a more specific list of queries, some quite straightforward ("What schools have you attended?"); some more provocative ("What character from a book would you most like to be?"). Don't worry, though; the former type far outweigh the latter, and your kid isn't expected to come off sounding like Barbara Walters or Billy Crystal, anyway.

Commonly, questions arise from student comments just as they would in a casual conversation. If your daughter says she's on the track team, the interviewer is apt to ask what events she does, how she fared last season, or perhaps what aspects of the training are most tedious. Here are some other typical interview questions:

- **What classes have you enjoyed most?** Your child should be ready to show enthusiasm for *something* (and it should be a recent course, not seventh-grade earth science). Another spin on this is "What do you like best (or least) about your high school?" or "Who is your favorite teacher and why?"

- **What do you do outside of class?** Whether your child's passion is soccer or ceramics, community service or a part-time job, showing interest in—and commitment to—*something* is far more important than *what* that interest actually is…unless the "something" is watching MTV or playing laser tag at the arcade.

93

- **What do you do in the summer?** Some teenagers have the luxury of studying overseas while others have to work long hours. As above, interviewers expect your child to be doing something constructive. When planning ahead, make sure that your child does have meaningful summer activities scheduled, not only because they "look good" on applications and in interviews but because summer choices can be an important part of an overall education.

- **What books have you found enjoyable but challenging?** This is an applicant's chance to show off academic proclivities. Let's face it...Jane Austen will make a stronger impression than Danielle Steel; Stephen Crane surpasses Stephen King. Your child may have favorite books that were great for the beach, while others demand more intellectual exertion. The emphasis should be on the latter. Another preinterview strategy: suggest that your child review favorite recent titles.

- **Whom do you admire?** Your child should be prepared to say why and to go easy on the soap-opera stars.

- **What are your postcollege plans?** It's fine to be unsure, but a student should be prepared to discuss some options or interests. Rather than simply saying "I dunno," your child might continue, "I like art and computers, and graphic design seems to combine both, but I want to study Japanese and economics too, so maybe I'll end up in international business." (That covers quite a few bases, doesn't it?)

- **What are you looking for in a college, and/or what brings you to this one?** Again, an academic emphasis is important. It's also fine to say, "I have a friend from home who loves it here," but applicants should add why a school seems right for them (size, location, majors, and extracurricular offerings may all be legitimate factors). Sometimes, however, the honest answer is, "My mother (or father) went here (or wants *me* to go here) and is bugging me." Our advice? A student can admit to admission personnel that someone on the home front is behind this choice, but it should be *stated;* not *whined,* and applicants ought to cheerfully agree to keep an open mind until the interview and visit are over and the experience sinks in.

- **What will you contribute to this college?** Students may be asked this explicitly; if not, it's certainly something they should *im*part before they *de*part. (See the section just below.)

Interview Hints

Many high schoolers have never been interviewed before. They're bound to be nervous and unsure of how much to sell themselves and just what to say. In addition to anticipating common questions, as above (and mulling over answers ahead of time), help your child relax and get ready by offering these suggestions from the pros:

- **Prepare.** Before every interview, an applicant should jot down the key points he wants to get across and then end the interview by adding, "There's something else I'd like you to know about me…" This may be the only way that the admission office learns about a summer art scholarship or a role in an upcoming musical.

- **Explain.** One critical function of the interview is to enable admission staff to read between the lines of a transcript. Although the application will tell them about grades and other activities, it's bound to be an incomplete picture. For instance, a C in calculus may not wow them, but do they realize that no one in the class did better? Or that Junior had been out with mono for three weeks and had to keep up on his own? He may have only pulled a B- in biology, but the teacher praised his term paper as the best she's read in years. Admission officers won't know that from a transcript…it's up to the *applicant* to tell them.

  Admission people can get pretty jaded. They've seen more than their share of cultural-exchange programs, regional orchestras, and debate awards. What makes your kid's special? Did she get a chance to go to China because Grandpa wrote a check, or did she have to submit an essay and be selected from hundreds of candidates? Was she the youngest flutist from her school to perform a solo with the state symphony or the first debater to make the national tournament?

  Furthermore, although interviewers are not therapists, they are accustomed to confidential information and don't shock easily. If health or family difficulties have affected your child, they should be explained succinctly in an interview. Your child shouldn't go overboard with details, but shouldn't be mysterious, either. This information is an important part of who an applicant is and may affect how a candidacy is evaluated.

  Problems, both academic and personal, can be sources of strength and self-knowledge. If your child doesn't feel comfortable discussing

95

these in an interview, but would like admission officials to know about them, consider a supplemental letter. (See Chapter 6.)

- **Boast.** Most of us have been taught not to, but at a college interview, a bit of bragging is in order, and admission counselors welcome it. For example, if asked about a chemistry class, it's fine to say "I was proud of the fact that I got the highest grade on the midterm" or "the teacher picked me to help with a special research project." If your child *founded* the environmental club and didn't merely *join* it, she should say so.

- **Expound.** Interviewers hate to pull teeth. They expect applicants to do much of the talking. Good interviewers usually ask open-ended questions: "What did you like most about your trip to Japan?" and not "Did you like Japan?" In any case, your child should offer information beyond the minimal.

  On the other hand, as impossible as it sometimes seems, teenagers need to know when to say when. Especially when they're nervous, kids can be inclined to rattle on with extraneous details. In particular, they should focus on events that occurred during high school. Unless they're extraordinary, fourth-grade trials and triumphs are not appropriate.

- **Question.** An interviewer is sure to ask if your child has questions. Even those who have memorized the catalog and spent a week on campus are bound to have *some*. An interviewer may construe a lack of questions as a lack of interest, but your child shouldn't feel compelled to fabricate queries ("How many books are in the library?") to impress the interviewer.

  Questions say a lot about the person behind them. The student who inquires about research opportunities in physics is bound to be viewed differently from the one who wonders if the dorms have cable television. Questions should also indicate that the candidate has done his homework. "What do students seem to like best about the geology department?" is a legitimate question. "Do you have a geology department?" is not. In general, good interview questions are any that *do* demand information that applicants genuinely want to know and that *don't* depict them as dingbats. The list of possibilities is almost endless. Some examples follow:

Questions Worth Asking at an Interview

• Will my choice of major affect my admission? • If I'm accepted into one department, how easy is it to transfer to another if I change my mind? • What is the average class size (especially in my field of study)? • How about the size of "intro" classes? • How easy is it to take classes in other fields, or are there some departments that are too crowded to accommodate nonmajors or underclassmen? • What are your internship options? • Where can I study or take classes off campus? • How competitive is admission to your study-abroad programs (or other special programs)? • Are there research opportunities for undergrads? • Tell me about your career guidance office. • What are the pros and cons of different housing options? • Does this school have a stereotype? How accurate is it? • What happens here on weekends? • Do fraternities and sororities dominate the social scene? • Who are the "minority" students here, and are they comfortable? • How does this college's religious orientation (where appropriate) affect campus life? • Do students of other faiths fit in? • What political issues concern students most? • How about campus issues? • What do students like best about this school? • What do they complain about? • What do you like about living and working here? (This is a good catch-all question that turns the tables on the interviewer and bails out the tongue-tied).

Additional Interview Q & A Tips

• Encourage your child to make a *written* list of questions before each college visit, to leave a space after each one, then answer as many as possible using the catalog and other publications. Those left are fair game for the interviewer. (The "College Bible" notebook is a perfect place for question lists.)

• The list can go right into the interview. When it's time for questions, they can be read right from the list. Interviewers appreciate organization, and your child won't forget anything (and should also feel free to jot down brief notes as each question is answered).

• The interviewer should be alerted to long question lists at the start of the session, so that time can be scheduled accordingly.

Q&A

Q: Should we plan a "practice interview" at a college we don't care about?

A: One family tried this strategy and discovered that their daughter liked the "practice" school far better than the "first-choice" college she saw three days later. While interviewing at a college that your child will *never* attend is really a waste of time for all concerned, it does make sense to plan interviews at one or two "safety schools" before visiting the long shots. You might also try role-playing at home where *you* play the part of the admission counselor. Better yet, if your child is charming to your friends (but barely gets beyond a grunt with you) ask another adult to serve as a warm-up interviewer. Let the "coach" and your child read the suggestions above and then stage a mock session.

Q&A

Q: How will an interviewer "grade" my child?

A: After the session, the interviewer will write a brief report. It will usually include objective details that will probably appear on the application later (e.g., "Is enrolled in 3 AP classes"), as well as other varied information that might not (e.g., "Dropped physics after hospitalization for hepatitis" or "organized city-wide clean-up campaign."). The write-up will become part of the student's "folder" and will assist admission officers in making decisions when the time comes. The interviewer is also likely to include some sort of personal evaluation such as "is articulate" or "reticent" or "will be a good candidate if senior grades continue to improve." At some colleges, interviewers also give a numerical or letter grade, and the vast majority of candidates get some version of a "B." Few fare truly poorly. Most interviewers are delighted to be on their own side of the desk and have enormous sympathy for their jittery victims. In fact, students tend to give *themselves* a lower grade than their interviewer will.

It's important to remember that an interview can go well, and an interviewer can be extremely impressed with a candidate who is still denied admission. "Jon loved his visit to Middlebury," his mother, Barbara, recalls.

"He thought that he and the interviewer really clicked, so when he ended up on the waiting list, he was demoralized because it made him question his own assessment of the impression he makes on others. Fortunately, I was able to learn from a friend in the admission world that Jon had indeed impressed the Middlebury interviewer. Even a good interview couldn't overcome deficiencies in his other credentials, but at least the inside information restored his self-esteem."

You, too, must help your son or daughter realize that a letter of denial doesn't mean that a seemingly successful interview session was really a flop.

By the way, some families expect to know a child's chances of admission by the end of an interview, but interviewers rarely give decisions in person. They may, however, point out if their college is a long shot.

Q: Does a long interview mean a successful one?

A: Parents and students often obsess when a session scheduled for 30 minutes lasts only 18—or celebrate if it drags on for an hour. In fact, "good" or "bad" interviews can be both long or short. Most commonly, an admission counselor's appointment roster—not a teenager's wit or wisdom—determines length, and a student can usually tell how things went without looking at the clock. Of course, there will be times when applicants and interviewers "connect" so well that they chat far beyond the projected period, but timing should never be used as a barometer of "success." There was once a laconic dean who was so unable to hold up his end of a conversation that he rarely saw students for more than 15 minutes, and many must have left the office downtrodden. On the other hand, one interviewer confounded her colleagues by keeping a prospect tied up for well over an hour on a busy Saturday. "She was such a boring, insipid kid," the counselor explained," that I kept thinking there must be something *I'm* missing. I asked a million questions, tried every angle I could think of, and finally just decided I'd gotten a dud."

A final "note"…

Someone (your Aunt Pearl?) may have told you that a thank-you letter to an interviewer is proper etiquette. While this is often true for job-hunters, it's polite, but hardly protocol, for college applicants unless *special* thanks are in order. One nice touch is for your child to follow up on an interviewer's suggestions ("We tried 'Jake's' for lunch and loved it" or "Professor Stein *was* interested in my bassoon composition"). It's also a great time to ask those two or three "crucial" questions that weren't remembered until the ride home. But most bread-and-butter notes get stuck at the back of folders and ignored, so don't insist that your child write thank-yous across the country. It's one less thing to nag about.

III. Second Opinions

Talking with current students is by far the best way to get to know a college, and any warm body is a likely source of information. Once you get to campus, put your inhibitions on hold. Feel free to approach passersby with your questions. They'll probably be delighted (if not, you'll figure it out fast enough and move on), and a range of perspectives will paint a more accurate picture than merely one or two. It can be especially enlightening to compare admission office "party-line" answers to what real students claim is the status quo. (Tip: Try this investigative-reporter routine while your child is being interviewed. Not only will it pass the time, but it also enables you to engage in an activity which is potentially mortifying to your offspring.)

Questions for students

• What is the average class size? • Do professors know your name? • Are professors easily available outside of class? • How are advisors assigned/selected? • Do they really *advise* you? • How many students are assigned to each advisor? • Is it hard to get into popular courses? • What's the workload like? • What's most stressful here? • Are students competitive? Supportive? • Do a lot of students apply to grad school? • Do they get in?

• Would you call this a "friendly" campus? • Is crime an issue? • What's the social life all about? • Is drinking prevalent? • Drugs? • Are there fraternities, sororities or other social clubs? • How important are they? • What happens on weekends? • What are the most popular extra-curricular activities? • Where do cultural events fit in? • How hard is it to make…(the orchestra, the volleyball team, the student government, etc.)? • What's dorm life like? • How's the food? • What are the strong points of the town/city where the college is located? • Is there much interaction with locals? • Where do students "hang out" on campus? • Off campus?

• Would you say the student body is diverse? • Is there a stereotype here? • What is the political climate, or is there one at all? • Who are the minority groups here? • How are they treated? • Are there tensions between different factions? • How are they handled? • Do women feel like second-class citizens? • Does anyone?

• Are internships really available? • Is the career-planning office effective? • Are rules (both academic and social) rigid or flexible? • Do you feel like a person or a number? • What do students complain about most? • What do they praise? • How did the brochures (or admission staff) mislead you? • Would you apply here all over again?

Professors' opinions are important, too, and making appointments ahead of time is recommended if your child really wants to meet a faculty member. However, a useful way to assess a target college is to wander the corridors where profs have their offices. Are doors often open? Are students in evidence? Are office hours posted?

How about after class? Do students linger to chat? Do professors appear to invite questions? Below are some that you or your child might try:

Questions for faculty

• What is your average class size? • Is the format lecture, discussion, or other? • Do students question or participate often? • How frequently do you meet with students outside of class? • Do nonmajors take your classes? • How many classes do you teach per term? • Who corrects and grades papers and exams? • Do you offer special independent-study or research opportunities? • May I see a syllabus from one of your classes? • What are some of your former students doing now? • Do you keep in touch?

Remember, whether you're talking with professors or students, alumni or administrators, counselors or coaches, the manner in which they respond to your questions can be as telling as what they actually say. Are they amiable, or are they aloof? Enthusiastic or apathetic? Well-spoken? Well-informed?

After all, a college is its *people,* as much as it is its catalog, classes, and campus, and without a visit to your target schools, it's difficult to determine just how your child will fit in.

IV. When You Can't Get to Campus

If cost or time constraints preclude a trip to campus, there are a few ways to "visit" anyway. They can't come close to replacing the real thing but can help to broaden your view of a college and promote your child's candidacy.

Connect with an alum

Colleges commonly utilize a network of their graduates who help with the admission process. These alumni may conduct interviews that are just as "official" as the ones held on campus (complete with an evaluation sent to the admission office afterwards), or they may provide less structured ways to learn about their former schools. The office of admission can give you the names of such alumni in your area. You may be surprised by how widespread—even international—these contacts can be.

Your child will go to the alumnus' home or office (or another mutually convenient spot) and should ascertain in advance if this is to be a formal interview and prepare accordingly. Be aware, however, that even when alums are trained to represent the college as interviewers, they are often better at answering general questions about their alma mater ("Are there cultural events on weekends?") than specific admission-related queries ("Can I take a test to place out of the language requirement?").

Alumni, too, are likely to paint a picture of the school that may be more subjective than factual. Recent grads *should* have the up-to-date scoop on a range of topics; older alums may offer enchanting anecdotes about the good old days but could have limited information about the campus that your child will encounter.

Make a virtual visit

Students with access to the Internet can "visit" almost every campus in the country. Hundreds of home pages will link you quickly to facts and figures, as well as to other information that can range from course syllabi to cuisine. Look back to Chapter 2 to review some strategies for getting the most out of the World Wide Web without getting lost or tangled.

At www.campustours.com you'll find a good starting point for virtual visits to hundreds of colleges and universities. Some are even set up to replicate armchair trips to campus ("On your right you'll see the field house...") But keep in mind that, just as travel brochures won't enable you to smell the coffee on the Champs-Elysées or feel the warm sand of Waikiki, photos found on typical Web pages can't compete with a real stroll through the library, dining commons, or "Stu U." More telling, however, are student publications that can usually also be accessed from the Web. At many institutions, student organizations have their own home pages, too, and these student-designed sites may provide more insight into a school's culture and climate than the official offerings. ("Prepare to meet the Phunky Pharaohs of the Nile" entreats one fraternity home page!)

From *Link* magazine's home page (www.linkmag.com) you can visit a "digital campus" where you'll find lists of—and direct access to—online college newspapers and magazines (click on the "Union" icon at the site), sports schedules (they're under "Stadium"...duh!), and other collegiate enterprises.

Make the scene by screen

Most colleges try to show off their best sides via video. Ask each admission office to mail you a copy of theirs. (You may be expected to return it.) High-school guidance departments often have a range of tapes available as well. Although celluloid tends to bring out the sameness—not the "specialness"—of most schools, the video will give a view that even the viewbook can't.

"The Road to College" is a PBS program that is updated and aired annually in many locations. It features highlights of varied college campuses, as well as information about college choices, applications, and financial aid, presented in story form. (If you don't blink, you'll even spot a plug for this book.) To order, call 800/672-9672 or check out www.roadtocollege.org on the World Wide Web.

Let the campus come to you

Ask your child's guidance office about area "college fairs" or "college nights" attended by representatives from a range of institutions. These vary from large and noisy all-comers occasions to smaller events, limited to students and parents from only one secondary school. Tables piled high with publications and festooned with catchy banners and displays are staffed by admission officials (maybe even the Big Cheese) or by local alumni (who are good at handing out brochures but can't be counted on for in-depth details). Don't rely on fairs as a time for your child to really get to know a school nor for the school to know your child. Yet, you might get lucky on a slow night, have lots of questions answered, and allow your child to feel he's made a connection with a particular school. At the very least, a fair is a good time to browse and see what's out there and to get on (yet more) mailing lists. Parents, as well as students, should try to attend and "work the room" from your own unique vantage points. (Hints: Bring stick-on address labels to fairs, and it will save you and your child from writer's cramp. Schedules for fairs sponsored by the National Association for College Admission Counseling can be found on the World Wide Web at www.nacac.com.)

In addition, representatives from hundreds of institutions make visits to high schools during the day. The guidance office posts schedules in advance, and students may have to obtain an excuse from class to attend. Sometimes college reps speak to a roomful of students; sometimes to only one. These talks are not official interviews, and candidates are not judged by their comportment, but they do offer up-close and accessible looks at colleges. Parents should ask guidance counselors for lists of upcoming visitors and encourage their children to attend appropriate sessions. If a top-choice college is on the list, you can call that school's admission office to see if the visiting rep will be attending evening events where parents are welcome. Your high school may also permit interested parents to sit in on school-day sessions. (And oh how your child will love that!)

Some college reps conduct official interviews while on the road; a few will even do so by phone. Always ask admission offices what your options are.

V. Drawing Conclusions

You've paraded through dozens of campuses, sampled coffee from Carnegie Mellon to Kalamazoo, seen more gyms than Bobby Knight. Each time you fish for the phone book, you come up with a viewbook instead. The "College Bible" brims with your kid's inscrutable scribbles: contacts and questions, pros and cons. Now what?

Now it's time to choose. The facts are in front of you, but there's more to this decision than the data. Sometimes, when all schools start to sound alike, it can be the little things that make a match work best. Cassie and Lissy, for example, were both strong students who wanted coeducational liberal-arts colleges and considered several similar-seeming institutions. Cassie especially liked the honor code at Haverford. It reminded her of the one that worked so well at her high school, and she knew that it would make her feel at home from the start. Lissy appreciated Carleton's "No Cars" policy, believing that it would help to put everyone there on equal footing. While both young women selected their schools for a range of reasons, it was a small and special quality—not the list of majors offered nor the student/faculty ratio—that led them to their final decisions.

Moreover, *don't discount gut reactions.* Two colleges might look about the same on paper, but your child may feel good about one and not so great about the other. This is quite normal. A small, subconscious voice that whispers, "It just doesn't seem right" can be a perfectly fine reason to eliminate a college from the ledger.

Let that same small voice remind you of what's really best for your child. It's easy to be swayed by a prestigious reputation or a fabulous football team; some schools are simply "hot," while others are practically unheard of. If such factors are important to you and to your son or daughter, by all means, don't dismiss them, but *do* pick those places that will meet your *child's* needs. Not yours. Not the neighbors'. Not anyone else's.

As you read earlier, aim for five or six applications. As you finalize your list, also keep these pointers in mind:

- The most selective colleges should be considered "long shots" by almost everyone. Too many candidates (with 1,400 SATs, excellent grades, and other extras) are turned away to make any of these schools a certainty.

- Although your child may like one college far better than another, that doesn't automatically make the latter a backup option. "Just because a college is *your* second or third choice, doesn't mean that it's *easier* to get into," warns a former dean of admission at Colgate University. "That's a dangerous type of transferal that's commonly made." Make sure to use statistics to determine "likely" and "safety" schools.

- These days, with so many families depending on financial assistance, no college is a sure thing until the tuition bills are paid. Don't forget that a sure bet is not only a place where your child will definitely be admitted but also one that he or she can afford to attend.

- For many students, first-choice colleges will often be likelies, not long shots. In such cases, fewer applications have to go in the mail— unless you need to compare financial-aid packages.

Did somebody say "application" and "financial aid?" That's right, no matter how extensive (and exhausting) your college search has been, it's not over until it's over—which means that there's a lot of paper-pushing still ahead.

CHAPTER

5

Money Matters: Financial Planning and Financial Aid

This is the chapter you have been waiting for, according to the responses from the questionnaires we circulated, asking "What are the major issues that you, as a parent of a college-bound student, are concerned about?" (The only item rated as more important was finding the proper fit between child and college.)

In this chapter, the focus will be on financing. You'll be able to set up a budget projecting college costs, start to determine what aid is available and how to qualify, and learn some tips for those who are ineligible for financial aid.

I. Estimating College Costs

Q: Just how much does college cost?

A: According to the College Board, 1996–97 average costs for *tuition and fees* at four-year public colleges were $2,966 and at four-year private schools, $12,823. The national average for tuition and fees at two-year public colleges was $1,394 and at two-year privates, $6,673. Based on recent history, it's safe to predict four- to six-percent annual increases.

Continues

Continued

Averages for books and supplies were around $600 and in the $4,000 to $5,000 range for room-and-board charges. If you went to college in the '60s or early '70s, you and/or your parents may have spent less on your college bills over four years than you and yours will spend for one year of room and board for your child. According to U.S. government statistics, in 1971 families spent 13 percent of their income on public-university tuition and 27.9 percent on private-college tuition. In 1993, families spent 15.2 percent on public-university tuition and 41.3 percent on private. It's no surprise that more families than ever are having to borrow for their children's education.

Read everything you can get your hands on about paying for college. The school guidance office, your local library, colleges, newspapers, the Internet, and government publications have information for you. Read them, reread them, and copy and underline what's important to you. Be sure the sources are up to date. Remember: You will pay for college with your past income (savings, investments, etc.), current income, and future income (loans). Figuring out the money end of college for your child will go a lot smoother if you are well informed, well prepared, and well organized.

The Educational Costs Budget on page 109 will give you a rough idea of what *your* child's college choices might cost. Consult college catalogs and guidebooks as well as financial-aid publications for estimated expenses. *Be certain that the costs you are comparing are current and official.* Chances are good that no two colleges will cost the exact same amount.

If you have absolutely *no* idea of which colleges will be appropriate choices for your child, you might just plug in figures from the *type* of school— i.e., the local community college or your state university. Don't add in scholarship aid or loans at this point; there is another budget on page 123 for that purpose. For now, we want a good, clean reading of what estimated costs will be.

Photocopy this form if you want to compare additional prices as you go through the more advanced stages of the college search. Also, cluster comparably priced colleges together under one heading.

Some parents are faced with "sticker shock" when first confronted with college costs. Indeed, for many people, paying for a child's education is second in cost only to the purchase of their homes. Depending on when and where you bought your home, financing a child's education may be even *more* costly. On the other hand, studies have shown that some parents *over*estimate the true costs of college tuition and fees.

BUDGET 1: EDUCATIONAL COSTS BUDGET

	Most Expensive	Top Choice	Financial-Aid Safety School
School name	_____	_____	_____
A. Direct Educational Costs			
Yearly tuition	_____	_____	_____
Required fees	_____	_____	_____
B. Books and Supplies			
	_____	_____	_____
C. Room and Board			
Living with parents or	_____	_____	_____
Living on campus or	_____	_____	_____
Living off campus	_____	_____	_____
D. Personal Expenses			
Medical	_____	_____	_____
Transportation: If *resident* student, round-trips home	_____	_____	_____
If *commuting* student, subway, bus fare, or automobile costs	_____	_____	_____
Other costs (clothing, lunches if not included under room and board, lift tickets, pizza money, etc.)	_____	_____	_____
Application fee, long-distance phone calls, and any other additional, one-time expenses related to the admission process	_____	_____	_____
TOTAL COST = A + B + C + D			
	_____	_____	_____

Budget 1 Explained

A. Direct educational costs

Tuition costs vary considerably from school to school, and higher costs don't necessarily assure a better educational experience for your child. While most public institutions cost less than privates, residency matters. If you are not a resident of the state that the public university is in, your tuition costs may be comparable to those of a private school. For example, '96–'97 tuition and required fees for out-of-state students at the University of New Hampshire were $14,231, and they were $14,550 at private Saint Anselm College, just a short drive from UNH. Sometimes, out-of-state tuition is even higher than private-school tuition. Out-of-state tuition at the University of Michigan, for example, is higher than tuition at Drake or Furman.

You may qualify for tuition benefits if you are employed by a college or even live in a college town. (Places like N.Y.C. and L.A. don't qualify as college towns!) Additionally, some schools like Catholic University offer tuition breaks for siblings who attend at the same time. Other colleges, like Bowling Green, offer non-need-based awards to children of alumni.

There are some very fine institutions *without* tuition—such as the service academies and Cooper Union. Cooper Union for the Advancement of Science and Art in New York City is, according to its catalog, "the only private, full-scholarship college in the United States dedicated exclusively to preparing students for the professions of architecture, art, and engineering." That's right—it's free! But, before you rush off to get an application (yes, there is an application fee) keep in mind that it is super competitive and for every spot in the freshmen class there are 10 applicants.

B. Books and supplies

Depending on your child's major, this figure can range dramatically. For instance, a personal computer, uniforms, and special lab equipment may be requirements for technically oriented fields of study. Evaluate whether these costs will be one-time investments (e.g., the computer) or if equipment needs (and costs) will increase.

Some majors lend themselves to taking advantage of paperback and used books. Shakespeare's work hasn't changed all that much in content over the eons but, with all the political changes in the world in recent past, a geography student could be on the way to academic disaster if second-hand textbooks are out of date.

C. Room and board

Consider variations in location of the schools (e.g., rents are more expensive in cities) and options in board plans (e.g., 21 meals a week or lunches and dinners only) when penciling in these estimates. While most students don't know where they want to live before enrolling in a college, some are sure that they want to live in a dorm, at home, in an apartment off campus, or in a fraternity or sorority.

If your child will be living at home with you, you will incur some costs (e.g., food and utilities) that you wouldn't if your child was away.

You can get estimates of local rents and fraternity and sorority charges from the college housing office. If renting off campus, consider a month-to-month lease at first, particularly if your child doesn't know anybody or may not be familiar with the area.

Many colleges offer flexible board plans, making it possible for students to determine how many on-campus meals they will eat (and pay for) per week. Meal plans are often offered to commuters as well as to resident students and may serve as a reasonably priced alternative to other eat-out options. They also provide a way for commuters to meet resident students.

D. Personal expenses

The numbers in this category can vary greatly, depending on geography, extracurricular interests, and your child's ability to stretch—or spend—a dollar. If your child goes to college 2,000 miles from home, airfare will be a big-ticket item in this section. Cities have treasures of museums and concerts, but ticket prices on Broadway can be extravagant on *any* budget, and city life brings with it parking costs. Thankfully, there are ways to get cheaper tickets, and student discounts are usually available.

If your child is going from a warm climate to a cold one, add in wardrobe costs. A winter coat and good waterproof boots can set you back hundreds of dollars—and that's not counting ski equipment and lift tickets.

A bicycle might be the best form of transportation around campus. Will your child insist on the latest model full-suspension mountain bike or pull the old Schwinn three-speed out of the garage? It's often not a bad idea to get there before making a major purchase such as this to find out what's really needed and to help keep transporting all the stuff to a minimum. Some colleges sponsor used bike sales at the beginning of the term.

Telephone costs can be exorbitant, although they can be minimized if your child will have access to e-mail. You might want to have some kind of agreement about who is responsible for what—you may pick up the tab on calls home, but late-night calls to girlfriends and boyfriends scattered all over the country should be the responsibility of the student.

111

If nothing else, if you have read this section in time, you may be able to make some suggestions to relatives for high-school graduation presents. Telephone-credit gift certificates, tickets to sporting or cultural events, and restaurant gift certificates are welcome and practical. A gift certificate to the college bookstore is always a winner.

Total costs

While you may be very surprised by the variations in costs among colleges, don't be premature about crossing a college off the list simply because prices are high. It may be that you will qualify for aid at the more expensive college and not at the other, and it may be that the less expensive school is really not a bargain because it doesn't offer your child as many opportunities or advantages.

Topics for round-table family discussions

- *Is there a certain amount of money that you are willing to commit to a child's education?* If your *ability* to pay is more than your *willingness* to pay, you should put your cards on the table as soon as you can in the college admission process. Some families agree to pick up the tab on tuition and room and board but expect their children to pay for books and personal expenses. This is a good time to work out the ground rules.

- *Are there sources of financial assistance that you should be investigating?* If a grandparent has always said, "I'll be willing to help out when the time comes," this might be the time. Often, grandparents are eager to help out financially—for tax reasons as well as altruistic ones. If grandparents pay tuition directly to a college, this money will *not* be treated as a taxable gift, and the grandparents would still be able to take advantage of making a $10,000 annual gift, reducing their taxable estate. Although the section of this chapter dealing with financial aid will detail aid available to all, there may be specific scholarships through your church or employer that you need to look into.

- *What sacrifices are you willing and able to make as a family to pay for college?* Vacations, new cars, and home improvements may be luxuries that you won't be able to afford with children in college. If these decisions are discussed and made together, they are usually easier to live with. In addition, if your child has assets such as stocks and bonds, will any or all of them need to be liquidated to pay for school?

112

- *Expect to borrow.* The number of families borrowing for education has risen dramatically in the last 15 years, and these days most college students borrow from *someone* or from *somewhere.* It's important for you to establish an idea of how much debt you are willing to incur. Make sure that your credit rating is healthy. If your family has not experienced any trouble with previous debts, you should be in good shape to borrow again.

- *Don't blackmail your children.* Far too many parents insist that they will foot the bill only if their children attend a school of the parents' choice or study a particular major. Janice unhappily enrolled at her parents' alma mater, and only after being miserable for two years was she able to convince her parents to allow her to transfer.

- *If parents are divorced, be certain that it's clear about who will assume what in college expenses.* Paul, a divorced noncustodial father, paid all the bills for his daughter's private college. Now his son is ready to enter college, and he's asked his ex-wife to split the cost since he hasn't recovered financially from their older child's bills. She has refused. The father plans to apply for financial aid this time around and may or may not qualify.

II. Applying for Financial Aid

➤ **THE GOOD NEWS:** Federal and state governments, educational institutions and private agencies are committed to making higher education accessible to students regardless of need, and a vast amount of money is available to help those who need it. According to the College Scholarship Service, more than $50 billion in financial aid were awarded to students in 1996–1997. At Smith alone, almost $20 *million* of the college's funds were awarded to our financial-aid recipients last year, and that doesn't even count federal or other outside sources.

➤ **THE BAD NEWS:** You will need to carefully and methodically complete a series of fairly complex forms in order to determine eligibility for these funds. If you've never been organized in your life, this is the time to begin.

Meet three families:

- First, there's Lynnette, a single parent of two, divorced when her older daughter was a toddler. The father has vanished. Lynnette earns $30,000 a year working at a bank. Her daughter, Brittany, wants to go to a college that costs nearly that much for a year.

- Then, there's Henry and Gretchen, a high-school teacher and a part-time nurse. Together, they earn $55,000 and have one child who is headed to a private school.

- Finally, meet Laura and Donny, who own their own business and jointly make $135,000. They have two undergraduate tuition bills to pay and a third child who recently graduated from college.

Each of these families qualified for financial aid, on the basis of need, at a private college.

Q: How do we know if we have a "demonstrated" need for financial aid?

A: In simple terms, *financial need* is calculated or "demonstrated" by taking the total cost of attendance and subtracting how much you and your family can afford to contribute. The *expected family contribution (EFC)* is calculated by weighing your family's financial assets against financial liabilities. This is done in a standardized needs analysis process using what is known, in financial-aid lingo, as Federal Needs Analysis Methodology. In addition, there are institutional philosophies that could make the calculation of your family contribution vary. For example, schools that go strictly by Federal Needs Analysis Methodology ignore home equity, but most private schools will take home equity into account when calculating family contribution. Additionally, aid officers sometimes use their own professional judgment to take special circumstances into account.

Colleges often have worksheets, computer programs, and financing and counseling sessions offered for parents to get a "ballpark" figure for the expected family contribution and to determine the likelihood of getting aid. Many schools have a staff member who is "shared" by the admission and financial-aid offices and will serve as a liaison between the two processes.

The "College Cost Explorer FUND FINDER," a computer program developed by the College Scholarship Service, provides reliable information about aid available and is used in many high schools, colleges, and community centers. Ask your guidance counselor or college financial-aid office how to gain access. If you are a World Wide Web user, sign on to The College Board's site at www.collegeboard.org and get up-to-date information about college costs as well as the chance to complete forms that will help you estimate your EFC and calculate estimated loan repayments.

In order to figure out how much (if any) aid you will qualify for, you will need to fill out more forms that you'd probably like to. Generally, to apply for need-based aid, you will need to be prepared to submit:

The Free Application for Federal Student Aid (FAFSA). Introduced in 1993 as a result of the 1992 Reauthorization of the Higher Education Act, the FAFSA is the form that any student wishing to apply for federal aid needs to complete. As the title suggests, there is no fee for processing. The FAFSA is available after December 1 at secondary-school guidance offices and cannot be filed before January 1 of the year in which your child starts college. If you applied for aid with an older child before 1993, the process will vary this time in large part because of the introduction of the FAFSA. See the Web site of the U.S. Department of Education at www.ed.gov and learn about the FAFSA Express which allows electronic transmission of the form, speeding up the process and automatically checking data, resulting in fewer mistakes. (Note: Not all schools have electronic-application capability, and some people have concerns about security when sending information about personal finance out into cyberspace.)

CSS/Financial Aid PROFILE™. This form is required in addition to the FAFSA by hundreds of colleges, private scholarship organizations, and other nonfederal donors of aid. It provides more information than required by the federal government to estimate aid eligibility. Some colleges will request PROFILE from all applicants, some from first-timers only, and others only from Early Decision or Early Action candidates. There is a modest registration fee, as well as a processing and reporting service charge for each college designated. Register for the service by calling the College Scholarship Service at 800/778-6888, connecting to College Board Online (www.collegeboard.org/profile.html), or via ExPAN, the College Board's electronic guidance and application network available at nearly 2,000 high schools and other sites.

College and university forms. Some schools have their own forms that need to be completed in addition to the FAFSA and PROFILE. In some cases, it is these forms that initiate an application for financial aid, so it is important that they be submitted on time. These are usually included with the application for admission.

Parent and student tax forms. Keep these records handy and try to file early; signed photocopies will be required as part of the aid application process.

Additionally, you may be required to submit a *Divorced/Separated Parent's Statement* along with both parents' tax returns. Colleges vary on their policies for dealing with noncustodial parents, so investigate. If the noncustodial parent is reluctant to complete forms at the request of a child or ex-spouse, the financial-aid office may be willing to intercede and to contact that parent directly or to waive the requirement. Don't hesitate to contact the financial-aid office for advice in dealing with parents' information.

A *Business or Farm Supplement,* along with corporate income-tax returns, may be required if one or both parents own their own business or farm.

Copies of both the Divorced/Separated Parent's Statement and the Business or Farm Supplement come with PROFILE.

About a month after you complete and return the FAFSA for processing, the SAR (Student Aid Report) will be sent to you. It will show your expected family contribution using the federal calculations. This standardized information will also be forwarded to the colleges your child selects.

While your expected family contribution remains relatively constant wherever your child goes to school (depending on method of calculation), financial need varies depending on educational costs.

For example: assume your family's contribution is calculated at $10,000 and two of the colleges your child is considering are College X, costing $25,000, and College Y, costing $15,000.

> **Financial Need** at College X is equal to:
> $25,000 **College Costs**
> *minus* 10,000 **Expected Family Contribution**
> _____
> **$15,000 Financial Need**

> **Financial need** at College Y is equal to:
> $15,000 **College Costs**
> *minus* 10,000 **Expected Family Contribution**
> _____
> **$5,000 Financial Need**

Consequently, even though College X is more expensive than College Y, your expected family contribution remains constant, and assuming that both College X and College Y award your child aid *to the full extent of need* ($15,000 at College X and $5,000 at College Y), both will be affordable.

116

While your calculated financial need varies at different schools (for the purposes of awarding "institutional monies," which comprise the bulk of financial aid awarded by private colleges), so do the colleges' philosophies of awarding aid.

Need-based aid

Need-based financial aid is money awarded to students on the basis of demonstrated financial need. Some colleges award aid to the *full extent of need.* That means your child will be offered $12,000 if that is what he or she qualifies for on the basis of need analysis. Other colleges spread their money further by practicing what is known as *need gapping.* In this case, students are awarded part of what they need so that more students can be offered aid. Asking about the philosophy of awarding aid will prevent surprises when award letters arrive.

In addition, some colleges exercise *preferential packaging.* That is, they will lower the amount of self-help and up the amount of gift aid for students they are trying to recruit. Be certain to analyze what percentage of aid is self-help and what percentage is gift aid when comparing financial-aid packages.

Some colleges also practice what may be called *front loading.* That is, they award a very attractive financial-aid package to first-year students to entice them to enroll, and then they either end all aid or reduce aid to a much lower rate after the first year. If your child is offered aid, be certain to ask if you can expect a comparable amount for the entire four years, assuming of course that your financial need remains consistent.

"Need-blind" admissions means that admission decisions are made without any regard to financial need.

Q: Do those colleges that claim to be "need blind" really treat the rich and the poor the same at decision time?

A: In a perfect world, yes. "Need blind" means that admission officers pay absolutely no attention to an applicant's ability to pay when making admission decisions. Admission officers enforcing a "need-blind" admission policy may not know (or care) if an applicant has applied for—or qualifies for—need-based aid. Colleges with vast resources (and there

Continues

Continued

are a few) are able to offer financial aid to the full extent of need to every-body who qualifies for admission, and who, through the standardized needs analysis, is deemed needy. Increasingly, the number of these schools is shrinking.

Colleges with more modest budgets may spread their money out by "gapping" (not meeting the full extent of need) or by offering admission to some students but not offering aid ("admit/deny"). Some colleges will, with or without confessing, use financial need as one of the criteria for admission when making "fine-tuning" decisions about equally qualified candidates. This is often called "need-sensitive" or "need-conscious" admission. More colleges are coming out of the closet and announcing that they are forced to exercise this option. Professional conferences host heated discussions about the variety of methods of administering aid, and the debates are likely to continue as colleges continue to distribute limited funds to growing numbers of students while using aid creatively to attract the best students.

Merit aid

Merit aid is money awarded for some sort of achievement—academic, artistic, athletic, etc.—and demonstrated financial need is not necessary to qualify. According to figures from the College Scholarship Service, merit awards are most common at public four-year colleges, where 93 percent of the respondents to a survey had no-need aid programs. Private four-year institutions weren't too far behind; 85 percent offered merit awards.

For example, at Rice University in Houston, where 80 percent of the student body receives some sort of aid, either need or merit based, there are academic scholarships ranging from the $1,000 annual Allen Awards to the full-tuition and room-and-board grants in memory of William Marsh Rice. While there is no special application for these merit awards, other colleges might require an interview, writing sample, or audition. Merit aid is discussed in further detail in section IV, "Non-Aid Advice."

In the state of Arizona, The Flinn Scholars Program offers a sought-after award that rewards top high-school students who continue their education *in-state* at one of Arizona's own universities.

Merit aid is not given just to brainy students, either. Ellen, an average student, came from a part of the country that is traditionally under-represented at her college. She was given a $1,000 break on her dorm costs since she was helping the college spread its marketing net wider.

118

III. Tips for Applying for Financial Aid

- **Deadlines may vary dramatically but *whatever* they are, stick to them.** Don't lose the opportunity to qualify for aid simply because you procrastinated. Keep financial-aid deadlines on the family calendar in the kitchen or in your date book. Some colleges operate on a "first-come, first-served" basis, particularly those that "roll" on decisions, so keep that in mind if your son or daughter is a procrastinator by nature.

- **Keep photocopies of all materials submitted, marked with dates sent.** That way if anything is lost in the mail or misplaced by the post office, the processing agency, or the aid office (yes, they are human), you can replace it right away.

- **Maintain a file for each aid application.** Hold on to all correspondence. Keep a record of phone calls (names and dates, too.) Happily, many offices have toll-free numbers and calling hours in the evening and on weekends. While some colleges will send reminders if any piece of the application is missing, many will not. It's fine to call the financial-aid office to check and make certain that the application is complete.

- **Try to file your federal tax forms in January if possible.** The FAFSA and PROFILE refer to the 1040 form and, if actual figures are available, the form will be more accurate and you won't need to update it later. If you cannot file early, you should use your best estimates. For example, the last pay stub for the previous year will show what total wages were. You should *not* wait to fill out the FAFSA or PROFILE for tax forms which will be completed later than the application is due.

- **Follow directions carefully.** Be certain that the writing is neat and clear on the applications and that each question is answered as carefully and completely as possible. The forms give very specific instructions. For your own purposes, underline deadlines and very important points.

- **Use designated space for comments and notes about special circumstances.** If necessary, add an additional letter to the college's own application.

- **Make an appointment to meet with a financial-aid officer** to discuss special circumstances. Offices often schedule telephone "visits." Remember, many admission offices "share" a staff member

119

with the financial-aid office, and this may be the person you will talk to. Be certain to write this name down and stay in touch when you need questions answered. Keep toll-free numbers handy.

- **Make certain that your son or daughter's name and social security number is on every form and document.** Be consistent and use formal names, not nicknames. Also, if your last name is different from that of your child, make sure *your* name and relationship are listed clearly on correspondence. Many colleges use computer-software systems that use the social security number as an ID.

- **If you need to revise information originally submitted to the federal processor, these revisions should be made on the Student Aid Report (SAR).** The SAR will be sent to you by the Department of Education, usually about four weeks after the FAFSA is sent in. If you have a change to make in your initial application, it needs to be made on the SAR. Follow the College Scholarship Services's own correction procedure for making changes on the PROFILE.

- **Follow-up.** Make sure that you, as a parent, have done your part of the job, and check up on your child's responsibilities. Keep in mind that procrastination may jeopardize your chance of receiving aid. Check with the financial-aid office, and find out if anything is missing from your folder. *Warning: Incomplete folders don't get considered at all at many institutions.*

- **Put plenty of time into the financial-aid process.** Students often spend months—and sometimes even years—corresponding with an admission office to get an application filed and completed. Usually, the time spent on the financial-aid application is a matter of weeks. Both application processes are important—keep that in mind, and spend adequate time preparing both sets of forms. Consider the time spent an investment. Myra Smith, director of financial aid at Smith, remembers, "A parent once told me he paid his son minimum wage to research and apply for scholarships and financial aid in order to reinforce the importance of the financial commitment." If you invest 40 hours in the financial-aid process and your child is awarded $15,000 worth of aid, that's a "salary" of $375 per hour!

- **Don't wait until after you receive an admission decision before applying for financial aid**—it may be too late. Students sometimes think that they won't be admitted so they don't "bother" to apply for aid or they hope that by not applying for aid they may be enhancing their chances of admission. If you think that your family might need aid,

120

apply *on time*. If you wait until too late in the admission cycle, you may be disqualifying your child only on the basis of timing. If you don't need aid now but may need it in subsequent years because, for example, your children's college careers will overlap, apply for aid when the older child is applying for admission. Some colleges won't consider an aid application from a student who didn't apply at the time of admission until the student has earned two years worth of credit.

- **Upperclassmen are generally expected to contribute more** in self-help loans and Federal Work-Study. Also, expected summer contributions rise from freshman year to senior year. Be certain to find out what the expectations will be for your child.

- **If your family applies for financial aid and is not awarded any,** either because your situation was assessed as "no need" or because there simply was not enough aid available, investigate the possibility of reapplying and being awarded aid at a later date. If you will never receive aid, you need to accept that fact and make appropriate plans. *Don't* get yourself into a situation in which you can't pay the bill or your child will have to work an exorbitant number of hours a week in addition to going to class. This is the formula for disaster.

- **Remember to apply to a financial-aid safety school.** That is, be certain that your son or daughter will have at least one choice for college that you can afford even if you receive no or little financial assistance.

- **Investigate additional sources of aid available to you through your employer, church, fraternal organizations, etc.** Call your company's human-resources office for suggestions, and keep your eyes and ears open for announcements.

Q: I have heard that there are millions of dollars of financial aid which go unused each year. Is this true? If so, how can we apply?

A: Some scholarships and loans *are* very specific and can be awarded only to students fulfilling certain criteria. For example, The Albanian Women of America makes a cash award to a student of Albanian descent. The

Continues

Continued

American Society of Mechanical Engineers Auxiliary, Inc. gives grants and loans to upperclassmen in accredited mechanical-engineering programs. In some cases, organizations will award their funds to a "non-specific" applicant if nobody with the stated qualifications applies, but others stick to their guns and wait for someone to come through the ranks meeting the established criteria. Keep looking in libraries and in the guidance office for opportunities that may be appropriate for your child.

Call 800-4-FED AID, the Federal Student Aid Information Center, operated by the U.S. Department of Education, with questions about their sources of aid. Among their resources is the free brochure, *The Student Guide*, also available online at www.ed.gov, which presents an overview of major aid programs available to students along with details about the application process.

Parents who try to "beat the system" and qualify for aid for which they lack income eligibility are often unsuccessful since so much official documentation is needed. Additionally, a process called *verification*, which randomly checks the applications of students applying for aid, catches inaccuracies. There are stiff penalties for cheaters. If you have any reason to suspect fraud, waste, or abuse involving federal student-aid funds, call 800/MIS-USED, the hot line to the U.S. Department of Education's Inspector General's office.

Financial-Aid Packages

If your child receives financial aid, a "package" is awarded, that is, a combination of the two basic kinds of financial aid: gift aid and self-help.

- Gift aid is a *present*—scholarships and grants that never have to be paid back. Sometimes there is a "string" attached—your child needs to be studying a particular subject or must maintain a certain GPA, etc. A financial-aid award letter should spell out all of this information.

- Self-help requires some effort from your child and, in the case of some loans, from you. Loans and Federal Work-Study jobs make up varying amounts of a financial-aid package, and that mix will be very important to you as you compare costs of one school against another.

Ideally, an offer of financial aid is mailed at about the same time as an offer of admission, and often it arrives in the same envelope. If your financial-aid decision is delayed and is not available by May 1 (Candidates Reply Date),

BUDGET 2: EDUCATIONAL-FINANCING BUDGET

	Top Choice	Middle Choice	Financial-Aid Safety School
School name			
A. Estimated family contributions			
Parental support			
Federal PLUS Loan (Parent Loan for Under-graduate Students)			
Child's savings			
Child's earnings			
Other family support (grandparents, aunts, uncles, etc.)			
B. Federal assistance			
Federal Pell Grant			
Federal Supplemental Educational Opportunity Grants			
Federal Stafford Loan			
Federal Perkins Loan			
Federal Supplemental Loans for Students			
Federal Work-Study			
C. State assistance			
Scholarships and grants for residents			
Loans			
Special programs			
D. College/university assistance			
Scholarships and grants			
Work aid			
Loans			
E. Private organizations			
Loans			
Scholarships			
F. Other sources			
TOTAL = A + B + C + D + E + F			

123

request an extension of the deposit deadline so that you can make an informed decision about attendance.

Budget 2, on page 123, will give you a chance to outline the amount—and types—of aid you might receive from different colleges. This exercise is most helpful *after* you have received financial-aid offers, obviously, but if you can project what might be available to you, it might serve as a good, rough guide earlier in the process. The various types of aid are described in the pages following the budget, so depending on what stage you're in now, you may just want to flip ahead to read about the programs—and later, come back to this "comparative shopper's" guide.

Budget 2 Explained

A. Estimated family contributions

The major responsibility for paying for your education belongs to you and your child. Parents' *ability* to pay—not *willingness* to pay—is what is measured by need analysis. And since your son or daughter will be the one to benefit from the education, he or she will be expected to contribute a percentage of savings as well as some earnings.

Gerald Krefetz, author of *Paying for College: A Guide for Parents,* says "Parents generally fall into two categories: those who have prepared to pay college bills from the day their children were born, and the rest of us." Paying for a college education is a family matter and you need to spend time reviewing family finances when planning for college.

A **Federal PLUS Loan (Parent Loan for Undergraduate Students)** is for parents who want to borrow to help pay for their children's education, and like a Stafford Loan (see below), is made by a lender such as a bank, credit union, savings-and-loan association, or even a college.

An *independent* student is required to report only his or her income and assets (and spouse's if married) unlike a "dependent" student, who must report parental assets and income along with his own. If you, as parents, are *able* to pay but are *unwilling* to pay, that doesn't necessarily make your child "independent," at least not according to federal guidelines.

Federal guidelines stipulate that a student is independent if she/he has reached the age of 24. If a student is not 24 but is one of the following, independent status will be granted for purposes of applying for federal aid:

an orphan or a ward of the court

a veteran of the U.S. Armed Forces

has legal dependent(s) other than a spouse

married, or a graduate or professional student

These guidelines are accurate as of this writing but may change. For updated information, or if you think that you have unusual circumstances not listed that warrant classifying your child as independent, consult the financial-aid office.

B. Federal assistance

In addition to having demonstrated financial need, students must be U.S. citizens (or "eligible non-citizens"—e.g., permanent residents, U.S. nationals); be enrolled and making "satisfactory academic progress" as a regular student working toward a degree in an eligible program; have a high-school diploma, General Education Development (GED) Certificate, or meet other approved state standards; and have a valid Social Security number in order to qualify for federal money. Men have to be registered for the draft.

- A **Federal Pell Grant** is an award from the government that generally serves as a foundation of financial aid to which aid from other federal and non-federal sources may be added. All students who qualify for a Federal Pell Grant are guaranteed receipt of a Federal Pell Grant at any school that participates in the Federal Pell Grant program.

- A **Federal Supplemental Educational Opportunity Grant** is an award to help undergraduates with *exceptional* financial need, as determined by the individual schools, with priority given to Federal Pell Grant recipients. FSEOGs are awarded above and beyond Federal Pell Grants, and there is no guarantee that every eligible student will receive one.

- **Federal Stafford Loans** are the federal government's major form of self-help and are available through the William D. Ford Federal Direct Loan Program (nicknamed "Direct") and the Federal Family Education Loan ("FEEL") Program. The major differences between a Direct and a FEEL Loan are the source of funds, some parts of the application, and the repayment plans. These loans must be paid back, and you can't borrow more than the cost of education at your school minus your family's contribution and any other financial aid you receive. Stafford loans are either subsidized or unsubsidized. A subsidized loan is awarded on the basis of financial need, and the government pays interest on the loan until the student begins repayment. An unsubsidized Stafford loan, an option introduced in 1992, is awarded to any student regardless of need and the interest is charged to the student from the time the loan is issued until it is paid in full.

- A **Federal Perkins Loan** is a low-interest loan for students with *exceptional* financial need as determined by the school. These loans are made through a school's financial aid office—your school is your lender. Schools have varying levels of Perkins money and may or may not be able to offer you one.

- A **Federal Supplemental Loan for Students** is for student borrowers and provides additional funds. It, like the Federal PLUS Loan, is administered by a bank, credit union, or savings and loan.

- **Federal Work-Study** provides jobs to students who need financial aid. The pay is at least the current federal minimum wage (and *can* be higher, depending on the campus and on the skills required for the job). Students are assigned a limit of how much Federal Work-Study money they can earn in a term. The amount awarded is based on financial need as well as on the availability of resources, and the program is funded by the government. Having a job is a great way to gain experience and to get plugged into the campus in another way. Jobs range from kitchen duty to conducting scientific research with a faculty member.

The federal government awards approximately 75 percent of all student aid, much of which is in loans. There are yearly limits and overall maximum amounts lent to borrowers. In addition, there are a variety of repayment plans as well as loan-consolidation repayment plans.

The programs listed on pages 125-126 are administered by the U.S. Department of Education. For more information and with specific questions contact:

Federal Student Aid Information Center
P.O. Box 84
Washington, DC 20044
800/4-FED-AID
www.ed.gov

C. State assistance

Loans, scholarships, and special programs are available through individual states, and application procedures vary. Some states, like New York, will *not* let you take state money out of state. Check into the transferability of your own state scholarship if you are investigating colleges in states other than your home state. Often you can be considered for state programs by completing only the FAFSA, but in some cases you will need to submit additional forms. Check with your local guidance office to get more information about state agency policies. State higher-education financial agencies serve as excellent sources of information about scholarships and financing information.

D. College/university assistance

The college or university may have its own resources to award to your child in the form of jobs, loans, or scholarships and grants. Some colleges have specific scholarships for children of alumni, merit awards for talent in the arts, and athletic scholarships that come from university funds and that may be awarded in *addition* to other sources of aid or may be the only sources of aid you receive. Generally, if you apply for financial aid, you will be considered for whatever special funds are available. In some cases, as in a writing competition or a talent scholarship, additional work such as an interview, essay, or a tape may be required. Stick to the deadlines!

E. Private organizations

Churches, employers, labor organizations, and fraternal groups represent just a few sources of aid for college students. Sometimes called "outside" scholarships and loans because they don't come from the government or college, these sources are calculated into your total financial-aid package.

F. Other sources

Although the bulk of aid comes from the government, the colleges, and private organizations, you may qualify for other kinds of aid not listed above. Examples include tuition exchange or other employee benefits and live-in positions in exchange for room and board and a stipend.

Tips for Comparing Financial Aid Packages

- *Find out how "outside" scholarships (that is, those not granted by the college or the government) will be handled.* Will the college financial-aid office deduct any or all of this amount from the loan? From the grant? From both? Colleges vary on this and will be willing to explain their policies to you.

- *Don't get carried away assuming that a less expensive school will cost you less.* Look very carefully at the amount of aid each place is offering you, and compare that to the total cost of attendance to find out what each college will cost you and your family.

- *If there is a discrepancy in the amount of aid you have been awarded at comparably priced colleges, contact the financial-aid office.* It might be that one application asked information that another didn't, and so your family contribution was calculated in a different light. If you are able to supply more information, you may be able to get a more generous award. Of course, there is the very real possibility that the offer will not change.

- *Colleges have different amounts of aid available and distribute aid with different philosophies.* These differences become very clear as you compare awards made by colleges able to meet *total need* with awards made by colleges practicing "need gapping." In addition, some colleges package their financial aid with merit taken into consideration—that is, they "sweeten the pot" by lowering loan aid and upping the grant for students with special appeal.

- Don't be surprised if you as parents don't agree with your child on the value of the varying awards and the value of the varying educational experiences. Be patient, be clear, and try to listen to your child to hear what he really wants and needs. Passionate arguments and lots of door slamming can be avoided by trying to communicate reasonably and calmly.

Q&A

Q: How reliable are scholarship search services?

A: Like anything else in life, some are good and some are bad.

Susan Grant, director of consumer fraud prevention in the Northwestern District of the District Attorney's Office in The Commonwealth of Massachusetts, wrote in the "For the Consumer" column in the *Daily Hampshire Gazette* on January 21, 1993, "My office once received complaints from two students against a company in California that advertised it would provide lists of scholarships tailored to each individual's eligibility and field of study. Both students got identical lists, though their majors and qualifications were entirely different. Furthermore, neither of them was eligible for any of the scholarships listed. They requested refunds of their $40 fees under the company's 'money back guarantee,' but they were ignored. We did eventually get their refunds."

Beware of organizations making promises they can't keep. Use (free!) sources of information: your public library, the guidance office, financial-aid offices at colleges, the Internet and universities, and read, read, read! Before you use any kind of scholarship search agency, ask your guidance office or a college financial-aid office for an opinion.

IV. Non-Aid Advice

One director of financial aid, who prefers anonymity, remembers a father describing himself as a member of the "disenfranchised middle class," who telephoned—in anger—when his daughter was denied aid. The financial-aid officer politely pointed out that since his annual income was in excess of $250,000 and he owned an expensive house in an exclusive neighborhood, he simply didn't qualify. The financial-aid director remembers, "Perception is everything. Perhaps compared to his friends he wasn't wealthy—but he was wealthy enough *not* to qualify for need-based aid."

➤ **THE BAD NEWS:** It *is* tough not to get any help with college bills. Some parents resent the fact that they are footing the whole bill while other families are helped because of financial need or merit.

➤ **THE GOOD NEWS:** While it *is* difficult to assume all college expenses, not needing aid *might* be a "hook" in the admission process and may give your child a slight edge over an equally qualified aid applicant.

Says educational consultant Bill Risley, "We are seeing some colleges go below their historic 'admit ranges' to get full-paid kids." However, it is a huge mistake not to apply for aid if you need it in hope of swaying an admission decision. The financial strain that can result is likely to undermine your child's college experience. On the other hand, never assume that *applying* for aid is a guarantee that you'll get it.

Parents who pay full freight for their children include those who *applied* for aid but didn't get any (either because they were deemed "no need" or because there wasn't any to give) as well as those who never filed an aid application.

Payment plans have helped to take some of the sting out of tuition bills by offering 10- or 12-month installments. Many colleges have a wide variety of creative financing plans for tuition payment. Parents are even offered the option of a prepayment plan—that is, you can pay the full amount covering four years' tuition the first year and be guaranteed no tuition increases. Be certain to read the fine print about what happens if a child transfers out or leaves before graduating.

People tend to be saving less and borrowing more these days, and most parents expect to borrow for their children's education.

Some of the more popular educational loan programs are:

The Tuition Plan, Donovan Street Extension, Concord, NH 03301; 800/258-3640 or 603/228-1161

Academic Management Services, 50 Vision Boulevard, East Providence, RI 02914; 800/556-6684 or 401/431-1490

Collegeaire, P.O. Box 88370, Atlanta, GA 30356-8370; 404/952-2500

Alliance Education Loan, c/o Bank of Boston, P.O. Box 1296, Mail Stop 99-26-11, Boston, MA 02105; 617/434-8971

Family Education Loan, MA Educational Financing Authority, 176 Federal Street, Boston, MA 02110; 617/261-9760, or, outside of 617 area code, 800/842-1531

Loans are also available from banks, credit unions, and generous relatives and friends. Business groups, churches, clubs, and professional associations sometimes have privately funded loan programs, often with interest rates below those at banks. Ask financial-aid officers for more details.

Some parents borrow against their life-insurance policies to pay college bills while others are willing and able to take out second mortgages or home equity loans. If you use an accountant, ask for suggestions that work with your financial situation in mind.

Final Warning: Don't forget that "financial-aid safety school"—one you can afford without any outside assistance. It may be that your child will attend a community college for a year or two, or commute to a local school, and then transfer to a more costly choice.

Merit Awards

There are some students grants available that do not require demonstrated financial need. Programs may be available through an employer, through a professional association or through corporations, and they may be renewable from year to year. Ask the financial-aid office for suggestions and consult a public library.

The majority of college students work for pay in addition to their school work, so even though your child may not qualify for the Federal Work-Study program, lifeguarding, baby-sitting, tutoring, waiting tables, etc. are still options. Colleges and universities generally have an office of student employment that will help students find part-time employment, including "spot" jobs such as helping out during registration, commencement, etc.

Some Very Helpful Financial Aid Resources

Paying for College: A Guide for Parents. A comprehensive and well-written guide by Gerald Krefetz, if you can't find it in a bookstore, order through College Board Publications, Box 886, New York, 10101-0886.

College Financial Aid. Written by John Schwartz and Wintergreen/ Orchard House, Inc., this book includes over 750,000 scholarships. Published by ARCO, it's available in bookstores everywhere.

The College Cost Book. A publication of the College Board, this very helpful guide is updated annually.

Paying for Your Child's College Education. Written by Marguerite Smith, this book was published by Warner Books, New York, in 1996.

Paying for College: A Guide for Parents and their Children. A free publication from SallieMae, a financial services corporation that specializes in funding education and currently funds about 40 percent of all insured student loans outstanding. Contact them at 1050 Thomas Jefferson Street, NW, Washington, DC 20007-3871; 800/222-7182; http://salliemae.com.

Web Sites to Browse

www.ed.gov   U.S. Department of Education

www.gov/prog_info/SFA/StudentGuide   *The Student Guide,* the Department of Education's very useful publication on aid, is available online at this site.

www.finaid.org   Financial Aid Information Page sponsored by the National Association of Student Financial Aid Administrators and FinAid

www.collegeboard.org   The College Board's Fund Finder, loan-repayment estimators, and estimated-family-contribution worksheet

www.studentservices.com/fastweb   FastWeb Scholarship Service database of 180,000 private scholarships. Free search using an online profile

http://fie.com/molis/scholar.html   MOLIS Minority Scholarships & Fellowships

6

Pushing Papers:
The Application Itself

If your child hasn't already received an application from every college that made the final cut, be sure to call for one right away, * and then steel yourself for a sinking sensation. Indeed, at first glance, an application packet may be enough to dash your hopes that your kid will *ever* go to college—those crowded cards that don't fit in a computer printer; the little lines that won't stay straight in a typewriter (and the memories that come rushing back of uncompleted jigsaw puzzles or abandoned *Lego* projects that littered the rumpus room floor for light-years). Relax. When it comes to the application itself, you'll find more flexibility than you might think.

Because colleges give greatest weight to high-school records (with test scores sometimes a close second), it may almost seem as if your child's fate is already sealed before an application envelope is even opened. Yet, a strong application *will* often make a difference in an admission decision. "It lets us see the person behind the paperwork and helps us to look beyond the GPA," claims long-time admission expert Bob Mansueto. "An excellent application *can* help overcome an average record." Conversely, notes an official at the University of Virginia, "We've denied admission to people with good grades who did a lousy job on the application."

Of course, as parents, your part in all of this is precarious. You can read the pages below and understand what makes a good application. You can share this information with your son or daughter and volunteer to act as a proofreader, a sounding board, or even a secretary. But, ultimately, this is your child's job to do—not yours.

* unless he or she will be using a Common Application or online application

I. Different Decision Plans

While some admission jargon seems standard from Seton Hall to Stockton State, when it comes to application options, known as "decision plans," even experts get befuddled. Most confounding are the early application offerings.

"Early Decision" usually means that a student has decided on one first-choice college and, in exchange for submitting all credentials by a deadline which is sooner than the school ordinarily demands, will receive an early reply. BEWARE: Such decision plans generally require a "statement of commitment" in which your child agrees to attend that college and to withdraw all other applications if accepted early. This is different from "Early Action" or "Early-Evaluation" alternatives where colleges will offer either tentative or definite admission decisions but the candidate need not commit until May. Among the Ivy League institutions, Harvard and Brown offer Early-Action but not Early Decision plans. The reverse is true at Dartmouth, Columbia, Cornell, Princeton, the University of Pennsylvania, and Yale, where eager beavers must agree to a binding decision if accepted early. Some colleges (e.g., Smith and Mount Holyoke) offer *two* rounds of Early Decision. Candidates can apply by mid-November and receive notification a month later, or apply in early January and hear in February. In both cases, these decisions are also binding. Confused? Be certain to check with each of your target schools to determine not only what their admission plans are called, but also what guidelines or restrictions apply.

"Rolling Admission" means that applications are evaluated as they arrive and decisions are mailed shortly thereafter—usually within two months. While this plan often catches the eye of procrastinators ("Look, Ma, no deadline!"), keep in mind that places are filled on a first-come, first-served basis. Note, too, that Rolling-Admission plans usually have financial-aid and/or housing "priority" deadlines. Try to apply well in advance of these. Latecomers may lose out.

"Open Admission" means that all students who meet minimum requirements (usually a high-school diploma) may enroll. This policy is most common at two-year public institutions.

Q: Is it harder or easier to get in via an Early Decision plan?

A: Common sense suggests that Early Decision applicants are top-notch students—not only more organized but also more qualified than the masses who, months later, will be racing to finish their "regular-decision" forms. While many admission officers do little to dispel this myth, in truth, the Early Decision option can be a good bet for more middle-of-the-road candidates as well. To some degree, the bird-in-hand-versus-two-in-the-bush theory is operating here. Only a fraction of the total pool will apply early, so admission officers can merely guess at how these early birds stack up against the rest of the flock that will follow, and they are likely to grab at sure things. "It is definitely easier to be admitted Early Decision here," says Lee Stetson, dean of admission at the University of Pennsylvania (where about one-third of the freshman class enters under the "E.D." option). "Everybody likes to be loved, and we're no exception at Penn. We want students who really *want* to attend, not those who are *resigned* to come."

➤ **THE GOOD NEWS:** Students who are admitted early only have to complete one application and may even avoid retaking standardized tests as seniors. Moreover, those candidates who are "deferred" (in other words, not accepted early but reevaluated in the spring), have sent a positive message that may pay off. An Early Decision application is one way to let a college know that it is your child's first choice.

➤ **THE BAD NEWS:** Early Decision plans are NOT advisable for late bloomers who didn't get off the mark until junior year, nor for those with poor junior standardized-test scores. Colleges will want to see first-semester senior grades and senior scores before committing and—if previous numbers were particularly weak—the Early Decision candidate may be rejected outright, not deferred, before having a chance to prove himself in 12th grade.

Early Decision can be tricky for some financial-aid applicants. Applicants will receive a tentative aid package at the time of the decision (based on estimates from the previous year's tax forms). However, if the aid isn't as much as you expected (or if you don't qualify at all), you might want to investigate other options, and your child may be forced to refuse the offer of admission, despite the signed commitment form. This mess can often be avoided by contacting financial-aid officers before the application deadline and asking for advice.

However, from a *parental* point of view, the real harm lies in a disappointed kid who must turn down a first-choice school after being admitted. Colleges aren't thrilled when E.D. applicants change their minds, but they don't "blackball" them at other schools, either. When done for financial reasons, it's often simply inevitable. However, when done because a candidate's interest wanes, it's not just unfortunate, it's unethical. When applying Early Decision, be as certain as possible that this is really a *first-choice* school, not the path of least resistance.

II. General Application Tips

Use the Correct Application

Some institutions have a different form (or a supplement to a standard form) for separate schools within a university (e.g., music, education). Read instructions carefully to be certain that your child has *all* required components. Some colleges also use different forms for international students and non-permanent residents of the U.S. (If you think your child may have completed the wrong application, don't panic, just call the admission office. They may require that the right one be substituted, but they may just let it slide.)

Some schools have a two-part process. Part I is a brief form requesting basic biographical data. When your child returns it to the admission office, Part II will be put in the mail.

HINT: It's a good idea to photocopy an entire application before beginning it to use as a rough draft.

Q&A

Q: Why won't colleges make life simpler by accepting the same application?

A: Some do. For example, the handy Common Application can be completed once, then photocopied and sent to any of the nearly 200 colleges nationwide that have agreed to honor it in order to minimize the efforts of their overtaxed applicants. The list of subscribing colleges and universities (and the application itself) is available in most high-school guidance offices or by contacting: The Common Application c/o The National Association of Secondary School Principals; 1904 Association Drive; Reston, VA 22091; 800/253-7746. *Some colleges will require an additional brief supplement* (and *occasionally* an extra essay), so if your child is using the "Common App," it is important to notify admission offices and ask if other forms are necessary. In addition, if your child is applying early-decision or to a special program or department, colleges should be alerted.

The Common Application can also be completed on a computer disk or downloaded from several different Web sites. Some high-school guidance offices provide disks for free. Otherwise they can be ordered for $10 by calling the toll-free number, above. Sites with links to the Common App include The National Association of Secondary School Principals (www.nassp.org/services/commapp.htm). In addition, many of the subscriber colleges offer links to the Common App directly from their Web pages.

Newer to the fray but equally helpful is the Universal Application sponsored by Peterson's—another familiar and respected name in the college search business. The Universal Application has about 600 subscribers and can be completed online by beginning at the Peterson's Web site (www.petersons.com).

You can also hook up with the CollegeLink™ program. About 800 institutions subscribe to this service that enables candidates to complete a *single* application on a personal computer. Students can either download the application from the World Wide Web (www.collegelink.com) or use diskettes available for both Macintosh or Windows. Completed information is then sent to the CollegeLink headquarters, where "customized" applications are printed for each member school for a small fee. For more information or to order diskettes, call 800/394-0404.

Q: Do admission officials accord the Common Application the same respect that they give their own?

A: Despite some rumors to the contrary, colleges subscribing to the Common Application pledge to give it equal weight, and they do. (Some, including Harvard, use it exclusively.) In fact, the Common App's essay question is actually three very general "Personal Statement" choices (asking students to either evaluate a significant experience or achievement; to discuss an issue of personal, local, or national concern; or to describe how one individual has had significant influence on their lives), and officials often find the results are a breath of fresh air after spending an evening with 106 other essays on some esoteric topic that their own Board of Admission cooked up.

The same is true for the Universal Application or any other format that your target school accepts. However, when sending paper applications or printouts, be sure to photocopy them neatly and clearly. Colleges *don't* appreciate getting an illegible, seventh-generation Xerox.

If you're still worried that bypassing an institution's own application will make your son or daughter seem like a less-than-serious applicant, here's a final bit of advice: Don't let the Common Application (or other generic alternative) be the *only* thing in your child's file. Include *some* indication of special interest in each institution. While a trip to campus and/or an interview are certainly the best bets in that department, they're not always possible. Even a brief note asking for specific information (e.g., the name of the Outing Club president) suggests to admission officials that your child has a genuine interest in their school and isn't merely mailing in a photocopied form as an afterthought.

Q&A

Q: We had to dust off our typewriter before starting the college applications. Can't we use a computer instead?

➤ **THE GOOD NEWS:** Many institutions recognize that "hard copy" got its name for good reason, since paper application forms are terribly cumbersome (and also probably the dinosaurs of the next decade). As discussed above, the time-honored Common Application can now be completed with a computer, and there are a growing number of other electronic alternatives. For example, when you visit a college Web site, you may find links to an online application. Some colleges even offer application-fee discounts (or waivers!) to those who apply electronically.

➤ **THE BAD NEWS:** Online application options are growing at such a rapid rate that the hours you might save by using them may be lost, instead, in a quagmire of Net-surfing confusion. For example, a number of the Web sites discussed in Chapter 2 (e.g., CollegeView, CollegeEdge, The Princeton Review) all have their own versions of electronic applications—but not all colleges accept all formats. You may also hear the term "ExPAN." A product of the College Board, ExPAN software is purchased by high schools and educational organizations, not individual families, and allows students to access applications and other information via computer. And from the College Board Web site (www.collegeboard.org) students can also download ExPAN's applications to more than 800 institutions. Another online service that is widely welcomed is "APPLY!" Students access the APPLY! Web site (www.weapply.com) and order a free CD-ROM with applications and other helpful tips and information. You can also call 800/93-APPLY.

A: Your best bet? Once you've identified target colleges, call (or e-mail) each admission office and ask which electronic applications (if any) are accepted. It doesn't hurt to ask if one is preferred. Find out, too, if fee discounts are available for electronic applicants.

Q&A

Q: My child has never won prizes for neatness (and gets it from me). How much does this really matter on an application?

A: "I, personally, am quite influenced by the neatness of an application," maintains one Duquesne University admissions official. "Sloppiness makes me wonder how concerned an applicant is with creating a good impression." "It makes me ask 'Are they seriously interested or are we just a backup?'" concurs an assistant director of admissions at Denison University. An application's appearance is, indeed, bound to make at least a *subconscious* impression. "Sloppiness never *helped* anyone get accepted," quips a top official at UVA.

On the other hand, don't be too much of a neat freak, either. One mother recalls a last-minute rush to replace an application because her daughter had gotten a small ink smear on one corner. Each form, in fact, is handled by so many admission-staff members that officials realize that fingerprints, wrinkles, and even coffee stains are more likely to be their fault than yours.

Ordinarily, applicants are asked to type or print. Your child should elect whichever can be done most neatly. If printing, use ink. Essays should not be written by hand unless you are given specific instructions to do so. (See "The Almighty Essay," later in this chapter.)

"In borderline cases, good spelling is especially important," insists an admission counselor at Ohio State University. "It tells us both about the quality of a candidate's education and about the amount of time and care put into the application." Even those counselors who offer amnesty for smudges, scratch-outs, and poor penmanship are likely to be less forgiving when it comes to spelling. Frank Crivello, former associate director of admissions at Beloit College in Wisconsin calls himself "a stickler" for spelling and cringes when he recalls the hapless prospect who misspelled the college's name!

Words commonly misspelled on applications include: business, medicine, psychology, architecture, archaeology/archeology, foreign, interest, profession, counselor/counsellor, and received. Capitalization is often omitted from English, French, and other proper nouns. Apostrophes are erroneously used to make plurals or omitted from contractions and possessives.

Grammar, too, can influence an admission decision. "When students use poor grammar on an application, we have to wonder if they are capable of college-level written expression," says an official from Duquesne.

If you don't trust your talents as a proofreader, urge your child to see a school counselor, teacher, or other "expert." Remember, though, clean corrections can be difficult to make on an application form. Your child should be urged to work carefully and to check out grammar and spelling uncertainties before plowing ahead.

The Deadline Isn't Always the Bottom Line

➤ **THE GOOD NEWS:** Observe application deadlines as closely as possible and NEVER BE LATE WITH FINANCIAL AID MATERIALS. Yet don't rule out a college because of a missed deadline (or total your Toyota on the way to the post office)—most schools are more lenient than you might imagine.

With college admission a buyer's market right now, many schools are accepting applications days—and even weeks—after they are due. If your child is behind schedule with paperwork or "discovers" a new school at the last minute, it's likely that there will be some leeway with closing dates.

Not even Harvard will heave out an application that's a day or two delayed, but an explanatory note is always helpful. If you will need an extension, request it *in advance* of the deadline whenever possible. Make a record of the staff member you spoke with. For long extensions (two weeks or more), follow up your phone calls with a note asking for a *written* acknowledgment of your extension. Keep in mind, as well, that an application is a complex affair, composed of many parts. If possible, submit at least the initial section on time—usually it's a quickie which asks for name, address, school (and fee!)—making the college aware of your child's intent to apply. The essay, recommendations, and so on can be sent later.

Express-mail companies make a bundle on 11th-hour applicants. Some colleges accept materials by fax, too—but many won't. (Always ask.) In most cases, if an application arrives only two or three days late, the tardiness will be ignored altogether. However, it's a risk you really don't want to run, when a brief phone call may assure you extra time. One admission officer remembers a beautiful bouquet of balloons that arrived with a very late application and a note of apology. She kept the balloons but refused the tardy application.

➤ **THE BAD NEWS:** There is no such thing as a standard deadline. They're all over the calendar.

To complicate life further, there are deadlines, and there are deadlines. Some schools have double-barreled dates like the University of Oregon. There, applications are accepted until March 1, except for those from prospective architecture students, which are due by *December* 1. At some colleges, financial-aid deadlines may be months before the application due date. And remember, as you read above, latecomers at "Rolling-Admission" colleges may miss out not only on financial aid but also on housing—and sometimes on acceptance altogether.

Always Ask if Sooner Is Better.

This is a key point. At many colleges, no application folders are reviewed until the due date has passed. Thus, the candidate who "completes" (admission jargon for finishing all application components) weeks in advance has no advantage over one who meets the deadline by only hours (although early applicants have more time to track down missing records). However, some colleges give priority to applicants who apply early.

Schools that don't "roll" on decisions usually notify all of their candidates at once. Don't expect that just because your child applied well before the deadline you'll hear sooner too.

Q: Must all parts of an application be mailed together?

A: Most applications are composed of separate forms, cards, and other components. It's impossible for all to be mailed at once because some parts, such as confidential recommendations and transcripts, must come directly from other people. Your child may want to mail in initial forms early and dawdle on an essay. That's okay, too. Just make sure that everything sent includes your child's full name, school, address, and social security number.

Q: How do we know if an application has arrived safely?

A: You'll find that some colleges include postcards in their application package which you self-address and which they will mail back when your child's application is received. Other colleges automatically send out a confirmation when forms arrive. If you don't get any sort of notification, feel free to telephone. It is the applicant's responsibility to follow up and make sure that all components—including transcripts and recommendations—have arrived.

One university admission official tells a sad (but not unique) story about a candidate who didn't call until after admission decisions had been made and she hadn't received one. She angrily blamed the office of admission for the oversight until she discovered her application—check and all—in her father's desk drawer. (Talk about panic!)

Above all, make copies. The inconvenience of photocopying everything you send out is nothing compared to the nightmare of rewriting even one application.

III. Tips for Tackling Specific Application Sections

All applications are not created equal. Each is just different enough from the next to keep candidates on their toes, but most are similar enough, too, to allow some universal truths. For instance...

Fill in All the Blanks

- Don't leave blanks blank. If a question isn't relevant, your child should say so by writing "N/A" (the standard abbreviation for "Not Applicable") or by using a dash.

- Family employment and education answers should be clear to those *outside* the family. Never abbreviate company names and/or colleges unless nationally known. (And your kids shouldn't worry if *you* didn't graduate from fancy colleges or if you didn't go to college at all. In fact, being "first-generation" can sometimes work in their favor.)

- Don't ignore the race/ethnic background question. By law, answers are optional, but a minority background is usually a plus and never a liability. A child who identifies at all with a racial or ethnic minority group should check the appropriate box. It is not necessary to have been born in a foreign country or have *both* parents belong to the group. Students from racially mixed backgrounds can check more than one box or explain in the "other" category.

- If English is not your child's first language and/or not spoken at home, make sure this is indicated on the application. Some forms will ask directly. Otherwise, your child should attach a brief separate statement explaining his language history or use an asterisk (*) in an appropriate spot on the form itself (such as in the racial/ethnic group section or next to the verbal SAT or ACT score). Find out also if a TOEFL exam (Test of English as a Foreign Language) is required or useful.

- Say "see attached" as needed. If the form does not provide adequate space to list extracurricular activities, job experience, etc., it is fine to include a separate page or résumé. (See "Consider Attaching a Résumé," below.) This is preferable to trying to jam too much information into too little space, but make sure that each additional page includes your child's name and a clear heading.

- Find out if "major" choices are binding, before committing. Most applications ask your child for an intended major. This helps colleges to see what departments are most (or least) popular among high-school students, to facilitate sending brochures or follow-up letters from faculty, and to ascertain that applicants are not planning on studying something that isn't even offered at that college (it happens!). While many students are undecided and say so, it's more impressive to list a range of potential interests. As discussed in Chapter 2, be aware of binding commitments (most often found at universities with preprofessional programs such as pharmacy, agriculture, business, etc. and rarely at liberal-arts schools) and determine in advance if, once admitted, switches are possible.

Above all, your child shouldn't be like one unfortunate aspirant who gave admission officials a chuckle. When asked for her "Probable Area of Study," she responded, "In my room or in the library."

Be "Cute" Cautiously

Madonna can get away with wearing undies in public; Sandra Day O'Connor can't. Likewise, some candidates can pull off cutesy gimmicks while, for others, they fall flat. Such attention-getters (like the Pomona applicant who wrote her entire application in alternating blue and orange, the college's colors) *do* make admission officers sit up and take notice, and even those who grimace and say, "Oh, *pul-eeze, spare me*," are apt to remember such an audacious applicant and maybe admire her pluck. Outrageousness is most effective if: a) it's appropriate to your child's personality (remember Madonna), b) your child is a strong candidate to begin with (or a long shot with nothing to lose), and c) can come up with an idea that is pretty darn clever (no hints here...it ought to be original).

Consider Attaching a Résumé

A growing number of applications now arrive at admission offices complete with elaborate student résumés that would humble Leonardo da Vinci. Not only is it easier to say "see attached" than it is to repeat activity information on each college form, but some students today do too much to put their best foot forward in the limited space provided. However, often the official form is fine.

Whether your child uses a separate sheet or the application itself, it's important to be sure that activities—and your child's role in them—are clear. In particular, leadership positions should be stated, and if your child started a club and didn't merely join it, then say so.

Maya tried to condense her life into seven lines, but it just wouldn't fit. She wasn't a team captain. In fact, she hadn't even played a sport since sixth grade. She wasn't a class officer either, but she *was* the only student in her entire school to be selected for the mayor's task force on crime. She co-chaired the subcommittee on youth affairs with a city councilor and helped design a pilot project that served as a model throughout the state. Add to that three science-fair awards, eight years of flute lessons, and an after-school job. Wisely, Maya typed "See résumé, enclosed" on each application and then submitted separate sheets.

When your child has been busy throughout high school or engaged in uncommon enterprises, there won't be room to list everything on an application form, and you won't *want* to list everything on a résumé, either. Be selective. Focus on those activities which have been most significant or long-term. If your daughter collected donations for the new playground one afternoon in ninth grade, it's not fodder for colleges. A year of varsity volleyball—however uneventful—*is*. Including too much can actually backfire. Colleges will question a student's commitment and priorities. They'll envision your Calvin careening down a corridor, sticking his head in every door while 16 clubs meet simultaneously—and with his chemistry notes lying fallow in his locker. They'll also be skeptical when activities look like application window-dressing that didn't get going until the start of senior year.

Following are more résumé tips:

- Don't worry if your software isn't state-of-the-art. Colleges don't care how many megabytes go into producing résumés, as long as they're neat and easy to read. Make sure your child's name, social security number (or address), and school are at the top of every page.

- Explain everything that isn't crystal clear. Avoid cryptic titles or acronyms. Even programs or organizations that are widely recognized like Girls' State or SADD should never be abbreviated and ought to be followed by a short explanation. (e.g., Instead of listing "AFS/U.K." say "American Field Service summer family homestay program participant in the United Kingdom.") Similarly, just like on a "grownup" résumé, work experience also requires a short description. Some students hold positions of real responsibility. Simply listing, "Clerk; Luigi's" doesn't tell admission officials that this applicant supervises six other workers and is in charge of opening and closing a busy grocery store every weekend.

- If your child has made a big time commitment to an activity, make sure it is clear. Admission officials often find themselves asking, "Did Jared volunteer at the soup kitchen for an hour a week or an hour a month (or an hour, period!)?"

- Use asterisks or similar symbols to identify those activities that your child has found most important and those which will be pursued in college. (Application forms will sometimes ask students to list the most important activities first.)

- Make sure that extra-special commitment or unique ventures stand out in some way. The essay or personal statement may allow this. If not, a supplemental essay—even a short one—is suggested. (See the section on essays later in this chapter.)

Short Subjects

➤ **THE BAD NEWS:** These are the questions from hell—those brief one-paragraph puzzlers that are a cross between a fill-in-the-blank and an authentic essay (and the worst of both worlds).

➤ **THE GOOD NEWS:** Many applications don't have them. They cut right to the chase scene and go straight for the essay without a warm-up.

Most students spend too little time on short-answer questions. They're saving their creative juices for the essay to follow. As a result, admission officers don't expect to be interested or amused by these items and are pleasantly surprised—and impressed—if they find otherwise. So, why not encourage your child to offer short answers that will stand out in a crowd?

Here are two typical short-answer questions followed by three responses: *exceptional, acceptable,* and *awful.* Note that the best answers take liberties with orthodox style and let the writer's personality shine through.

Which of your extracurricular activities is most important to you and why?

Exceptional: You can't miss us. We're the ones with the ink stains on our shirt sleeves, the ever-furrowed brows. Yes, we're the newspaper staff, the folks who live on too little sleep and too much coffee so we can get that tabloid on the lunchroom tables every Tuesday. I guess it's in my blood. I need to know what's going on around me, and I maybe even harbor hope that I can (sometimes) challenge it or change it through my writing.

Acceptable: I am most interested in my involvement with the school newspaper. I like to write, to try to present information in unique or unusual ways, and to stay in touch with what's going on in my immediate surroundings.

Awful: Newspaper. I like writing and news.

How have your academic experiences in high school contributed to your intellectual development?

Exceptional: "Physics!" My classmates covered their ears as I shrieked. "I can't believe I'm taking *physics.*" I'd never been a "science person," and now here I was in a room full of pocket protectors and tiny calculators. The other thing I couldn't believe was how closely physics was connected to a subject that had always intrigued me—philosophy. My physics teacher introduced me to the ties between seemingly discrete academic disciplines, and it fueled my enthusiasm to study both in college.

Acceptable: I have come to appreciate the ways in which different subjects are connected to each other. For example, I reluctantly took physics my senior year and found that it includes issues that touch on another new area of interest, philosophy.

Awful: By showing the way different subjects are connected to each other (like physics and philosophy).

146

Other tips for short subjects

- *Practice makes perfect.* Urge your child to perfect answers on scrap paper before printing or typing on the application.

- *A separate sheet is acceptable.* Application forms aren't computer-friendly. It is permissible to say "see attached" beneath short-answer questions and type both the question and reply on a separate sheet. Proper labeling (including your child's name, in case the sheet gets detached) is imperative. Each answer should be about the same length as the space allocation on the original form.

IV. The Almighty Essay

The irony of college application essays is this: students are informed (and rightfully so) that a good essay can gain admission for an otherwise average applicant; a bad one may scratch a contender from the list. Entire books are devoted to telling teenagers how to create compositions that will "work." As a result, applicants are so intimidated by the thought of such a make-or-break endeavor that some procrastinate until the last possible minute and then dash off a stack of mediocre efforts.

Admission officers use essays not only to assess a candidate's writing, spelling, and vocabulary skills, but also to get a look—sometimes their *only* look—at the personality behind the prose, at a prospect's interests, sense of humor, values, and goals. For this reason, college essay topics usually emphasize the personal—not merely academic—side of their authors. Yes, some colleges still ask applicants to unravel obtuse quotations from eminent alumni, but those who pose such questions often offer other options as well. More typical of today's topics is this one from Sarah Lawrence which simply says: "Tell us something about yourself that we might not learn from the rest of your application."

Typical Essay Topics

Here are some of the essay topics that have appeared on recent college applications:

- Describe the person whom you would choose as your hero or heroine. Please explain how this person exemplifies the ideals which you value. (Tufts)

- What are your expectations of a college education? In what ways do you hope to grow or change? (Mills)

147

- If you were given the opportunity to leave a time capsule for posterity in the cornerstone of your city hall, what one book, one mechanical object, and one other item of your choosing would you have as a statement about life in the late 20th century and why? (U. of PA)

- Describe what you would consider to be the perfect adventure. (Hollins)

- You have answered many questions on this form, all asked by someone else. If you yourself were in a position to ask a provocative and revealing question of college applicants, what would that question be? (Dartmouth)

Some colleges demand *several* short essays; many allow applicants to select *one* of three or four topics. However, given the very open-ended nature of these questions, it's tough for most teenagers to decide how to best respond. Reassure your child that there are never "right" or "wrong" answers, nor are there "trick" questions. Any response that is well supported and well written is the correct one.

Stay Away from Overworked Topics

Strictly speaking, a good essay can be written about *anything,* and college officials certainly appreciate unique and imaginative entries. However, when informally polled, many such officials agreed that there are some subjects that crop up over and over and which rarely spawn essays that are creative and memorable. These subjects are included in the following list:

- winning (or losing) the "big game"

- boyfriend or girlfriend problems

- religious epiphanies

- telling troubles to a "journal"

- anything that suggests that the applicant doesn't see the world beyond the boundaries of the high school (e.g., the pressures of prom planning)

- oversimplified solutions to world problems ("People need to realize that people are people wherever you go and have to try to understand one another.")

"We realize that these issues are important to our applicants," one admission counselor observes, "but only the most able writer is likely to be able to turn such commonly chosen topics into a strong personal statement."

And speaking of taboo topics that should only be attempted with great caution, an Ivy League admission official proclaims that she's "just amazed by how *stupid* some students are when it comes to picking essay subjects. This year I read two essays on throwing up, one on constipation, and one on nose-picking! Actually, Seinfeld did a thing on his TV show about nose-picking that was quite funny, but it's something that most high school students aren't going to be able to pull off as successfully. We realize that they're trying to find a topic that will stand out, but they've got to remember that this essay will be read by a committee that may include the dean of admission, the dean of students, and faculty members."

Aim for Originality

What, then, are "good" essay subjects? Again, anything goes; the more original the better (let sound judgment prevail when it comes to the bodily functions), but admission folks seem to always warm up to those which are included in the following list:

- overcoming adversity (e.g., recovering from a serious illness; struggling with family substance abuse; living with a disabled sibling)

- insight into an uncommon lifestyle, experience, or achievement (growing up on a commune; being raised by a grandparent; attending school in Saudi Arabia; climbing a challenging mountain)

- information about an unusual hobby (building Victorian dollhouses; raising goats; collecting political campaign buttons)

- lessons learned from literature

While, perhaps, great writers are born, not made, and even months of preparation won't transform your child from Hem N. Haw to Hemingway, there is some essay advice worth heeding. Begin by reading the two examples below. Both were written by the same author and address the topic: *"If you could have dinner with anyone, living, dead, or fictional, whom would you choose, and why?"*

Essay #1

There are many, many people who would make interesting dinner partners and for a number of reasons. If I had to pick only one person, living or dead, I would choose my Aunt Rae. Unfortunately, she's the latter, having died when I was just eleven, and, actually she was my great, great aunt—the sister of my father's grandmother, if you can follow that. Aunt Rae was always important to me because she instilled in me my love of reading and, especially, my appreciation of literature by and about women.

I first met Aunt Rae when I was eight. It was October of fourth grade, and my teacher, Mrs. Millan, was encouraging her pupils to read by offering us a gold star each time we finished a biography from the classroom bookshelf. I proudly told my "new" aunt that I had already completed seven books. She asked about whom I had read and was surprised (and a bit perturbed) that all of these subjects were male. She urged me to borrow her books about Helen Keller and Jane Addams, and I was quickly mesmerized.

Soon, Sunday afternoons with Aunt Rae became a regular routine, and I plowed through her extensive collection of biographies, each detailing the fascinating life of a different woman, from Juliet Ward Howe to Florence Nightingale; from Harriet Beecher Stowe to Harriet Tubman. Afterwards, we would share tea and strange cookies she called "madeleines."

Aunt Rae, like the heroines in her books, had had an interesting life herself. She was a native of England and flew supply planes in World War II. She married an American man who died during a Navy mission in the Pacific, so she left her homeland and came here, taking the reins of her late-husband's hardware supply business.

I wish I could say that all of my time with Aunt Rae was special but, like many youngsters, I grew impatient with her prodding and with her insistence that I share her passion for literature and history and other adult affairs. It is only now, as I look back on what she taught me and inspired in me, and as I look ahead to my goal of one day becoming a writer myself, that I most appreciate my Aunt Rae, and miss her, and long to see her again, even if only for one brief dinner.

Essay #2

My Dinner with Aunt Rae

"Ah. You remembered the madeleines. I knew you would." She brought a delicate biscuit to her lips and sighed. "Milk and honey is much overrated, I'm afraid." Everything was indeed in order. For weeks I had planned this reunion, careful with each detail. Most important, though, were the madeleines—the shell-shaped French tea cakes that used to be part of every meeting with my Aunt Rae. In those days, of course—I was no more than eight or nine at the time—I secretly longed for more familiar fare—butterscotch brownies perhaps, or lemon squares. But Aunt Rae had never treated me like a child—even then—and that was part of her allure.

"You look like you've seen a ghost," she announced as she reached for another biscuit. Certainly, I hadn't known what to expect—a white sheeted Casper like a school boy on Halloween? The ephemeral Elvira of *Blithe Spirit* that I'd struggled to perfect as a sophomore? Aunt Rae chuckled heartily, and a decade melted away. In fact, she looked exactly as I had recalled her so many times: the sturdy shoes and cotton shirtwaist dress; the sand and silver hair drawn up in an earnest bun. I was suddenly grateful that my mother had kept me from the hospice in those final weeks.

Technically speaking, she had been my great, great aunt—my father's grandmother's sister. I suppose this would not make her a close relative by some calculations but, to me, she was all-important. Born in England, Aunt Rae had piloted a supply plane in World War II and, when her American sailor-husband was lost in the Sea of Japan, had installed herself in Savannah to oversee his family hardware business. I found her life as unfathomable and as enthralling as the faded photograph of the long-gone spouse on the mantle piece.

"Now, tell me, again, why I'm here," she implored. "What they said wasn't entirely clear…up there." She cast her eyes toward the ceiling. "It's an essay, Aunt Rae," I explained. "For college. I get to choose someone to have dinner with. Famous or fictional. Living or, uh, dead. I picked you."

"Well, my dear. I must say I'm flattered," she replied. "Was Helen Keller unavailable? Jane Addams, as well?" Aunt Rae surely never missed a trick. She was harking back to our earliest encounter—the one that had precipitated so many others. I had just begun fourth grade. My teacher, Mrs. Millan, was awarding us gold stars for each biography we finished from the classroom shelf. Eric Eisenberg and I were neck and neck. Already seven stars apiece. When Aunt Rae met me for the first time, I was winding up *Wyatt Earp, U.S. Marshal.* She questioned me on other titles I'd completed. "Why, they're all *men!*" she proclaimed when I was through my recitation. Although I hadn't given it much thought before, she was right. Nowhere on Mrs. Millan's shelf was there even a single female's story. But Aunt Rae had had her own collection, and before that weekend was over, I had befriended both Helen Keller and Jane Addams. The following Sunday, she introduced me to Harriet Beecher Stowe and, the next, to Sacajawea. Always a contented reader, under Aunt Rae's tutelage, I became an insatiable one.

For most of that year, my Sundays were spent in Aunt Rae's cluttered library. Afterwards, there would be madeleines and tea. Eric Eisenberg got left in the dust as I clamored for more insight into myriad women's lives. Yet, those afternoons with Aunt Rae were never easy. She was an exacting mentor and had no patience for my childish complaints or whims. For my birthdays she gave me hand-blown glass from Venice, papyrus from Sicily—never games or toys. She spurred me to read Jane Austen while my friends were touting *Nancy Drew*. I could recite the Brontë sisters by name, but not the Brady Bunch. My visits slipped to once a month—and then to every other—but books still routinely arrived in the mail, and I consumed each one with fervor.

"So, why me?" again Aunt Rae insisted. "Have you run out of literary recommendations. Do I still need to tell you what to read?" "Actually, no," I answered, more shyly than is my usual nature. "It's not *reading* that's the issue here. Now, it's my turn to *write*." And so, I admitted to my great, great aunt my dream of becoming an author. I told her of my project on Susan B. Anthony that had made such a stir at school ("the best work I've ever seen," my junior humanities teacher had maintained) and of the workshop on Maya Angelou that I had run for pre-teen girls last summer at the Y. "I want to write a biography, a full-length one," I confided. "Nobody renowned; just somebody special." I took the last madeleine from the plate. "I want my subject to be *you*."

The cookie surprised me with its sweetness. It was richer than I had remembered; far more interesting than a brownie or a lemon square. It was an acquired taste, I decided—not unlike Aunt Rae, herself.

The two essays tell the same story: the first is solid, but the second has more spark. With both, the applicant is admissible, but, while #1 is hardly memorable, #2 might be enough to prompt a positive decision from an otherwise ambivalent admission board.

Some Valuable Essay Tips

Even if you hardly consider yourself a literary critic, you can offer valuable editorial assistance—and the tips that follow—to your child:

- **A title is a nice touch,** especially if it's catchy. The title of Essay #2 is a clever pun, an allusion to a well-known and rather intellectual film, *My Dinner with Andre.* In only five words, and before the essay has really begun, this applicant has shown off her witty and sophisticated side.

- **The introduction is crucial.** If your kid does only one thing right in the essay, this should be it. Never let the reader doze off at the first sentence. Note that the start of Essay #1 is a real snoozer. How many others must begin almost identically? Essay #2, however, immediately engages. Curiosity is piqued: just who is this Aunt Rae, and what about these madeleines and milk and honey?

- **Good writers take risks with style.** Observe how Essay #2 plays with intentionally incomplete sentences ("Already seven stars apiece") and with phrases set off by dashes and parentheses.

- **Vocabulary should be varied and interesting.** Teenagers tend to use the same boring words (like "varied" and "interesting") over and over and over. Check for repetition. Suggest more colorful alternatives. On the other hand, don't encourage your child to use words he's not comfortable or familiar with. He should use a thesaurus for suggestions, but his writing shouldn't sound as if he swallowed one.

- **Humor is a big plus,** especially when one considers those beleaguered admission officers plodding through piles of applications as the clock ticks past midnight. Just because an essay will be taken seriously, doesn't mean it has to be a serious essay. Essay #2, above, uses touches of humor judiciously (e.g., "You look like you've seen a ghost;" "Was Helen Keller unavailable?"). Nonetheless, if a kid has never been Rosie O'Donnell or Eddie Murphy, this isn't the time to start.

- **Sentimentality, too, can be an asset** if used sparingly. Both essays, above, end on a note that is slightly sentimental but not maudlin or melodramatic.

- **Show off an academic side.** Your kid does have one? Essay # 2 hints at the author's familiarity with writers Jane Austen, the Brontë sisters, and Maya Angelou as well as with historical figures like Susan B. Anthony.

153

- **Be revealing.** Essay #2 craftily tells us *much* about this applicant. We certainly learn that she's an excellent writer, one who uses subtlety well. (We see, for example, from references to ghosts and "up there" that Aunt Rae is deceased). Moreover, we also learn that this author is an actor (she had the lead in *Blithe Spirit*); an avid reader; a strong student ("the best work I've ever seen"); and a community leader (the summer workshop at the Y). We even find out that she's not especially timid ("more shyly than is my usual nature"). Clearly, the admission officials who read this essay will get some genuine insight into the person behind it.

- **Finish strong.** While not as critical as the introduction, an essay should end with a bang, not a whimper. The reader should have no doubt that it's over and shouldn't be left scampering around the floor searching for a nonexistent second page. *Essay #2 successfully uses the "full circle" style of writing.* The concluding paragraph neatly brings the reader back to the madeleines in the first sentence and explains their significance as a symbol of Aunt Rae's nature.

- **Check and recheck spelling and grammar.** Computerized check systems are valuable tools, but most don't pick up the types of common errors that most of us make (using "on" when we mean "one;" "that" for "than," etc.). Even parents who don't trust their own spelling skills can recognize a "form" that should be a "from."

- **Neatness counts.** Remember that a separate, well-labeled sheet of paper can always substitute for the form provided, especially if your child (or you, as typist) has blighted the initial document beyond recognition.

- **Unless directed otherwise, aim for one to two typed pages.** When instructions do set length restrictions, be aware that there is always leeway to go somewhat shorter or longer.

- **Use a computer or typewriter** for the essay section unless instructed otherwise. Brown University, for example, requests *handwritten* essays. "We think it helps to personalize the application process," explains a Brown official, "but we don't have handwriting analysts hidden in the basement as some applicants may fear."

- **Sleep on it.** Most students wait until the bitter end to tackle the essay. Urge your child to let it mellow and then review it, days later, with a fresh perspective.

- **Get a second opinion.** It's not "cheating" for your child to ask an advisor, teacher, etc. to review an essay *after* it's written. Key questions to ask: Is it grammatically correct? Is it clear? Does it answer the question being asked? Is the introduction inviting? Will it stand out in a crowd? As parents, you should be available to offer suggestions but shouldn't *insist* that you see an essay at all. Remember, this is a *personal* statement and teenagers are somehow more comfortable baring all to a total stranger than to Mom or Dad. You know how that is.

- **Don't seek out the toughest topic.** Some applicants believe that, if given several choices, they will earn extra brownie points for choosing what appears to be the hardest one. In fact, sophisticated essays can spring from simple subjects, and essay topic offerings are never a test of an applicant's ambition.

- **Consolidate.** Help your child "recycle" essays. Although admission officials don't appreciate submissions that are clearly answering *another* college's question, not their own, there is often enough similarity among topics that an essay can be used again at least once, with few or even no revisions. (Be sure that you edit out any references to Oberlin on the Carleton essay!) Try to gather all applications together before your child begins to complete any, and then determine topic overlaps. For instance, both sample essays above could be recycled to respond to questions such as "Who is your hero or heroine?" "Who has had a great influence on you?" "What is an important interest of yours?" "What is your career goal?" or any open-ended query that says "Choose your own topic," "Make up your own question," or "Tell us about yourself."

  Of course, those who use the Common Application, the Universal Application, CollegeLink, etc., are able to share one statement among several schools—a good reason to elect generic formats when possible.

  The fewer essays your kid has to crank out, the easier it will be to produce strong contenders. Or…

- **Bail Out.** Some colleges, even nationally-known ones, don't require any essay at all. Among these are Purdue, Penn State, Fairfield, and the U. of Oregon—good bets for those suffering from term-paperitis.

155

Q&A

Q: We've heard rumors about applicants who "cheat" on applications. They don't write their own essays or they invent extracurricular achievements. How do colleges guard against dishonesty?

A: Very carefully and not always successfully. When a student with abysmal test scores and average grades submits an essay that Robert Benchley would be proud to claim, officials are suspicious. They'll scrutinize recommendations for signs of literary achievement and, perhaps, call a guidance counselor for further information. But, when *good* students write especially polished essays, admission people have no choice but to give the benefit of the doubt. As for embellishing "extras," heaven help the student who gets caught—and it does happen, rarely. If Johnny lists "Class President" on his application, and the counselor only mentions his leadership as a bathroom monitor, most astute officials will pick up on it. Students have been denied acceptance for making false statements. It's hard, however, to spot exaggeration. The once-a-month hospital volunteer can list a once-a-week commitment, and no one is apt to be the wiser. Like many things in life, it's a question of personal ethics and responsibility.

Recommendations

Most colleges require a recommendation from your child's guidance counselor, as well as from one or more teachers. Private schools often pride themselves on presenting long, informative, anecdotal counselor "recs," while some overworked public-school counselors submit those which say little more than "Melinda is a hard-working and personable young woman who will succeed at the college of her choice." While admission officers won't discriminate against students whose school references are brief and vague, strong and personal recommendations certainly give a clear-cut picture of the candidate. If your child does attend a school where counselor loads are large, provide the guidance staff with a résumé (even a very informal one) and a summary of achievements, interests, and goals. Stress qualities that you want colleges to see (e.g., community service involvement, team leadership, willingness to seek academic assistance, etc.) As you read in Chapter 2, you may also wish to include personal information that may help to explain bad grades or other problems. This will make appreciative counselors more able to write a revealing recommendation.

156

Never feel that you are bothering teachers by asking for references. This is part of their job and most are actually flattered to be asked (and asked and asked!). Don't feel, either, that you have to "spread the wealth." If Joelle has done her best work in Ms. Smiley's class, then, by all means, let Ms. Smiley write all of Joelle's recommendations. (But be fair, give her the whole stack of forms at once so she can reuse her well-turned phrases.) Be sure, also, to give teachers plenty of time before deadlines and to provide stamped, addressed envelopes.

Select teachers for whom your child has done good work (and that doesn't always mean "A" work. A C- in advanced chemistry may have been the result of enormous determination and effort). It's also preferable to choose those who have taught your child a major subject in the junior or senior year. Sometimes the teacher who knows a student best is a club advisor or coach (who may not have had your child in class at all). Activity advisors may be asked to write supplemental letters (see below), but should not replace academic references.

Supporting Materials and Optional Information

Some candidates are convinced that even the most enormous application just doesn't tell the whole story. In such cases, consider providing additional "supporting material" that may be a plus at decision time.

Admission offices often receive such extras. Most commonly they include slides of artwork; tapes (video or audio) of music or theater performances; samples of poetry, fiction, or other written work; newspaper clippings about past achievements; recommendations from family friends, employers, coaches, alumni, etc.

Many a modern parent has been traumatized by tales of *other* parents who engage professional production companies to present *Junior's Life as Colleges Want to See It,* via thirty or so minutes of carefully selected celluloid. How heavily do admission counselors weigh these additions? Should you indeed be humbled by those who have the time, talent, (or money) to get such addenda all together? Our suggestions follow:

Arts (visual, music, theater, dance)

Specialized schools/programs usually require slides, tapes, etc. as an integral part of an application. When not required, however, these are often overlooked by busy admission counselors. If you believe that your child's artistic abilities are *exceptional,* ask admission offices if they automatically forward *all* submissions to faculty evaluators. If the answer is no, consider sending copies of slides or tapes *directly* to appropriate faculty members. (Use course

157

catalogs for guidance.) Make sure that tapes are of good quality and clearly labeled with the candidate's name and a *brief* description of content. Don't count on getting the material back (although if you enclose a prepaid addressed envelope, you might). Include a cover letter in which your child expresses wishes to study under this chosen mentor. Follow up by telephone in a couple weeks. A prof who is truly impressed is usually willing to call the admission office to put in a good word, and this can definitely help your child's candidacy.

Writing samples

When verbal SAT scores are low or English course grades are only average, an additional writing sample, such as an English class essay or history term paper, can be beneficial. Send just one. Some schools, like Wheaton College in Massachusetts, actually require *all* applicants to submit a *graded* writing sample. "We want to see both what a candidate considers good work and what a school considers good work," explains a Wheaton admissions official. "If a paper is weak and the grade is good, it tells us that this applicant comes from a place where expectations are not high." Whether requisite or not, including an "A" paper (with the grade and comments on it) is an A+ idea. If the work is truly excellent, admission officers will be impressed. If it's not, they will be more likely to put poor test scores or a not-so-hot application essay in perspective.

When an application touts your child's passion as a poet or a budding novelist, an ecology columnist or a theater critic, then an example is in order. Writing samples should be sent to the office of admission, along with the application. (Committed creative writers can also consider contacting faculty members, as in "Arts" above).

...And more essays

Some students have special situations which warrant explaining in an extra essay. Did your family only recently emigrate to America? Has your child been diagnosed with a learning disability or hospitalized for several months? Are parental problems to blame for a semester of Cs? Any significant experience, from attending six schools in seven years to trying out for the Olympic diving team, can be fuel for a supplementary personal statement. (See also "Unsolicited Letters," below.) Sometimes these statements need be only a few sentences in which your child explains transcript irregularities like:

> "After finishing British Literature as a junior, I knew I wouldn't survive my senior year without taking Ms. Stone's Shakespeare seminar. I didn't want to miss out on the Advanced Placement English class

158

either, but the schedule conflicts that resulted meant that calculus got lost in the shuffle."

But admission officials are wary of those who "doth protest too much," so advise your child to avoid a whiny tone. ("My French teacher was really awful, and she didn't like me, and neither did my calculus teacher, so my bad grades were really just due to those personality conflicts....")

You or your child may also have to make a judgment call about how much you want to reveal about personal issues. For instance, if a child suffered from a clinical depression, and his grades suffered along with him, it probably makes sense to tell admission officials about the situation—and, especially, about how it is being treated. On the other hand, if your daughter is struggling with a serious eating disorder but still managing to pull down straight As, should you tell all in an application? And what about the applicant who was arrested for shoplifting in his senior year?

Colleges aren't *supposed* to make decisions based on such personal matters, but sometimes they do anyway. Some admission officials find an applicant's efforts to overcome personal problems especially admirable, but others may be reluctant to accept candidates who are going to bring serious problems with them to campus. It's usually to your child's advantage to tell admission offices about ongoing health or psychological problems, so that he or she won't be heading to a place that can't handle them. However, if the crisis is clearly behind you, this becomes another one of those moral dilemmas that you're going to have to decide for yourselves.

Newspaper clippings

These should be included with an application only if the applicant is the author or if the clipping is recent (within two years) and your child is its featured subject (and the achievement is outstanding or unique). Two clippings are always sufficient.

Gotta getta gimmick?

In the race for space on selective campuses, some students resort to including a variety of unexpected extras in their application packages. Lee Coffin, dean of admissions at Connecticut College, concedes that a "No" decision became a "Yes" when the admission office received an extraordinary animated video that an applicant had drawn and produced himself. "We all sat down and watched the tape together," Coffin recounts, "and agreed to admit this candidate after all, on the strength of his creative genius—and then he turned *us* down!"

Even less talented prospects have successfully cashed in on ideas that are longer on novelty than on artistry, such as the Bard College hopeful who enclosed two photographed self-portraits. One, which showed a grinning candidate was captioned, "This is me, if I'm accepted." The other depicted a frowning counterpart labeled, "This is me, if I'm denied."

The majority of applicants, however, *don't* go in for gimmicks. Even those who do find that they don't necessarily work; they just never hurt. And they are, for sure, a way to garner at least fifteen minutes of fame in an admission office.

Unsolicited letters

Supplemental letters that are most helpful to admission staff show an important side of an applicant that other credentials have not. These may come from physicians, counselors, clergy, and others who can shed light on a medical, psychological, or family situation that may have affected your child, or from a club advisor or employer who recognizes your child's special nonacademic strengths. (See also, "...And more essays," above.)

Some parents beat the bushes to drum up support from other, often distant corners. Is your uncle an alum? The next-door neighbor a trustee? Your sister's boss the former dean? Is anyone in any way linked to you also linked to your child's target schools? Admission officers *sometimes* give credence to such endorsements, especially if the author really knows the applicant. (And don't worry if your connection turns out to be a *persona non grata* at a target school—it won't reflect badly on your child.)

Don't worry either if you have no such rabbits to pull out of your hat—most other candidates won't either—and keep in mind that there's an old saying in admission circles: "The thicker the folder, the thicker the student."

Parent letters

Some schools, like Smith, have finally wised up to the fact that if anyone can offer a close-up look at a candidate, it's you—the parents. Indeed, whether a college invites it or not, a short letter of support from an applicant's mother or father can add a dimension that no other form will provide. Some parents are hindered by their own writer's block or by fears that poor grammar or spelling may hurt their child's chances. In fact, some of the most poignant and effective parent letters have come from those whose inexperience—but sincerity—shines through.

Parent letters are bound to offer platitudes like "responsible," "hard-working," and "good-natured," but be sure to also include anecdotes or examples that illustrate your child's special traits, as in the letter below.

This may also be the time to explain serious medical problems or other personal issues, if any, that have affected your family and your child.

Dear Board of Admission:

It's been a long while since I've written anything besides a grocery list, and just thinking about the task ahead makes me appreciate what Jessica and her friends have to go through all the time. Please bear with me while I tackle this challenge of sharing the most important person in the world to me with strangers.

Jessica is an only child. We lost her little sister at birth. Because of this, it might have been easy to spoil her, but she has never allowed it. For instance, in eighth grade, when a less fortunate friend signed up for a paper route to finance gymnastics lessons, Jess insisted on getting one, too, and, from that day on, has paid all of her own gymnastics fees.

As you can see from Jessica's application, she has been so successful with her gymnastics that she now competes on a statewide level. Yet, despite the cost of costumes, travel, and classes, she has never gone back on her decision to pay her own way. Since delivering newspapers didn't put a dent in mounting expenses, Jess found her first "real" job at a nearby nursing home where she helps with morning meal service. Her application probably tells you that, too. What it won't tell you, though, is that she gets up at 5 A.M., three days a week, and rides her bike a mile to work and, then, two miles to school at 8. Often, on weekends or in the evening, she returns to the home again, this time as a visitor. "There are so many patients there who have nobody," she tells me, "and I can't spend time with them while I'm working."

For most of Jessica's school years, she has also been a top student. She was selected for advanced math and science as a freshman, took accelerated chemistry as a junior (usually a senior class) and was one of three who helped implement an AP American history course last year. I hope you will focus on that, and not on the bad semester she had as a sophomore. That fall, my father was diagnosed with cancer and moved into our house. Jess quickly volunteered her room to "Pop-pop" and slept on the couch in the basement den. It wasn't relocation that hurt her grades, but the enormous stress that all of us were under which ended with my father's death at home. I think that, as a result of this experience, Jess learned an enormous amount about the importance of family and about strength and hope and faith. But I'm not sure how much French and geometry she learned during those months!

I could go on and on with examples that point out this wonderful young woman's determination, her optimism, and her generosity. But, better yet, discover this for yourselves by offering her a place in your freshman class.

Sincerely yours,

Yvonne P.

Financial-Aid Forms

Financing a college education is such a tricky topic that it rates a chapter all its own. (See Chapter 5.) Remember, always take financial-aid deadlines and requirements seriously.

Application Fee (or Waiver)

Ordinarily, an application will not be processed and your child will not formally be considered an applicant until an application fee is received. (A few lucky families stumble on target schools such as Case Western Reserve University in Ohio where there is *no charge* to apply.) Such fees range from about $25 up to $70, a pittance compared to the tuition bills to follow, but still a problem for those with limited resources. Fortunately, most institutions grant "fee waivers" to needy candidates. However, the process of obtaining one will vary from school to school. Some colleges include fee-waiver information, or even a short form, with application materials. Generally, a fee waiver is granted if, along with the application, your child sends a statement or form from the guidance department (or a social worker, clergy member, etc.) confirming financial need.

You won't be penalized for requesting a waiver, but keep in mind that they're designed for genuine hardship cases, not for those whose credit cards are overused or who don't want to pay to apply to "safety schools." (Once financial-aid forms are in, colleges may check to see if the waiver was really needed. If not, you will be billed for the application fee and your integrity might be questioned.)

As discussed earlier in this chapter, some institutions may lower or waive fees for those who apply electronically.

Q: I fear that admission officers won't get to know my daughter from reading her application. How can we make the "real" Elizabeth come through?

A: Admission staff probably will spend less than 30 minutes reviewing your child's credentials. Don't expect them to know—and love—her as much as you do after 17 or 18 years. Even the best applications don't tell everything about the candidates who submit them, but here's a quick and easy exercise that you and your daughter can try:

Write down 20 words that describe Elizabeth (e.g., "daughter," "swimmer," "friend," "book-lover," etc.). The first six or eight usually come pretty easily; it's the last 10 or so that are tough but often more revealing ("dreamer," "procrastinator," "perfectionist," etc.) Parents and children should do this exercise separately and compare notes.

When Elizabeth finishes the application, take stock of which characteristics have been revealed. Have any important ones been left out? ("diplomat?" "gourmet cook?" "class wit?") If so, how can they be included? This game is also a good one to play as you are making college matches.

For example, a risk-taker might want to consider unusual colleges or those far from home. A procrastinator might not do well at a place without enough personal attention and structure.

Now What?

The applications are finally in and the waiting process has begun. So, what are admission officials up to while *you're* waiting? Read the next chapter.

CHAPTER 7

How Admission Decisions Are Made

➤ **THE GOOD NEWS:** Admission decisions aren't made by tossing applications down the stairwell and accepting those students whose folders reach the bottom step. The process is fair and thorough, and admission professionals take this part of their job very seriously.

➤ **THE BAD NEWS:** So many factors go into these decisions that the results can sometimes seem unpredictable and maybe even off the mark.

How are decisions made? Who makes them? What "counts"—and what doesn't? What parents *really* want to know, when they sidle up to admission-officer acquaintances in the Shop 'n Save, or back them into break-fronts at countless potluck dinners, is *"What looks good on a college application?"* The subtext here, for sure, is "How can my child get into not just *any* college, but those popular and picky places where all the applicants seem to be Junior Achiever clones? What will give *my* kid a competitive edge?"

First, all application materials are collected in a folder. Every scrap of paper which bears your child's name—from supplemental essays to phone-message slips and thank-you notes—is likely to end up there. Then, each folder is read carefully. (WARNING: Incomplete folders stay on the shelf.)

At tiny schools, the entire admission staff may evaluate each applicant (and at great length); at larger ones, a single official may be the sole judge. At many places, decisions are made by more than one person, including admission officials and often faculty representatives and other administrators. The committee with which your child's folder lands may be determined alphabetically, geographically, departmentally (e.g., school of business applicants) or by the date an application is completed. The individual who interviewed your child, visited your local high school, or spoke so reassuringly to you on the phone may—or may not—be among the arbiters. Typically, committee members examine each folder independently (and commonly assign it an overall rating) before the committee meets to make decisions.

I. Transcripts

In evaluating each candidate, the high-school transcript is almost always the most important component. (Exception: specialized schools in areas like art, music, and drama look more carefully at portfolios or audition tapes.) As you read in Chapter 2, included in every candidate's application folder is a "school profile" which details the curriculum available at that high school, explains the grading system, and sometimes even lists median grades for each class. Admission officers are skilled at understanding the discrepancies among schools and the ways that grades are awarded, recorded, etc. They know, for example, that at some schools only those who walk on water will earn As while, at others, anyone who hands in the homework is an honors student! They read between the lines of transcripts and school profiles to ascertain a school's strength (e.g., What percentage of graduates go on to four-year colleges and where? What advanced classes are offered?). They recognize that good students at challenging, competitive high schools (public or private) may have lower grades and class ranks than their counterparts at "easier" ones (and that some students may not be ranked—or even *graded*—at all). Admission staff are also seeing a growing number of candidates who have been homeschooled and submit detailed narratives in lieu of transcripts.

What are officials looking for? Parents and students may underestimate the importance of secondary-school course choices. Decisions made as early as junior high might have affected what classes a child was eligible to take later on and, thus, how a college application will be evaluated, especially by the most selective institutions. Minimum high-school graduation requirements vary, but most are less stringent than those expected at the more competitive colleges. Colleges normally have *recommended* secondary-school programs, not *imperative* ones.

Commonly, high schools grant diplomas to those who have completed a curriculum comparable to this:

English: 4 (full-year courses or equivalent)

Social Studies: 2

Mathematics: 2

Science: 2

(usually plus physical education, health, and often keyboarding and electives)

While these minimum requirements are sufficient to allow admission to many not-so-selective schools, the more competitive institutions expect a program that looks closer to this:

English: 4

Social Studies/History: 3

Mathematics: 3

Science: at least 2, preferably 3

Foreign Language: 3 years of 1 language or at least 2 years of 2.

Such "suggested preparation" will vary from school to school. For example, The University of Michigan at Ann Arbor favors four years of English, math, science, foreign language, and social studies/history, while other U. of M. campuses (e.g., Dearborn and Flint) make less stringent requests. Johns Hopkins also recommends four years of math but just two of language. Predictably, schools with a technology emphasis look more closely at math and science backgrounds. Massachusetts Institute of Technology (MIT) "highly recommends" four years of both math and science (and only one of foreign language). Most entering MIT students have taken calculus before enrolling. If it's not offered at their high schools, they find it elsewhere. Similarly, Rensselaer Polytechnic Institute in Troy, New York, "strongly encourages" applicants to take physics and chemistry in secondary school, as well as calculus or, at the very least, pre-calculus.

Here is an example of a strong four-year academic program:

English: 4

Social Studies/History: 3 or 4

Mathematics: 3 (at least through 11th grade, even if algebra is taken in grade 8)

Science: at least 2, preferably 3 (with 2 or more lab sciences)

Foreign Language: 3 or 4 of at least one language

Q&A

Q: My daughter's high school is on a "block system." How will college admission officers evaluate her transcript?

A: With so many high schools operating on a block system (where students take fewer, longer classes each term), this is not big news anymore. Admission officials realize that they have to make decisions before they see final grades (or *any* grades in some cases) in some important senior subjects. However, it's essential that they know which classes are planned. For example, if your daughter submits a first-semester transcript that includes English, foreign language, and social studies, but expects to start calculus and physics in January, it should be made clear on her application.

Similarly, if your child's school uses a block system, make certain that this is made clear to admission officials so they'll realize that what may look like a single semester of a subject was really the equivalent of a full-year course.

Admission officers expect to see a minimum of 5 "solids" or major subjects per term, plus at least one elective or minor subject—e.g., band, art (a "major" in some schools), yearbook, etc. (At schools on "block" or "trimester" systems or at some independent schools, fewer solids per term will be the norm.) No matter how "high" your child is aiming, he or she will be well served by pursuing a secondary-school program that exceeds the basic requirements.

The most competitive colleges also expect that applicants will select the most challenging courses available. If there is a "tracking" system at your child's school, where students are grouped by ability, the transcript should indicate if classes have been at the highest level (e.g., "Honors," "Enriched," "Level 1") or at a lower one ("Standard," "Level 2").

While such names vary from school to school, one coast-to-coast constant is the "Advanced Placement" designation. Schools that list "AP" classes (usually for juniors and seniors, or just for seniors) are participating in a program offered by The College Entrance Examination Board based in Princeton, New Jersey that enables high-school students to take classes which may lead to college credit. Some secondary schools offer Advanced Placement courses in over a dozen subjects; others offer far fewer (or none at all). More information on this program will appear in Chapter 9.

Increasingly, too, International Baccalaureate programs are turning up, even in unlikely places, far from foreign shores. Initially designed for those who might be heading to non-American universities, this system is gaining stateside popularity among high schools interested in providing a widely acclaimed and challenging curriculum for strong students who can also gain college credit through "IB" participation and testing. (Again, see Chapter 9.)

Ordinarily, AP and IB classes, if offered, are the top-level courses taught in high schools and are well respected by all college officials. Because of their universal recognition, they jump off a transcript and put a spring in admission counselors' steps.

Q&A

Q: Are Bs in honors or AP classes "better" than As in less demanding ones?

A: Bs in first-string classes *are* more impressive than As in easier ones. Even an *occasional* C won't rule out a career at a highly selective college. (But tip-top applicants often have all or mostly As in tip-top classes. We're not trying to ruin your day; we just want you to know what your son or daughter may be up against.) Yet, while the most competitive colleges do prefer the most competitive courses, there *is* room for fluctuation, and a second-level class in one or two weaker areas may work better for your child.

When computing class ranks, most high schools now use a "weighted" system where extra points are allotted for higher level classes, so the "B+" student in honors courses is likely to be ranked above the straight-"A" student in the second tier. Colleges, too, are careful to note those high schools which do *not* use weighted ranks and take this into consideration when evaluating and comparing candidates. So, if your child attends such a school (and it's a good idea to ask), he won't be penalized for taking a tough load.

Admission pros know that many high schools don't have AP or IB programs and that some don't even have advanced or accelerated classes. Your child will be evaluated in light of what opportunities were available.

Q&A

Q: My son wants to take part in a "dual-enrollment" program at our local community college. How do admission officers view this?

A: Dual-enrollment programs allow students to take some courses on a college campus for credit while they remain enrolled in high school classes. Admission officials are always pleased when students take advantage of challenging opportunities. However, while they will "credit" your son with making a wise choice, their institution may not necessarily award college credit for his work.

You may have grown up in the sixties, when there weren't as many opportunities to take AP or IB classes or to head to a local college for high-school credit. But what you *might* remember from your era is that some schools abandoned courses like "Biology II" for those with a more "relevant" ring, like "The Ecology of the Okefenokee." And while, in some schools, such selections still live on, their jazzy titles may be misleading. A tough and very serious class with a funny name may appear to admission officials to be what some dub "fluffy," "flimsy," or "lightweight." Unfair as it may seem, it's sometimes hard to convince admission boards that classes with names like "The Big Bang," "Visigoth Visionaries," or "Montezuma's Revenge" are equally as arduous as their time-honored counterparts: physics, world literature, and history.

➤ **THE GOOD NEWS:** Some high schools have an entire curriculum that sounds like Timothy Leary devised it during his first LSD trip. Fear not. Older admission officers understand this and even smile with appreciation or sigh with nostalgia when English turns up on such transcripts as "Utopias and Dream Worlds," or science as "Were Wilbur and Orville Right?"

➤ **THE BAD NEWS:** It may be up to you to point out the difficulties of benign-sounding offerings. Sometimes good guidance counselors will alert colleges to killer classes that masquerade as filler classes, but if Angie's "A" in astrology was her finest hour, let admission officers know—via parent letter or supplementary essay, etc.—just what it took to land it.

However, there are cases out there like Cassandra's. She took a heavy schedule through her junior year and worked hard to knock off graduation requirements in order to "enjoy" her first senior term. She chose long-awaited electives like ceramics and photography in place of math and science. Her top-choice college viewed her transcript with disdain. Many families dwell on the importance of 11th grade without realizing that 12th grade courses are just as crucial.

Although the overall Grade Point Average (GPA) is important, colleges realize that it is calculated on the basis of all four high-school years. Class ranks are often cumulative (based on three- or four-year records) but sometimes broken down by year (e.g., "Junior Rank," "Senior Rank," etc.) Admission officials tend to be believers in what they dub the "rising record," and are willing to forgive freshman (and even sophomore) foibles when a student has shown impressive improvement as a junior and senior—the two years which get scrutinized most closely. They may be likewise willing to overlook one awful grade (or an entire catastrophic semester) if followed by a strong rebound (and, remember, this is also where an explanatory letter or essay can help).

Colleges are also impressed by students who have sought enrichment opportunities outside of their school, both during the academic year or in the summer. Make sure that these are noted on the application.

Q: **Don't admission officers from highly selective colleges prefer private-school applicants?**

A: Colleges, even the choosiest ones, do *not* prefer *either* private-school or public-school candidates. Since most students attend public high schools, the vast majority at *all* colleges are public-school graduates. "Diversity" is now the clarion call, and that means drawing students from all sorts of backgrounds.

Parents sometimes believe that paying for private school is like buying an insurance policy that promises that their child will be admitted to a "name" college. However, while admission officers recognize that the top independent schools are excellent proving grounds for top colleges, they are also aware that there are some crummy private schools and many outstanding public ones. Being a preppie can also backfire. Imagine what it's like to be one of 46 in a senior class to apply to Princeton or among 57 to aim for Brown. Of course, if you're at the head of such a list, the odds are with you, but those down the line a piece might have had a better shot from Sheboygan!

Q&A

Q: My child switched high schools, and the move has meant some transcript irregularities. Will admission officials figure it all out?

A: Be certain that each college will receive a transcript (or several) that covers your child's entire high-school career. This may be the perfect time to add an extra statement explaining why moves were made, and what impact they had on course choices (e.g., "Velma missed biology" or "Louie took math courses out of sequence"). Parents who anticipate relocation should look ahead, where possible, and check into curricular differences at the transfer school.

II. Test Results

All of Chapter 3 is devoted to standardized tests and explains in detail how colleges use them. Test scores are intentionally listed in *this* chapter *after* transcripts, to emphasize that they are less important, but they are also used *in conjunction* with transcripts. For example, Annie scarcely squeaked by when her first-choice college made its decisions. She had terrific test scores (1,400 SATs) but her record had more than its share of Cs. Kirsten, on the other hand, would never have been admitted to her favorite college on her sorry scores alone, but admission officials were impressed with her A average and interesting choice of activities. In general, admission officials prefer students like Kirsten who have demonstrated their ability to perform well in school.

Additional considerations that admission officers keep in mind when reviewing test scores include:

- Is the testing pattern consistent? Did a student clearly have an "off day?" Are scores compatible with academic achievement? If not, why?

- Are there strengths in one area (e.g., language, math, etc.) while others are weaker?

- Were tests taken under special conditions (e.g., untimed)? Does the student have a diagnosed disability?

- Does the student come from a disadvantaged background?

- Is English spoken at home?

- Were SAT II tests taken close to course completion or a year or more later? If language test scores were low, how many years of study has this student had?

Some colleges also use test scores for placement purposes, once a student has enrolled. Even those colleges that do not demand standardized tests may ask students to submit scores, if available, after admission.

III. Essays/Personal Statements

Chapter 6 covers the ins and outs of essays. Remember, a great essay can really make an admission official sit up and take notice. However, subjectivity prevails here. Some readers are biased toward content, some toward writing style and mechanics. One applicant submitted an ambitious essay that compared the works of three eastern-European writers. Two of her evaluators were impressed by her literary sophistication and the insight of her analysis; a third couldn't get beyond the errors in spelling and sentence structure.

IV. Recommendations

Quality and depth vary tremendously. Colleges don't penalize students when the recommendation is not well written or offers only superficial information. However, a clear and comprehensive letter of recommendation *can* make a difference. Specifics that admission folks seek from recommendations include:

- Comparisons to others in the class; to those with whom the teacher or counselor has worked in past years; or with students who have enrolled at the college in question ("In twenty years of teaching, I have encountered few students as determined as Evan" or "Jamie reminds me of Susannah Leone whose test scores were equally dismal but who went on to graduate with honors from your college").

- Information about grading and/or competition ("Mr. Jones rarely gives above a B" or "This year's AP English class was the most able this school has ever seen").

- Illustrative examples or anecdotes ("Jennifer is the swim-team captain and a state record holder in the backstroke. However, her sensitivity is another special strength. She stays late after every practice to help a far weaker swimmer, to keep her from being cut from the team").

- Personal information ("Ian struggled with his mother's drinking and finally caused an 'intervention' which led to her enrollment in a treatment program").

- Other personal traits or study habits (e.g., maturity, response to criticism, acceptance by peers, timely completion of assignments, willingness to go beyond what is expected, participation in class discussions).

The law entitles students to see completed recommendations. However, reference forms include a clause which most students sign to waive this right. This enables counselors and teachers to be candid, which is what admission officials prefer. (Recommendations normally do *not* become part of a student's permanent file once enrolled).

V. Extracurricular Activities

➤ **THE GOOD NEWS:** Colleges aren't terribly picky about how your child spends non-class time, as long as it's doing something meaningful. It isn't necessary to have a long list of activities, either. Commitment, some level of accomplishment, initiative, and leadership are far more important.

➤ **THE BAD NEWS:** With so many high-school students doing so much in so many programs, organizations, teams, clubs and causes, it's hard to predict what will make a splash anymore. However, some activities *do* stand out more than others, and proper presentation can help admission officers look more closely at Davina's debate awards or Roger's rock climbing.

When evaluating an applicant's "extras," these are considerations that crop up during committee meetings:

- How much time does this student devote to an activity? How significant is the contribution? Admission folks often favor depth over breadth. Phillip, for instance, attends most weekly chess-club meetings. Coral, on the other hand, organized a chess clinic and tournament at a nearby junior high. It was such a success that she ran a second one at a homeless shelter, persuading local merchants to donate prizes.

- "Evidence of leadership" is a phrase that comes up often at admission committee meetings, and it can be what separates an accepted student from one who ends up on the wait list. There's a world of difference between the student who *joined* the Geography Club and the one who *founded* it. The more selective a college is, the more carefully this leadership role is examined. Some colleges are impressed by

French-Club presidents and yearbook business managers, while it takes a *student-council* president or *editor-in-chief* to make a mark at others.

- Some balance is best. While there may not be as much talk of "well-roundedness" these days as there was back when Dobie Gillis and Ricky Nelson (and maybe *you*) went to college, varied ventures appeal to admission officers. The student who participates in the science club, the drama club, and is also on the tennis team usually stands out more than the one who chooses only athletics as extras. The good—yet not *exceptional*—player should also have other, *different* activities on the roster. Similarly, a balance of school-related activities (clubs, teams, choirs, etc.) and those which take place elsewhere (volunteering, scouting, church groups, community theater, etc.) suggests that your child's horizons extend beyond the school yard. "Seeking out and participating in off-campus activities shows initiative and is likely to capture our attention," maintains Karen Pellegrino, associate director of admission at Boston College.

- "Volunteerism is very important," stresses David Donovan, former admissions counselor at Allegheny College in Meadville, PA. "It especially impresses us when a student from a more affluent background goes into an inner city to volunteer in some way." The key here is real hands-on *involvement*. Admission people are usually able to differentiate between the candidate who spends every Saturday tutoring at a storefront literacy center and the classmate who served on the Students Against Styrofoam Dance Decoration Committee.

- Specialists are exceptional. As Lee Coffin, dean of admissions at Connecticut College, points out, "The ideal of the well-rounded student is important, but so is the well-rounded *class*. So, within a class of 450 students, we have those who aren't the least bit well-rounded, but will bring something unique to the community." A few collegiate candidates will up their stock in admission officers' eyes by being extraordinarily talented in some area or with a truly off-the-wall interest or experience. This may be the prima ballerina who dances six hours a day, pirouetting all the way to Prague with a national company, or the downhill skier, just one run away from a gold medal. Admission annals, too, are filled with stories about adolescent entrepreneurs who started home-baked cookie companies or computer-software services and prodigies who published their own novels or built fighter jets in the garage.

Colleges appreciate uncommon undertakings: hand-bell ringers, Morris Dancers, magicians, sky divers, or dog trainers. Says B.C.'s Karen Pellegrino, "It's exciting to see unusual activities on an application— not always the student council, the newspaper, or the yearbook."

A final note: *You* recognize how much effort went into planning the Booster Club barbecue; how tough it was to sacrifice a season of soccer for a semester in Sweden; how many lines your son had to learn for *King Lear.* But admission officers have heard it all before. Be sure that your child presents extracurricular activities and accomplishments well and *differentiates* between meaningful and minimal contributions.

VI. Interviews

Interview evaluations often confirm the impression made by other credentials in a folder. However, as you read earlier, an interview may also help a committee to see another side of a student, to understand why certain choices were made, to appreciate the extent of a commitment. Interview write-ups may even contain comments like "TAKE HER!!!" or "a solid student but I'd hate to have to room with him." In some cases, even a favorably impressed interviewer who isn't on a candidate's committee may go out of the way to lobby those who are for a "yes" verdict.

VII. "Hooks"

A "hook," in admission parlance, is any additional advantage that makes a candidate attractive to a particular college. This will vary from school to school and from year to year. Some candidates may try to hide their hooks, preferring to be admitted only on merit (parents tend to discourage this) while others will fight furiously to exploit even the most inconsequential connections. Such hooks may include: athletic ability; minority status; veteran status; alumni connections; special talent (e.g., art, music, theater, writing, etc.); underrepresented socioeconomic background (e.g., first-generation college); geography; gender; area of study; VIP status; ability to pay full tuition.

Having a hook can give a candidate a higher rating from the get-go or can pull an application from the "deny" pile and put it into the "admit" (or "wait-list") stack. Hooks come into play most often when judging equally qualified candidates. For example, if a college has to select one of two students who "look the same on paper," and one is the daughter of an alumnus and the other is not, the daughter is probably going to get in over the nonconnected student. However, no matter how well connected or how gifted a student is *outside* of the classroom, if he doesn't have the grades or the ability, he won't—or shouldn't—be admitted. And, if he does get admitted for "special" reasons, those connections won't guarantee that he'll succeed. One college even had to turn down its own president's son!

The hooks below are the ones discussed most often—and most passionately—in admission committee meetings:

Alumni Connections

While you shouldn't assume that your child is a shoo-in just because *you* went to the target school, you *can* assume that the folder will be reviewed very carefully and, if denied for any reason, the decision will be painful for the college.

Smith, a college with an extensive alumnae admission effort, takes about 70 percent of its alumnae-connected applicants, as compared with only about 50 percent of its regular pool. If there is a particularly well-connected marginal applicant, the folder gets extra special attention.

Athletic Ability

➤ **THE GOOD NEWS:** Playing a sport can be an excellent way to give your child a boost at decision-making time. A superstar can earn a full scholarship; a less exceptional enthusiast can still up the odds of an acceptance.

➤ **THE BAD NEWS:** Some students (and parents) *overestimate* the weight that athletic ability carries in the admission process—and they overestimate their ability period. Dave Shelbourne, head football coach and guidance counselor at Warren Central High School in Indianapolis, affirms that the "absolute first thing that I am asked by college recruiters is 'What about his grades?' 'Who are your *best* players who qualify *academically*?' When I worked in admissions at Wabash College, lots of parents weren't objective about their children's academic and athletic talent."

Q: How can families capitalize on athletic accomplishment so that it pays off at decision time?

A: A good place to get information and solid advice on the ins and outs of eligibility and distinctions among recruiting rules in Division I, II, and III schools is the *NCAA Guide to the College-Bound Student Athlete.* If your

Continues

Continued

high school doesn't have an up-to-date copy, write to: The National Collegiate Athletic Association; 6201 College Blvd; Overland Park; KS 66211-2422, or phone 913/339-1906, or visit www.NCAA.org on the World Wide Web.

If your child is interested in playing a sport in college, after talking with his or her own coach and guidance counselor, it's a good idea to contact the college coach as soon as the search process begins or—better still—ask the high-school coach to initiate the contact. However, remember these key points:

- **Just because your child is recruited by a coach, don't assume admission is a given.** Generally, there is an admission officer who serves as a liaison with the athletic department and, while decision-making may be collaborative, remember that admission people admit the applicants—not coaches, not athletic directors, and not sports writers who can only offer input.

- **A coach's interest, at any level, is not a promise of playing time, either.** This can especially affect Division III athletes. Coaches, at all levels, encourage more athletes than can ever fit on the bench. However, in Division I and II programs, athletic scholarships are awarded. If your child is given one, it is certainly an indication that he or she is slated for playing time...at least eventually. At the Division III level, however, since no athletic scholarships are allowed, some coaches woo athletes by promising playing time that may never materialize. On a more positive note, although Division III institutions can't award athletic scholarships, students who are athletes can receive aid on the basis of need.

If your child is talented enough to play at *any* level—and even qualifies for an athletic scholarship—there are still decisions to be made. Your child may "ride the pines" at a Division I college for most of four years or start every season in a lower division. In addition, remember that your child is a student first and an athlete second when making college choices.

Students of Color

Colleges normally give students the *option* of describing themselves as members of these "minority" groups: American Indian or Alaskan Native; Black or African-American; Mexican-American or Chicano; Puerto Rican;

178

Other Hispanic-American or Latin American; Asian-American or Pacific Islander; or multiracial.

Many colleges aggressively recruit students of color, and financial-aid opportunities are great. Some even set aside funds to pay travel expenses for these students to visit campus. Most admission offices have a counselor who is in charge of this effort, and this person can serve as a good source of information as well as an advocate in the process. While all admission counselors work together to attract a diverse student body, one may be charged with reading all folders of students of color—or at least have a major say in who gets admitted.

If your child has checked one of the categories above, he or she may get special consideration by admission committees—just how much consideration depends on the institution in question and your child's racial, ethnic, and socioeconomic background. For example, Spelman College in Atlanta is a predominantly Black college for women which is eager to encourage Latina applicants. Some families, especially Asians, are concerned that they have become an overrepresented minority on many campuses and that their cultural background may actually work against them. This is not true. What *is* true, however, is that while they are *never* discriminated against, they may lose their "hook." They have essentially melted into the American melting pot. When a minority student (or *any* student) is from a disadvantaged family or community, credentials such as test scores, writing samples, and course selection are evaluated with that in mind.

Talent in the Arts

Being a painter, a poet, a musician, a dancer, and so on can really make an application stand out. A conservatory or art school will carefully examine each applicant's ability. For instance, Rhode Island School of Design requires a slide portfolio, in addition to three drawings (a bicycle, an interior or exterior environment, and a subject of the applicant's choice). Instructions are specific about what to draw, what size the paper must be, and how it should be folded, so students need to follow directions carefully. In contrast, more generalized institutions may use such strengths to counterbalance weaker areas but don't necessarily have tapes, slides, or other submissions reviewed by professionals in the arts.

Geography

At a public college or university, being an in-state resident is obviously a hook. However, at many institutions, coming from an underrepresented region can also be an advantage. Southeastern colleges love to see North

Dakota and Montana zip codes on applications, while southwestern schools welcome candidates from Vermont and Maine.

Parents, however, often worry when it seems as if *too* many of their child's classmates are aiming for the same colleges. They wonder if admission offices set quotas and ask how their child's decision might be affected when stronger cohorts have also applied.

Some high schools are known as "feeder schools" for certain colleges which means that many students typically apply and many, too, may be accepted. In such cases, your guidance counselor is familiar with the college in question and can help predict how your child will stack up. On the other hand, the more competitive colleges often want to cast a net broadly and include many different high schools in each entering class. In such cases, it may be a liability if your child is not as impressive a candidate as the others from his school—although just what impresses a college will vary. Decisions can likewise depend on which program within an institution your child desires. She may be turned down from the School of Engineering while her less able beau will be accepted by the School of Education.

Gerry Carnes, guidance counselor at Brockton High School in Massachusetts, which graduates over 600 seniors a year, is no stranger to this dilemma. "If a student from BHS is applying to nearby Bridgewater State College, being one of 20 applicants is not a hindrance. However, if a student is one of only three or four applying to Brown, then having multiple applications from Brockton High could be a factor in who gets in. However, students shouldn't shy away from applying—even someone who is #10 in a class from which #5 is also a candidate. Depending on major and extra-curricular activities, the college would not necessarily take the student with the higher rank."

VIII. Thumbs Up or Thumbs Down?

If you were a fly on the wall while an admission committee was meeting, this is what you would be likely to hear:

Readers begin by sharing the ratings they have given an applicant independently. Commonly, there is consensus. If not, the dickering begins, as one committee member exclaims "Look how well she plays the harp!" while another is pointing to a 330 math SAT.

At the most competitive colleges, candidates are not even discussed in committee unless they are firing on all cylinders, and excellent grades and scores must be a given. According to Patricia Wei of Yale, "Then in committee, we say, 'This is a good student. Now what is *special*?' A lot of times we call an applicant 'solid.' It translates into 'fine, but nothing distinctive.' At other colleges where I've worked, 'solid' meant admissible, but here it's the kiss of death."

The goal is to assign an overall rating that every reader can live with. Contrary to what you might suspect, committees often give numerical or letter grades, rather than voting "In" or "Out," "Accept" or "Reject." For example, where an "A" to "F" scale is used, while readers may realize that A and B applicants are likely to be admitted and that C applicants stand a good chance as well, they won't know for sure until all folders have been rated and compared as a group. Since competition and space availability are not constant from year to year, cut-off points likewise vary. It's a serious and sensitive undertaking, but hardly an exact science.

There are always clear-cut decisions at the top and bottom of the pool. The toughest to make are about those students who fall in the middle. Here is where hooks really come into play. Moreover, colleges don't always go by the book when finalizing choices. There is room to make adjustments for "wild cards"—those candidates who, on the basis of statistics or in the light of tight competition, might be far from the top of the pile, yet have that "special something" that really impressed the pants off the readers.

There are also other "fine-tuning" issues such as shaping the overall composition of the class. Says Dean Lee Stetson of Penn, "Eighty-five percent of those who apply would thrive here, but we have to choose among them. We're not looking for only the best numbers, but also for those who will make each freshman class the most interesting, the most 'yeasty,' the most representative of the broad-based society we live in…and there is *some* element of crap shoot in the whole process."

Each institution must determine how many offers of admission to make in order to "yield" the desired number of entering students. For example, while one college must accept 1,000 candidates so that 500 will enroll, another may need to make only 750 offers to net the same total. In any case, colleges always admit more students than they expect to actually enroll. (Financial-aid offices do the same thing.)

Although colleges are pretty good at making such estimates based on experience, it's impossible to always be right on the mark. Thus, your child may receive a letter of acceptance, a letter denying admission, or one which explains that he or she has been put on a "wait list." (For wait-list advice, see Chapter 8.) Other specific "admit" decisions can include:

- admission to the institution but not to the program of choice within it (programs, majors, and departments also use "wait lists").

- admission without housing and/or financial aid
- "conditional acceptance" such as "contingent on receipt of SAT II scores" or "on completion of summer physics course"
- admission to a later term (e.g., acceptance for second semester)

While most decisions are announced in a form letter, special personal "deny" letters may be sent to offer counsel or to soften the blow.

For instance, an applicant from a disadvantaged background may be encouraged to reapply after strengthening the academic record elsewhere.

Lest you think that admission officers are hardened and cold-hearted adjudicators, impervious to the feelings of applicants and their families, consider the words of William H. Peck, a former college admission dean and current director of college counseling at Santa Catalina School in California, "Remember that however disappointed you may be about an adverse decision on your child, the admission staff has experienced even more disappointments: those legions of wonderful students who looked at the college and never applied; who applied but were regretfully denied; who were admitted but chose to go elsewhere. We call them 'admissions' offices instead of 'rejections' offices for a reason—admitting students is, after all, the real goal and is a pleasure; denying them is a necessary element of the process, but an unpleasant task."

CHAPTER

8

We're In—We're Out— What Now? (After Decision Letters Are Received)

After all the letters are mailed—the ones that say "yes," which may be thick with forms to return, or the thin ones with only an apologetic "no"—there are whoops of joy and, unfortunately, many tears of disappointment. In addition, although there may be *good* news from the admission office, there may be *bad* news from the financial-aid office. Whatever the news, at least there's closure (and that's a relief)—well, for everybody except those on the wait list, that is. More about that later.

➤ **THE GOOD NEWS:** Most students get into a college that they like, feel pretty good about their choice, and head off with a bit more excitement than anxiety.

➤ **THE BAD NEWS:** Unfortunately, some students are bitterly disappointed by admission decisions. Often, it's the first time they've experienced a major rejection—and it hurts (...not only your child, but you, the parent, too).

First and foremost, it's important to remember that the college admission decision process does not make any kind of value judgment about how good, strong, special, or successful your child or your family is. Sometimes the nicest kids aren't the highest achievers in schools, and sometimes the most ornery ones—and the real challenges for parents—are the superstars in class and make out very well in the college admission game. Remember that success in life is defined lots of ways and getting into—or not getting into—one of the "hot" colleges is not going to make or break your child's hope for a happy and successful future.

Dr. Thomas J. Cottle, psychologist, and Edward M. Gillis, director of admission at University of Miami, hit this nail on the head in their article, "Surviving the College Admissions Maze," by observing, "Students are not being *judged* by the colleges that accept or reject them. In personal terms, college admission and rejection don't say much about you at all. Also, parents should not view college admission as a test of their success at child rearing. If academic status or report cards stand as the final proof of good parenting, then we're all in a lot of trouble."

In part, because this generation of parents knows more about college than their own parents, and because they feel pressured to provide more and better opportunities to their children, there is a lot more hysteria surrounding the admission process than there needs to be. Remind your child to, "Keep things in perspective," wisely counsels Bill Peck from Santa Catalina School. "If I don't get into my first choice college, and this is the worst disappointment I suffer in my life," Peck observes, "then I am indeed fortunate." Most students are sensible and realize that a *reach* college was just that. As a parent, you may have to help your child work through the disappointment if the *reach* college was also the first-choice college. Whatever school your child attends should *become* the first-choice school. And, please, don't imply that your feelings of love for—and approval of—your child have anything to do with college decisions or choices.

Having said that, it's time to consider the very practical issues that need to be handled after the thick and thin letters are mailed from admission offices.

I. Deposits

When your child is admitted to a school, that's when the shoe gets put on the other foot and *colleges* have to wait for a decision. Candidates' Reply Date is May 1, and your child has the *right* to wait until that date to let the colleges know if it's thumbs up or thumbs down, even though some places may put pressure on students to respond earlier. A *non-refundable* tuition-and-room deposit of several hundred dollars is required at most places.

In the old days, most very selective colleges mailed decisions on April 15, which gave students only two weeks to decide what to do and to negotiate financial aid. Even the Ivies mail earlier now, and most colleges have the bulk of their decision letters in the mail at the beginning of April.

Try to attend the open houses and similar functions planned for parents and students. Colleges will often invite admitted students for one last "look-see" on campus and might offer overnights, classes, meals, etc. This can be especially helpful if your child has never visited a particular campus or is having a really hard time deciding between two. Some "competitor" colleges even consult with each other when setting dates for open houses, so that students admitted to more than one place can plan to spread their visits around. (See "'Crunch-Time' Visits" in Chapter 4.)

If you need an extension of the deposit deadline, contact the admission office. If your financial-aid offer is not final or you have a persuasive reason to get a few more days to decide ("We're out of the country until May 7," etc.) call and ask for an extension. Generally, if a student is waiting to hear from another college, an extension *won't* be granted.

Q: If we pay a deposit by May 1 and, later, our son is taken off the wait list at his first-choice college, what happens?

A: If your child is accepted off a wait list *after* May 1, another deposit will be required for the admitting college, and the deposit paid to the original college will be forfeited. After colleges hear from all admitted candidates on May 1, they can make a decision about whether to take students off the wait list. If your child gets into one college off a wait list and decides to attend, be certain that he notifies the original college of his intentions in writing.

If the deposit poses a tremendous financial burden, ask the admission office if a payment plan can be worked out. Some financial-aid offices will waive the deposit in the cases of families with extraordinary financial need. For other families, it's just impossible to get together several hundred dollars by May 1. Colleges may be willing to accept partial payment by the deadline and then set up extended deadlines for the remainder. Example: $100 by May 1 and $50 every week afterward until total is received.

Don't "double deposit." It's not ethical to pay tuition deposits to two or more colleges. Students sometimes are tempted to do this if they can't make up their minds about which college is a more appropriate choice. May 1 is the time to fish or cut bait. Your child will be taking a space away from another student and just protracting the decision process if you don't stick to that deadline.

II. Wait Lists

➤ **THE GOOD NEWS:** Your child didn't get rejected.

➤ **THE BAD NEWS:** Your child didn't get in, either—at least, not yet.

Somewhere between the despair of rejection and the elation of acceptance is the uncertainty of the wait list. The college remains interested in your child but isn't ready to make a final decision. After May 1 (or sometimes before), when the college knows what kind of yield (i.e., the percentage of students admitted who pay their deposits) there is on the class, a decision will be made on who, if anybody, comes off the wait list.

Follow instructions about what to do about staying on the wait list. If a card needs to be returned to indicate interest in remaining on the wait list, have your child do so promptly. Updated transcripts or additional information about awards won or accomplishments not mentioned in the application should be submitted for review.

Some colleges rank order the wait list, while others don't. Your child may get his number written right on the wait list decision letter, which is better news for number 3 than number 333. At many schools, ranking doesn't take place until students respond to the offer. A phone call may be able to give your child a sense of how high—or low—he is. Also, a college may tell you how many they usually take off the list. Don't be surprised if they fudge and tell you that the number varies year to year. It probably does.

Many colleges plan to use their wait lists every year. Some are more erratic—some years they take a lot off, some years just a few or none.

Almost every parent of a wait-listed student asks how many students were taken off the list last year. A better question might be, "Over the last three or four years, how many students were taken?" Popularity of colleges changes, (when you're hot, you're hot; when you're not, you're not). It's not good news to find that a school hasn't used a wait list much in the past several years.

There may not be financial aid available for those on the wait list. Just ask to find out if there might be—or has been in the past—any money set aside for wait-list candidates. In all probability, they won't know until they have heard from other candidates. Colleges float more aid than they expect to have accepted by entering students, but variations in the yield influence availability of aid for wait-listed students. Not needing aid may end up as a hook for students on the wait list.

Hooks help determine who gets off the wait list. All sorts of lobbying goes on for wait-listed candidates, and the mix of the class is considered when choosing students off the list. For example, if the yield of students of color for this class is low, that will make a student of color on the wait list even more appealing. If there aren't enough alumni children, kids from the West, males or females—whatever—that will be considered by admission staff when looking at the list.

Is it helpful to try to be creative or try to make yourself stand out in any way to get noticed on the wait list? A student takes a risk when going out on a limb by trying to be zany, particularly if that's not a natural style. However, at wait-list stage, a little creativity or risk-taking can pay off.

Yale's Patricia Wei remembers, "A wait-listed student sent me a package and in it was a sneaker elaborately decorated and including her name and the year she hoped to graduate from Yale. With the shoe came a note saying, 'My foot is in the door—the rest is up to you.'" She got in. Of course, the sneaker wasn't the only reason she was tipped in off the wait list, but in this case it didn't hurt.

The vast majority of students do nothing more than send in their wait-list response cards and perhaps call once or twice for updates and advice. Plenty of them get good news, so don't assume that doing more is better.

If your child had an especially good interview in the admission office, or had been recruited by a coach or corresponded with a faculty member, this is a good time for him to get back in touch with that person so that a 'good word' can be put in. Some very wise advice comes from Richard E. Steele, dean of admission at Bowdoin College in Maine, "Unfortunately, far too many students and parents regard the offer of a position on the wait list as simply another form of rejection. The applicant who tends to be successful in getting *off* the wait list is the student who sees the wait-list letter as a call to action rather than a death knell. This is the moment when a thoughtfully written letter from the heart can move an admissions officer or a selection committee. A sensitive letter from a parent testifying to the son's or daughter's interest in the college can also help. Whatever you do, don't attempt to badger, threaten, or coerce the admission team. They won't want to present their dean of students with a four-year parental problem."

Occasionally, students taken off the wait list are offered admission for mid-year (January) rather than fall entrance. If this option sounds appealing, be sure to find out if credit will be awarded for courses taken elsewhere in the fall (continuing-education courses, community-college courses, etc.), if there is a good orientation program at mid-year, and if registration for appropriate freshmen-level classes will be difficult in January, especially in the case of year-long classes (elementary languages, introductory sciences, etc.).

III. Not Getting in Anywhere

➤ **THE GOOD NEWS:** Your child was excited about all the colleges he applied to.

➤ **THE BAD NEWS:** He didn't get into any of them.

Sadly, this does happen to students every year. In the case of very selective colleges, more students are denied each year than admitted, even though the bulk of the applicant pool is capable of doing the work.

Rule of thumb: Personalize the application process, but depersonalize the decision process.

Not getting into a college doesn't mean that your child is not bright, or is incapable of academic success or even unworthy of higher education. What it *does* mean is that the colleges selected may be very competitive, or that space was limited or that the college believes your child is not ready right now. Lots of wonderful, successful adults were once rejected from a college or two.

Q&A

Q: Can we appeal a "deny" decision?

A: Sometimes a college will review the folder of a denied applicant if some additional information has become available since the time decisions were made. Call and ask the admission office. Better still, have your child call and ask. Occasionally, if additional information submitted is persuasive, a deny decision may be overturned or a conditional acceptance might be offered. Don't get your hopes up, though, as this is a relatively rare happening.

Investigate Other Options

Realistically, in most cases it's best to accept the decisions and go on to investigate other options. Matthew, a gifted high-school senior, had talent in track and music, and his SATs were the envy of all his friends. Cockily, he assumed every one of the highly selective colleges he liked would want him too, so he passed up the chance to go to optional interviews, didn't spend much time on his essays, and generally "blew off" the seriousness of the application process. In April, he received two wait-list letters and three denies. And he was crushed.

The pile of thin letters from the admissions offices served as a wake-up call, and Matthew had no choice but to make an application in May of his senior year (this time he tried harder) to a less selective college with a "rolling-admission" policy. Not only was he admitted, but he was awarded a very generous financial-aid package. He liked the place when he got there—and didn't feel the need to transfer as he thought he might when he was originally admitted.

There is a place for just about anybody who is ready for college. If your child doesn't get in anywhere, consider a college with a later filing deadline or with an open admission policy (that is, everybody gets in) such as a community college. (Don't be surprised if housing or financial aid is not available at this point.) Your child may consider "trading up" by transferring elsewhere after a year or two. Community colleges are great places for a formerly unmotivated high school student to "pour it on" academically. "You have to make a lie out of your high school record, and one of the ways you can do this is by going to a community college," asserts John W. Vlandis, former director of admission at the University of Connecticut.

Talk to an Admission Officer

No matter what you do, don't do anything without asking an admission officer about chances of admission at a later date. Most institutions will not admit an applicant they've denied until new (and improved) academic credentials are available. Olivia, a very stubborn resident of Massachusetts, applied only to the universities of New Hampshire and Vermont, even though admission is more competitive for out-of-state students. She was denied at both schools. Convinced that UVM was her "dream" school, she took a year off, and reapplied *only to UVM* without having consulted the admission office to ask for advice on strengthening her record or enhancing her chances for admission in any other way. She didn't get in the second time, either, and wasn't too happy about it.

Often, there is no way a student will *ever* be admitted, and it's wise to ask the admission officer if chances for reapplication are good, slim, or non-existent. If you child is stubborn or willful, you're probably used to behavior like this. Unfortunately, a child can be hurt by his own inability to be objective and reasonable and can get his college career off to a false start by not being realistic.

On the other hand, some students know what they are talking about when they ask that a deny decision be reconsidered. Henry Mackal was denied admission to the University of Rhode Island and then admitted on a "trial basis" after he convinced the university's president that he could do the work. The risk paid off—he graduated with a degree in engineering four years later, and after amassing a fortune designing and manufacturing miniature precision valves, he donated lots of money to URI and they named a field house after him.

Consider a PG (Post-Graduate) Year or Time Off

Ask your child's guidance counselor for suggestions and contact the transfer counselor at your local community college for additional options. The reasons for disappointing news will guide you in making a sensible choice. Is your child ready for school? Does he need to look at less competitive choices? Does he need to work on any personal problems before he can concentrate on schoolwork? (See Chapter 9.)

"Time off should be more than space between high school and college," according to Jacqueline Murphy, director of admissions at Saint Michael's College in Vermont. "It should be productive—even if you are working, if college is the ultimate goal, a course or two will help admission people see improvement in your school work."

Each May, annual surveys of vacancies at two- and four-year colleges and universities are available. If your guidance office doesn't have them, contact NACAC (National Association of College Admission Counselors), 1631 Prince Street, Alexandria, VA 22314-2818 (or at www.nacac.com).

IV. Not Wanting to Go Where Accepted

➤ **THE GOOD NEWS:** Your child got several letters of acceptance from colleges.

➤ **THE BAD NEWS:** She doesn't want to go any of them—anymore.

Students apply to some colleges as backup or safety schools and never in their wildest dreams (nightmares?) do they plan to attend. However, in many cases a student will reluctantly go off to a "safety" school and end up happy as a clam, and this *last* college choice may soon become the number-one choice. Or, a student may be able use the backup school as a springboard to a better choice. As a parent, you can help your child look at the bright side of the story. After all, there must have been *something* your child found appealing enough to inspire an application.

A student shouldn't apply to a college that she doesn't like, but for lots of reasons that happens all the time. Some colleges are "hot" in a high school—tons of students apply to them, and so your daughter did, too, without really figuring out if the college was right for her. Many times, students wish that they had applied to tougher schools—and are envious when their friends who took the risk got into more competitive places.

It may be that she simply has cold feet about leaving home and high school. Take her for a visit to campus, if possible, to examine the areas she's doubting. She may not realize what's available. Have her review the "pro" and "con" list she made when she was exploring. Call the admission office and ask for the names of alumni and current students from your area and ask your child to contact them to get the scoop on what the campus is really like.

The choices basically boil down to the following options. Your child can:

- "put up and shut up" about the colleges that have accepted her; choose the least offensive of all of them, and hopefully become more enthusiastic after getting on campus.

- make late applications to other colleges with rolling deadlines. Options will be limited and financial aid and housing may not be available, but those might be sacrifices your child and you are willing to make.

- attend a prep school as a PG (post-graduate) or take a year off and reapply to more palatable choices.

Generally, before any major decision is made, there is some amount of doubt. Remember what it was like before you got married? Even the happiest couples admit that they wondered if this really was the right person, the right time, the right match. Of course, if you are divorced, you also know how miserable one can be after making a wrong choice. So, be sympathetic and try to help your child determine how serious the doubts are and how best to allay them.

Summer orientation or a cheerful letter from a future roommate or information about fall sports can get a reluctant prefreshman geared up for a less than enthusiastic college choice.

Another option for your child to consider is taking some time off from school. Classes in the School of Hard Knocks can often motivate an underachiever and light a fire under a lethargic student. In addition, "adult" students are flooding college classrooms, and they enter with a sharper sense of purpose than they would have had right out of high school.

Rob Yacubian, coordinator of transfer at Greenfield Community College in Massachusetts advises, "I think it's important not to push children towards college just because it's the best way to rise on the career ladder or because everybody else is going. Let the youngster work a while—six months, a year, two, or three or go into the service. Soon some youngsters tire of mundane jobs and see that they are smarter than others (in some cases, even their supervisors!) They will also realize that what they thought was a well-paying job no longer is. In other words, give them time; they'll soon find out and turn toward higher education. Good public and private colleges aren't going anywhere; they'll be waiting for them when they are ready."

V. Campus Security

Next to financing and finding the right "match" in our research, parents asked the most questions about campus security.

➤ **THE GOOD NEWS:** The Campus Security Act of 1990 Title II—Crime Awareness and Campus Security legislates that campus crime statistics be available to the public. A comprehensive report listing the incidents of crimes should be posted somewhere central on campus for you to review. If you don't see it, ask at the admission or security office.

➤ **THE BAD NEWS:** Some awful things can happen on college campuses, and you've probably read about some of the most horrendous in the newspapers. You worry, understandably, that your worst fears might be realized as your child leaves the nest and won't have you around to monitor locks and enforce curfews.

➤ **MORE GOOD NEWS:** Violent crime is not a problem on most college campuses.

Theft is the biggest issue at most schools. Unlocked bikes get stolen, leather jackets disappear, and CDs walk away. Beyond cautioning your child to lock the room, bike, or car, and to be really careful with special items, one of the best things to do is check what kind of coverage your homeowner's insurance policy offers for loss of items belonging to a child away at college. Also, find out how safe computers, TVs, and other expensive items are in dorm rooms over term breaks. If the dorms aren't secure and home is far away, is there adequate, secure storage provided on campus?

When looking at a campus, check the door locks. Are there locks on inside as well as outside doors? Are there working locks on windows? If a visitor comes to a dorm, is he let in without identifying himself? Who is in charge of the daily activities within residence halls? Is there a monitor or a head resident available at all times to keep an eye on what is going on?

Ask what kind of security force is on campus. Is it on-site? Do they have police powers? Have budget-tightening measures curtailed any staff or services? How involved is the security force in *preventing* crimes? Are they actively involved in the orientation process? Is there ongoing education? Are students instructed about personal safety and their responsibility to their dorm mates? Are students kept informed about rashes of thefts or seasonal prowlers? Are sketches of suspicious people posted in the cafeterias or in the dorms for students to be on the lookout for flashers, burglars, stalkers?

If you are aware of a well-publicized crime that has taken place on a campus, don't assume the campus isn't safe. Ask the security office about it. What happened? What did they do about it? What are they doing to educate students and prevent it from happening again?

Especially in schools located in an urban area, find out if there is an escort service for students at night. Is transportation provided from the library to dorms or to commuter parking lots? Car theft can be more of a problem in urban areas, too. If your child is going to take a car to campus, what kind of overnight parking is available? Is a car really needed? Should you invest in a car security system? If your child is going to be driving at night to a part-time job or class, perhaps a car phone might be a good graduation gift.

Buy a copy of the local paper when visiting a campus. What stories are published about crimes—are there murders mentioned on every page or is the theft of a mountain bike given front-page coverage? If the area the college is in is very different from the area of your home, be certain that your child understands the differences. What might be okay at school might not be okay at home—and vice versa.

Investigate the college's alcohol and drug policies. Unfortunately, alcohol abuse and misuse are major problems on most college campuses and car accidents, date rapes, and fights happen too often when students are under the influence. Continue to talk with your child about drinking responsibly.

Dorms and fraternity houses have burned to the ground and students' lives have been lost because somebody fell asleep with a candle lit or left a burning cigarette in a trash can or misused an electrical appliance. While you don't want to be a nagging, hovering parent, you *do* want your child to come home from college safely—so be sure to calmly and reasonably discuss safety habits. Also, find out the school's policy before you send microwave ovens, refrigerators, etc. Prohibitions are often for safety reasons—not due to concerns about utility costs or theft.

VI. Planning to Transfer

➤ **THE GOOD NEWS:** Lots of students transfer.

➤ **THE BAD NEWS:** Lots of students transfer.

You probably thought that once your child got accepted to college and decided to go (and you figured out how to pay for it) that everything would be all set for four years. That's not always the case.

Almost 900,000 students transfer each year from one college to another. In the old days, students, particularly those at competitive colleges, transferred more out of duress than any other reason and more often than not (since transferring was so difficult in terms of credit, housing, etc.) most students didn't dare try.

Fortunately, times have changed. On campuses from coast to coast, transfer students repeatedly turn out to be top scholars and leaders, faculty favorites, and graduation award winners. Indeed, these days, students are no longer satisfied with sticking it out at a college where they don't fit in, aren't happy, or can't study an area of interest. High tuitions and fees also spur many students to build a transfer deliberately into their college career. They attend a community college for two years, save money, develop academic strength, focus on a career path, and then transfer. Others, "trade up"—that is, after not being admitted to their dream school the first time around, they work on polishing academic skills and reapply for admission after a year or two of college-level work. Interestingly, many colleges and universities don't require standardized tests as part of the transfer application, and that can open up many new opportunities to some students.

Some parents are not wildly enthusiastic when their child mentions making a move. They worry when offspring don't stick to things—or wonder if they will be penalized credit-wise, or lose out on financial aid or housing. Keep in mind that transferring is not quitting or failing—it's changing—and colleges and universities are more welcoming and more accommodating to transfers than ever before. Wise enrollment-management officials at colleges rely on transfers to keep beds and classrooms full. Policies on financial aid and housing are more liberal than in the past, and at many colleges, transfers tend to be among the most satisfied graduates.

With so many college students transferring—and with even more *considering* it—there is a decent chance that you might at some point discuss with your son or daughter, the possibility of a switch. Read our book, *The Transfer Student's Guide to Changing Colleges* (ARCO) for all the details about making a change.

CHAPTER

9
Special Situations

➤ **THE GOOD NEWS:** All students are special—just ask their parents.

➤ **THE BAD NEWS:** When it comes to college admissions, there are special situations that require additional planning, preparation, and paperwork.

The following six relatively common, but "special," situations are grouped together in this chapter and presented alphabetically:

- **Advanced standing:** Advanced Placement (AP), International Baccalaureate (IB), and other precollege credit

- **Deferring admission to college:** postponing entrance to college for a year after high-school graduation

- **Early enrollment at college:** entering college before completing high school

- **International students:** students entering U.S. colleges from foreign countries

- **PG (post-graduate) year at a secondary school:** prepping for a year after high-school graduation

- **Students with disabilities and special needs:** people with learning, physical, and psychological disabilities

I. Advanced Standing

Advanced Placement (AP)

The AP program, administered by the College Board, offers Advanced Placement (college-level) courses to high-school students. The Board reports that about 51 percent of high schools in the U.S. offers AP courses to about 20 percent of their college-bound students and that more than 2,900 colleges recognize AP scores of 3 or better.

Thirty-one standardized exams which include multiple-choice and essay questions—in addition to portfolio evaluations in studio art—are administered in 16 fields of study each May and are graded on a 5 (high) to 1 (low) point scale. While the cutoff for acceptable scores is generally 3, many colleges—especially the highly selective ones—will accept only scores of 4 and 5 (and this may vary within the college depending on the student's major as well as other considerations). Check each college's policy in the catalog, since some are much more restrictive than others.

While most AP courses are taken senior year, not all are. Consequently, since AP exams are administered each May, students should take the AP exam the same year that the AP course is taken. For instance, if AP Biology is taught in 10th grade, the exam should be taken sophomore spring. That way, the subject is still fresh in students' minds. In addition, an AP exam may be repeated so your child can have another shot at the same exam junior or senior year.

As of this writing, students pay $74.00 to take each test, which is a pretty good deal when you calculate how many hundreds—or thousands—of dollars you might save if scores are acceptable for college credit. The College Board reports that more than 1,300 institutions will grant *a year's worth* of advanced standing to students with adequate AP scores. So, if your child is interested in one of *those* schools and wants to accelerate in college and graduate in less than four years by applying AP credit toward degree requirements, that could save you roughly between $10,000 and $20,000 in tuition and room-and-board fees. Don't push things, though. Many students don't want to—and are not required to—graduate early, even if they have extra credits. If your child doesn't want to push ahead and finish up a degree sooner, he or she might be able to take more advanced classes, fulfill core requirements, take a lighter load, or switch majors by having AP credit on the record.

College admission officers like to see students challenge themselves academically, and having AP courses on a transcript indicates that a student wants to stretch. However, if your local high school is in the 49 percent that doesn't offer AP courses, don't feel that your child will be penalized in the admission process. Remember, colleges evaluate what is available to the student and how the student took advantage of what was offered—if AP wasn't an option, that's not the student's fault.

For more information on AP, contact your guidance office or contact: Advanced Placement Program, The College Board, 45 Columbus Avenue,

New York, NY 10023-6992, 212/713-8066 (or www.collegeboard.org/AP/html/indx001.html).

International Baccalaureate (IB)

The International Baccalaureate (IB) is a two-year academic curriculum designed for students ages 16 to 19 and developed to meet the requirements of a variety of educational systems throughout the world. Founded in the mid-1960s, the IB has over 700 member schools in 81 countries ranging from Australia to Vietnam, and nearly 300 high schools in the U.S. and Canada currently offer this option to their students.

Exams are administered and graded, and if a student earns the IB Diploma, many colleges and universities will grant credit and/or advanced standing. IB students take six exams—three at the *higher* level and three at the *standard* level. Typically, college credit is awarded for *higher*-level exams only. (Some institutions may award credit for standard exams.) The best grade a student can earn is 7, and, while normally results of 5 and above are necessary for college credit, many institutions will award some credit for lower scores, especially in languages.

As with AP exams, colleges have their own specific policies regarding acceptable scores on the IB and placement rules. At Kansas State University, higher-level scores of 5 through 7 receive *varying* amounts of credit, and in some instances standard-level scores of 5 or better are also considered. Consult each college for individual practices.

Standards and policies vary, and if you are interested in more information as well as a comprehensive listing of IB educational programs in the United States, contact International Baccalaureate North America, 200 Madison Avenue, Suite 2007, New York, NY, 100016-3903; 212/696-4464 (www.IBO.org).

Q&A

Q: Is it better to have IB or AP credit?

A: Since both provide good, solid academic challenges, and since college credit can be awarded for both programs, one is not necessarily "better" than the other. With AP courses, students get to pick and choose what they're good at and what they enjoy most—sort of like ordering à la carte from a menu. On the other hand, the IB is comparable to ordering a

Continues

197

Continued

complete meal from a menu and, while there are some choices within the meal (Spanish instead of French, for example), no course in the meal can be skipped. Students must take the full curriculum including subjects that may not be their favorites or their strong points.

In the past, IB was an appealing choice if foreign travel was in a family's future. According to Lorna R. Blake, director emeritus of admission at Smith College, "The IB might be the best bet if you think that your family may be spending time abroad for international business or the military, or if your child has plans and dreams of his own to work or study abroad in the future. The IB is internationally recognized and, with good results, your child could gain acceptance into most universities abroad. Another advantage of the IB is that students finish with a solid *liberal-arts* education since courses are required among a variety of disciplines. A student isn't able to take just sciences or languages, for instance."

Times appear to be changing and, as of this writing, 40 percent of students taking the IB exams do so in secondary schools in the U.S. and Canada and most of them are going to American or Canadian universities.

Either way, both IB and AP offer great academic challenges to high-school students and college credit may be awarded for appropriate scores.

Other Types of Precollege Credit

Other than AP or IB credit, colleges have a variety of policies governing what credit—if any—will be awarded for work completed before matriculation at the freshman level.

While some colleges will not award any college credit to entering freshmen (except for AP and IB), others are quite generous. Some tend not to award credit for college courses taken in high school that count toward high-school graduation requirements. Opportunities for high-school students to take courses for credit at local colleges have increased, and colleges vary dramatically on how they view the credit earned.

➤ **THE BAD NEWS:** If your child takes a physics class at a local college during senior year or a summer course at a community college, he or she may—or may not—be awarded credit when enrolling in college.

➤ **THE GOOD NEWS:** While college credit might not be awarded, your child may be able to "place out" of a class on the basis of the information covered in the college-level course. In addition, if your child is able to take an AP exam that parallels the college course content and scores well enough, credit may be granted.

Consult current college catalogs for particulars, and ask your child's guidance counselor for specific advice about specific courses. While not all students wish to accelerate and graduate early, most hate to be bored and if they have mastered subjects in high school, they can go to deeper levels in college. If your child has taken college-level courses in high school, save the course syllabi, papers, and exams. They may come in handy when your child is seeking university credit or determining appropriate departmental placement.

Other types of credit accepted at some colleges include College Board's CLEP (College-Level Examination Program), American College Testing Program's PEP (Proficiency Examination Program), the Department of Defense DSST's (DANTES Subject Standardized Tests), correspondence courses, and in some unusual cases, "Life Experience." Normally, these options are offered to "adult" students returning to the classroom, but if your child has any of these credits, for one reason or another, consult individual colleges for their policies. Don't be surprised if credit is denied.

Predictably, the more selective the college, the more stringent the rules regarding the transferability of outside courses for entering freshmen. Naturally, a college wants entering freshmen to take full advantage of courses offered there…and so, understandably, there are restrictions on what comes in from the outside.

II. Deferring Admission to College

Many students ask colleges to "gimme a break" for a year before enrolling. They are not ready to go straight from high school to college for a variety of reasons. Some study abroad for the year after high school, some travel, some work, and others wish to pursue art or a sport or another skill full time without the "distractions" of the academic year. Other students choose this time to take care of a health problem or to work on personal or family problems.

Currently, 35,000 to 40,000 students take a year off between high school and college, and only about 20 of the nearly 3,000 colleges and universities in the U.S. will not allow students to defer enrollment for that year, according to Robert Gilpin, faculty member at Milton Academy in Massachusetts and coauthor of *Time Out: Taking a Break from School to Travel, Work and Study in the U.S. and Abroad.*

If your child plans to stop out of school for a year, encourage him to apply to colleges during senior year rather than waiting until the year off to do so. It's easier to get application materials together while enrolled in high school, and—particularly if the year off is spent abroad or in a remote area in this country—the mail service may not guarantee meeting deadlines. Also, if he or she has a change of heart and decides *not* to take that time off, there will be the option of enrolling at college.

Generally, to defer admission, an accepted student needs to put his/her reasons in writing to the dean of admission and submit a deposit by the *published deadline* to reserve a place in the following year's freshman class. Colleges vary on their policies about what is an appropriate reason—the major source of disagreement seems to center around credit for academic programs completed during the year off. Smith, for example, will not allow a student to enroll in another degree-granting program and will not give college credit for any work completed during the year off. If a student wants to enroll elsewhere in the year off, she would need to reapply as a transfer student.

Many colleges and universities will discourage—or just won't allow—students to defer for just one semester or one quarter. Orientation can be difficult in the middle of year. There may not be on-campus housing or financial aid available, and enrolling midyear may prohibit your son or daughter from enrolling in some required, year-long courses which might be prerequisites for higher-level courses. Elementary language and sciences are often especially difficult to enter in midstream.

Don't be surprised if your child's goals and college plans change during the year off. Kevin deferred admission to Colby College in Maine to have knee surgery for an injury sustained playing football. During his rehabilitation, he became very interested in physical therapy. Since Colby didn't have a program, he reapplied to colleges during his year off and entered the University of Vermont where he could study PT. Colleges expect some "melt" on the students who defer and, while they are disappointed to lose a freshman who postponed enrollment, nobody is totally stunned by that turn of events.

It is wrong to "double deposit." You should not put in nonrefundable deposits at two colleges hoping your child will make up his mind during the year off. That takes a space away from somebody else and, if financial aid is offered, that money is unavailable to another deserving person.

Be certain to check with the financial-aid office and find out what impact—if any—taking a year off will have. If your child has been offered financial assistance, ask if it will it be guaranteed the next year. How will you have to update the aid application? If a student earns any money during the year off, how will that affect eligibility for aid? Geraldine, a bright and ambitious young woman, took a year off to do some fashion modeling and earned enough money to pay for her college tuition.

There are hundreds—thousands even—of opportunities for high-school students during their interim year ranging from the familiar AFS (American Field Studies Intercultural Programs) to "Up with People" to living on a kibbutz in Israel or serving as a "Willing Worker on Organic Farms." Many charge tuition and a few come with a stipend. Some have financial aid available, and some offer room and board as payment. All offer students chances to mature and learn.

Students can work before, during, and after college in the national AmeriCorps program which provides educational awards in return for community service. For more information, contact The Corporation for National and Community Service, 1201 New York Avenue, NW, Washington, DC 20525; 800/942-2677 (www.cns.gov).

If your child wants to take time off but doesn't know what to do, ask around about good programs and look for guidebooks and brochures in the guidance office or library. There are plenty of Web sites to visit including Gilpin's www.stoppingout.com.

Some parents worry that the child who takes time off will never go back. While some *do* drop out of the academic world for awhile, most who take time off with a purpose or plan return to school with a new vigor and focus, and they become better college students than they would have been without the "pause that refreshes." Sounds tempting, doesn't it?

III. Early Admission, Early Enrollment, Early Entrance

A relatively small, but steady, number of high-school students find that they have exhausted academic and extracurricular options at their high schools well before they are ready to graduate.

So, since they feel that they will be spinning their academic wheels until graduation, they leave high school—with or without a diploma—and enroll at college, usually after the junior year. Admission people take extra care in evaluating early-admission candidates to make certain that they are *socially mature*—as well as *academically ready*—for higher education. To determine how ready an applicant is, the admission office may request a personal interview (even if it's not required for other applicants) or ask for an additional writing statement detailing reasons for wanting to enroll early.

Consult your child's guidance counselor to discuss whether Early Admission is a reasonable option. Carlene Riccelli, college advisor at Amherst

Regional High School in Massachusetts, is careful to make sure her students have exhausted the high-school curriculum and have taken full advantage of the opportunities available before leaving early. Since Amherst Regional offers the option of taking college courses at UMass/Amherst as well as at Amherst College, only two or three opt to leave early out of a class of 250. "Frequently, I hear reasons that are *not* legitimate for early admission. 'All my friends have graduated' or 'I don't want to live with my parents anymore' are examples."

Social adjustment to college life is often more of a challenge for students who are quite a bit younger than others. A precocious 15-year-old might be smart enough to tutor her 21-year-old classmates in physics, but might find herself very lonely when roommates are selected and party invitations go out.

Rather than severing ties completely with the high school, some students opt for a compromise and try for a dual enrollment program. For example, Rockland Community College in New York, has developed programs for high-school seniors who may elect to attend full time in lieu of the senior year in high school or part time while attending high school. Several states have developed cooperative agreements between high schools and two- and four-year colleges. With educational funding as tight as it is, it makes sense to coordinate resources, and more of these kinds of collaborative programs are popping up.

Simon's Rock College of Bard in Great Barrington, Massachusetts is the only "early" college in the country, and students enroll after completing the sophomore or junior year in high school.

➤ **THE GOOD NEWS:** There are plenty of good options available to high-school students who feel *underwhelmed* by their school's offerings.

➤ **THE BAD NEWS:** Colleges treat the options differently. For instance, if your child enrolls in a dual program with a community college while still taking courses at the high school, some colleges may consider your child a transfer student and some a freshman applicant. It can add a touch of confusion to the admission process, so your best bet is to consult with colleges first about the options your child is considering.

If your family is interested in financial aid, be warned that in order to qualify for federal funds, students need to:

- have a high-school diploma or
- earn a GED certificate (General Educational Development—a standardized test taken by those who haven't graduated from high school) or

- pass an independently administered test approved by the U.S. Department of Education (e.g., PSAT, SAT, ACT, Army Entrance Exam, etc.) or

- meet other standards your state establishes that are approved by the U.S. Department of Education

Even if your child applies to and is admitted to college at the end of junior year, he can always defer admission if he needs extra time before leaving home.

IV. International Students

➤ **THE GOOD NEWS:** International students are welcomed to U.S. colleges in large numbers and not only do they enjoy academic challenges at American institutions, but they grow culturally by experiencing life in a country different from their own.

➤ **THE BAD NEWS:** Students must be U.S. citizens (or eligible noncitizens, such as permanent residents) to qualify for federal financial aid. Consequently, funding from colleges and universities—as well as from outside sources—is limited, and competition for scholarships is often brutal.

Admission officers travel all over the world to recruit top international students, and studying in a country other than a homeland has never been more popular. While many of the questions are the same for domestic and international students, some are different.

- *International students who are not citizens of the United States should mention this fact when they request college information. Then schools can send these students the appropriate application and specific information about any available aid.*

- *Follow deadlines and, if possible, follow up by phone, fax or e-mail about the receipt of credentials.* The mail in some parts of the world is painfully slow and unreliable, so it's advisable to post mail to admission offices one month ahead of the deadline. If you have access to a fax machine or e-mail, include specifics on the application. Many colleges send decisions by telegram and follow up with a letter, and that can be a help. If your child hasn't heard from a college by the expected time, call—but be sure to check time differences first. In addition, although international calls are expensive, you might be spending your money well by calling to make certain that an application has been received and completed by the deadline.

- *Many colleges will waive the application fee if it imposes too great a burden—read application instructions for details.* Some may ask that a school official verify the financial necessity of a waiver; some may simply take your child's word for the fact that she can't get money out of her country.

- *International students whose language of instruction is other than English are required to take the TOEFL (Test of English as a Foreign Language) in addition to, or in some cases in place of, other standard-ized tests.* This standardized test is offered, for a fee, throughout the year, all over the world. Some colleges may post their preferred scores. (For more information about TOEFL see Chapter 3.)

- *Some international students choose to take an intensive summer course in English right before enrolling to brush up on skills, especially conversational English. Some colleges may offer a conditional acceptance, requiring such a program.* "Contact the college your child plans to attend to ask for recommendations of which English language programs might be appropriate," counsels Nicholas Senecal, assistant director of admission at Bryant College in Rhode Island. "I will only suggest programs that I trust and ones that are well-governed and will consider the student's specific needs and goals, as well as our relationship with the program, when helping to select one."

It's especially important that international students make a comfortable match for themselves, since college will be a home away from home. Some international students, because of finances, aren't able to go home in the summers, and a large number don't go home for holidays. The office of international students or the dean's office can help make suggestions about housing during holidays and summer. Also, there will probably be an international students' association that will serve as social and cultural support for your child while abroad.

Often, international students are surprised by how informal students are here and how relaxed the relationship is between faculty member and student. The international students' office may have a guidebook for students and/or an orientation program which will help familiarize your child with social mores and customs. Sometimes, slang and money are the biggest adjustments. With McDonald's serving all over the world now, U.S. food is not as foreign anymore, but many students have to adjust to some new flavors and smells.

If climate is totally different, consider having your child buy clothes after arriving on campus to find out what styles are appropriate on campus. Tag sales (sales of used materials usually on lawns of private homes) as well as used-clothing stores will have many bargains.

- *The I-20 Form (Certificate of Eligibility) will be issued to your child after acceptance and will enable a student to apply for a student visa at a U.S. Embassy in your home country.* Your child will need to get a passport and apply for a student visa. The college or university admitting your child will correspond with you regarding details for obtaining a student visa.

Read *The International Student's Guide to Going to College in America,* by Sidonia Dalby, Sally Rubenstone and Emily Harrison Weir (ARCO, 1996), for more details.

V. Attending a Post-Graduate (PG) Year at a Secondary School

A very sensible option for many students not ready for college right after high-school graduation is spending a PG year at one of the more than 80 independent secondary schools in the United States and Canada offering this option. While some students take an extra year of high school just to polish up academic skills and reapply to colleges that rejected or wait-listed them, others use it as a year to sharpen athletic prowess and not "waste" a year of eligibility playing a sport at a college that doesn't interest them while they try for admission to a high-power school.

➤ **THE GOOD NEWS:** Prepping for a year can polish up academic skills, help a student mature socially, broaden horizons for college choices, and give a student a chance to retake standardized tests.

➤ **THE BAD NEWS:** Depending on what the student hopes to accomplish in a year, it could be little more than a waste of time and money.

Rosita Fernandez-Rojo, associate director of college counseling at Choate Rosemary School in Wallingford, Connecticut, stresses that "a PG year works well in some cases and not in others. The success of the experience depends on the expectations of the students."

Jay, father of three and a veteran of the college admission process, advises, "Some people are not ready for college at the usual time. My son applied only to schools he wanted to go to—no safety colleges the first time— and was rejected by all three. He then went to prep school as a PG, had three terms of highest honors, graduated cum laude for PG year, reapplied to his first-choice college that had turned him down and was accepted! Life is not a sprint; it is a long distance run. There is no rush or deadline—go at *your own pace,* not the colleges.'"

Hmmmm...*your own pace.* Sometimes parents hope that their children will turn around in a PG year and become the students that they never have been. While that is the case sometimes, in other cases, pushy parents with unrealistic expectations send their kids off to a PG year hoping for a miracle in the classroom.

Tryna, a wonderful young woman but not a terrific student, went off to a PG year, kicking and screaming, at the insistence of her parents. School is not her strength, and she hated every minute of the experience. Although she was admitted to a junior college at the end of her PG year, she probably would have been admitted out of high school, and if she had it to do over again, she wouldn't. She could have saved her parents an awful lot of money and herself some heartache if she had skipped the PG year.

A PG year is a time for enrichment. Courses are taken above and beyond high-school graduation requirements, weak areas can be focused on, strong areas can be polished, SATs and ACTs can be retaken, writing skills can be sharpened, and in the case of boarding students, dorm-living survival skills can be developed. Some students are very young at the end of high school, and one additional year at the secondary level might make a difference between an okay freshman year and a great freshman year. To get the most out of a PG experience, a student needs to be well-motivated.

"Since it's a relatively short period of time, PGs need to hit the ground running," according to Devon Schlickman, a former admission officer at Northfield/Mount Hermon School in Massachusetts, which has a very competitive PG program with 70 to 75 students each year.

Athletics often motivate students to try a PG year. Paul, a strong hockey player at a large public high school, was encouraged by all the college coaches who recruited him to consider a PG year, especially since he would be just 17 when he graduated from high school. "They counseled me that after a year at a prep school, I would be bigger physically, more mature emotionally and mentally, and better prepared for the academic rigors of college," he remembers. "I covered my bases and applied to the PG program at Choate as well as to several colleges." Although admitted to a few schools (but not his top choice), he decided to go to Choate. "The college counselor at Choate advised me to apply to Bowdoin but since they rejected me previously, I was bitter and didn't want to. However, since there was no fee charged to reapply, I figured that I had nothing to lose and tried again." Happily, he was admitted, enrolled, and became captain of the Bowdoin hockey team.

You can look into PG years at the same time you are looking at colleges, but don't worry if you consider this option after mid-April of senior year since many independent schools continue to accept applications for PGs throughout the summer. Check a guidebook, such as *The Handbook of Private Schools* by Porter Sargents, Inc., to get names of some schools with the option of a post-graduate year.

VI. Students with Disabilities and Special Needs

➤ **THE GOOD NEWS:** Colleges are prohibited *by law* from discriminating against a student with a disability.

➤ **THE BAD NEWS:** Free, appropriate, special education is mandated by law *only through age 22 or high-school graduation, which ever comes first.* Consequently, since the rules are different in higher education, colleges vary dramatically on the resources—financial and human—they are willing and able to commit to students with disabilities. What is available to your child at one college may not be at another.

The bad news isn't all that bad, however, since the Americans with Disabilities Act (ADA) of 1990 guarantees civil rights and prohibits discrimination against persons with disabilities, and Section 504 of the Rehabilitation Act of 1973 requires that institutions receiving federal funds provide "reasonable" accommodations to students with disabilities. Reasonable accommodations include accessible classrooms, untimed exams, note takers, and books on tape.

Depending on the extent of your child's disability, you will have to add more "look-sees" to your list when considering different campus options. Every disability is different—and whether your child's is learning, physical, or psychological—you need to spend time as a family deciding exactly how much support will be needed at the college level. Any specialist you have worked with (physical therapist, speech-language pathologist, social worker, etc.), as well as your child's guidance counselor, can offer helpful suggestions.

When corresponding with a college or visiting the campus, contact the office that deals with students with disabilities. The office of admission or the college's affirmative-action officer can point you in the right direction. Not only do you want to find out how accessible and accommodating the campus is *technically,* but you want to get a feel for how sensitive administrators are about making housing assignments, what kind of special academic support is available (readers, interpreters, tutors, etc.), and generally what is the "feel" of the campus for a student with a disability. You want your child to fit in, as well as to get the support needed to make college the best experience it can be. It's helpful if your child can meet with a student with a comparable disability and, by doing so, get the "inside scoop" on accessibility. An overnight visit is a must if your child plans to board. Even though the gym is listed as wheelchair accessible, is there a lift in the pool? What kind of climate is there in the dorms? Does the campus community accept and integrate people who are different? Is there any extra charge for special services? Will you or your child get assistance in hiring a personal-care attendant? How many other students have similar disabilities? What kind of medical care is available?

Offices dealing with students with disabilities can provide a tremendous amount of information to prospective students and help them determine if they will fit in on campus. Although Arizona State University has nearly 30,000 undergraduates, there is nothing impersonal about the way its Center for Disability Resources treats students. Staff members contact each applicant identifying himself as a student with a disability by phone and letter. These applicants are asked more about their specific needs and are told—among other things—that the Center has physical therapists on staff as well as a powerhouse wheelchair basketball team which included a former U.S. Olympian.

Parents of students with disabilities often are more involved with the education of their children than other parents. This is a good time to do some heavy-duty thinking and talking about how independent your child is. If he is going to live away from home, how skillful is he in taking care of business such as laundry, arranging for transportation, and sticking up for himself?

Your child will need to be able to accurately describe his disability and service needs. You know how you have told your child over and over again that "I'm not always going to be around to do this for you?" Well, college is one of those times, and your child will be a better self-advocate, knowing how to articulate his situation accurately and clearly.

Accurate and recent documentation will be required to obtain support services at the college level. This sort of documentation can be very expensive when obtained privately. Consider having your child evaluated by the public school system before graduating, since colleges often require documentation that is not more than two years old. As long as they haven't graduated from high school, even students enrolled in private schools may be eligible for an evaluation through the public school system.

Consider a college such as Gallaudet which deals exclusively with deaf students or Landmark College, specializing in working with students with learning disabilities. Gallaudet University, located in Washington, D.C., is an internationally renowned school whose chief mission is to educate people who are deaf and hard of hearing. "We have students from diverse backgrounds which include those who were educated in residential school settings, mainstream programs, oral programs, and those who attended school with no support. At Gallaudet, everyone is made to feel at home because of our unique identification of deafness," according to Deborah E. DeStefano, director of admissions.

Landmark College in Putney, Vermont, is the nation's only accredited college exclusively serving students with dyslexia or specific learning disabilities. Credit courses lead to an associate degree in general studies, and a noncredit curriculum gets students ready to enter or return to degree-granting undergraduate programs. "Landmark serves as a launching pad for those who wish to go on to a more challenging school than they might have been able to handle right out of high school," maintains Carolyn Olivier, director of admissions.

Investigate how the college will help students get oriented and how they will be plugged into any special activities after enrollment. Idaho State University's Cooperative Wilderness Handicapped Outdoor Group (C.W. HOG) provides unlimited physical activities including adaptive water-skiing, therapeutic horseback riding, white-water rafting and dog sledding! While these activities are not for everyone, it's terrific to know that students with physical disabilities have all sorts of options, and offerings like these give you a sense of how committed an institution is to students with special needs.

Some students, for a variety of reasons, are reluctant to admit that they have a disability or are shy about asking for special treatment. "Self-identifying as disabled is *not* asking for special treatment; it is merely asking to be treated fairly. At the same time, evidence of a disability is not a guaranteed ticket of admission; you have to be able to demonstrate a satisfactory level of academic accomplishment to justify your admission," contends Jonathan P. Reider, associate director of admissions at Stanford University in California.

Self-reporting a disability of any sort can help *explain* rather than *excuse* some parts of an application. A student with a serious—but unmentioned—sight impairment completed her application by hand and it was a mess. Before knowing she was nearly blind, evaluators thought she was sloppy and careless. After a guidance counselor mentioned her disability, those same evaluators thought she was spunky and remarkable to do as good a job as she had done. It was *still* illegible—which isn't the best first impression to make—but nevertheless, it was authentic.

A bright young man with a learning disability, and the younger sibling of three high-powered, high-testing college graduates, did not want "special" treatment because of his LD. He chose not to have untimed SATs, and consequently his scores were—predictably—low. Hoping to continue to hide his "secret," he applied only to colleges that did not require standardized tests, limiting his choices considerably. Had he taken untimed SATs or documented his learning disability, an admission office would have had valuable information with which to interpret his testing pattern. Further, he could have taken advantage of the support services available to him and probably have had a more productive college career.

If your child has a physical disability that could make a traditional campus visit difficult, encourage him to let the admission office know before arriving on campus. Arrangements can be made to ensure that the visit is as productive and comfortable as possible. One young woman, a person of small stature, arrived at the admission office of a large, urban campus planning to go on a tour. She wasn't expecting a group tour and felt that the busy city streets and huge campus would be impossible for her to negotiate on foot. Had she called ahead, a personal guide could have led the tour at her own pace, or arrangements for a driving tour could have been made.

Untimed standardized tests or special accommodations, such as large-print test booklets or accessible testing sites, can be provided for students with disabilities. (See information numbers at the end of Chapter 3.)

"How to Choose a College: Guide for the Student with a Disability" is available for $1.00 from the HEATH (Higher Education and Adult Training for people with Handicaps) Resource Center at One Dupont Circle, Suite 800, Washington, DC 20036-1193; 202/939-9320 (this number is Voice/TDD) or its Web site http://ACENET.edu. This guide provides an excellent outline for getting into the college-selection process, and the office couldn't be more helpful and welcoming to questions. The staff is knowledgeable and friendly, so don't hesitate to call.

10

Words of Wisdom: Advice from Educators and Once-Panicked Parents

While your sons and daughters will learn the best lessons by doing things (including making mistakes) *on their own,* another good (and safer) way to learn is through the experience of others. Below you'll find advice from admission professionals, guidance counselors, and other parents on topics that range from A to, well, V.

If it makes you feel any better, the admission pros who are also parents of college-bound children are not immune to the concerns that plague "civilian" parents going through this process. "I am knowledgeable about college admissions, I understand my kids' strengths and weaknesses, we do not have financial problems, and my kids had good guidance counselors. Even with these advantages, the process was difficult, time-consuming, uncertain, and stressful," confides Elaine Kaplan, assistant vice provost at the State University of New York at Stony Brook.

Admission Madness

"College has achieved a symbolic importance so out of proportion to its actual meaning, and the admission process has evolved into such a Byzantine ritual, that it can make normal people act nutty, and nutty people act quite crazy," writes Michael Thompson, a clinical psychologist, in his article, *College Admission: Failed Rite of Passage.* He goes on to observe, "From a psychologist's point of view, college admission is infected by irrational forces exactly proportional to the extent that the participants believe it is only about getting into a 'good college.'"

Bribes

One director of admission remembers a father who opened his son's letter of denial and immediately called the admission office informing them that he would be in the director's office in half an hour. The father hung up the phone, got in his car, and showed up as promised. A successful, self-made business man, he opened the conversation with, "What will it take to get Gary in? Would $100,000 do it?" The long and short of the matter was that Gary wasn't qualified and might not be happy and successful at that college, but by hook or by crook, his father was going to great lengths to make it happen.

Barbara, now a mother of a college-bound daughter, sadly recalls, "As a high-school senior, I was bribed to attend a school my mother and grandmother wanted me to attend and received gifts all during my stay. I had decided that I would never do that to *my* child. I do not agree with my daughter's college choice (actually it was my *last* choice for her), but I will be here to support her because I feel if she is not comfortable and happy she will not succeed in life."

Budget Cuts at Colleges

Richard E. Steele, dean of admission at Bowdoin College in Brunswick, Maine, advises, "Today's concerned parent has a newly formed responsibility when it comes to assisting in the college search. Faced with a troubled economy and reduced sources of financial support, many colleges and universities (public as well as private) are scrambling behind the scenes to trim budgets and to cut costs. As this trimming and cutting occurs, parents need to discover the extent to which budget adjustments will affect the quality of the undergraduate experience. Today, parents need to ask a whole series of questions which were rarely needed just a few years ago: What cuts in services, personnel, or programs are taking place? How will these cuts affect the quality of my son's or daughter's educational program? Will it take longer for my daughter or son to complete the degree? Will graduate students replace faculty as instructors? Which programs or majors will be dropped? Will any important services be eliminated in the future? Most high-school students are reluctant to ask such tough-minded questions, but this is where a concerned parent needs to come to the rescue. Colleges and universities which have gone about budget cutting with care and creativity will welcome such questions."

Essays

Wally Lamb, author of *She's Come Undone* and teacher at Norwich Free Academy in Connecticut shares, "I frequently assist students struggling with the application essay. My best advice is to avoid writing an 'Eddie Haskell' essay—adopting that smarmy, see-through tone that tries to *impress* adults rather than speak honestly. It didn't work on Ward and June, and it won't work with the college admission office either. Be yourself when you write the essay; write about what's important to you so that you'll write from the heart. *Revise!* Don't settle for your first draft."

Stanford University associate director of admission, Jonathan P. Reider observes, "Parents, who are older, wiser and more experienced writers, are frequently tempted to help their children write their application essays. As long as the student is willing, some kinds of help are normal; brainstorming, giving an honest reaction to a first draft, and proofreading for spelling and mechanics—these are all practices of any thoughtful writer, adult or adolescent. But some parents want to go farther: they want their daughter to leave out that she's a vegetarian because they think it might make her look flaky, or they want their son to include the name of the father's company because it will lend status. These forms of help are mistaken because they keep the applicant from sounding natural, like eighteen-year-olds, with all the innocence that implies. The only adult who can write successfully like a teenager is J. D. Salinger, and I know he won't write an essay for your child. And *you* shouldn't try either. Admission officers can't claim that they can detect an adult-assisted essay every time, but I honestly doubt that the help actually helps. So let Sarah sound like Sarah, and Eddie like Eddie. They will feel better, too, knowing that the work is really theirs."

Fathers

"I remember two fathers in two different years, both of whom absolutely lost any sense of composure while ranting, railing, raving, and raging to me by phone about why their C- student did not get into a 'reach' school. Counselors deserve politeness and respect—pushy, demanding parents can really damage the whole process, making a difficult situation unbearable for the student," according to Gregory Tuleja, director of studies/college counselor at Williston Northampton School in Massachusetts.

Mistaken Identity

Admission maven Tom Anthony writes, "A number of years ago the mother of a student I had just interviewed told me this story: Their next-door neighbor had done the summer college tour; they visited about twelve colleges in ten days and *of course* got an in-depth view of each! As luck would have it, the young woman found 'the college of her choice.' *It was so exciting.* She returned to high school in the fall, filled out her early decision application and sent it in. *It was so exciting.* She was deferred—*much less exciting.* But she worked hard, her midyear grades were strong, her new SATs showed improvement, and in April—an acceptance. *This was really exciting.* They sent in the deposit, got the housing and registration materials, heard from her roommate, and *it was almost unbearably exciting.* Even the tuition bill was exciting—for some of them. Then in September they loaded up the family bus and set off for the promised land. They drove expectantly to the college and found the *wrong* campus! In the course of the previous summer vacation they had confused the name of one college with the campus of another."

Mothers

David Thompson, college counselor at Northfield Mount Hermon in Massachusetts comments that "it's almost always a mom" who gets too involved with the process. He muses, "One mother was so proud of herself that when she mailed off her son's fifteen applications (having done most of all of them except the essays), she sent out announcements, congratulating herself. She's a wonderful woman and a good mother, and she did all the work with humor and charm, and the announcements were funny. But her son may have suffered in subtle ways (despite his expressed gratitude) and certainly missed the most rewarding moments in the process. Who really applied to college and got in?"

Pamela Batchelder, former assistant director of admissions at Trinity College in Hartford, Connecticut, recalls, "We received a letter from a student who informed us that 'me and my mother have decided to attend Dartmouth,' which left me wondering A) how his roommate will feel about his mother staying in their room and B) who really made the decision to attend Dartmouth."

Reacting

"I think that one of the things that parents must remember—which I have tried to teach since my eldest daughter went through the college search— is that kids need time to react to schools their own way without any input from parents," Phyllis S. Steinbrecher, educational consultant and coauthor of *You Can Say "No" to Your Teenager,* suggests. "A gentle 'ah hum' or 'huh' or a terribly unobtrusive neutral sound is far more effective than a comment. I think parents need to trust their kids to do their own reacting and hold off on input until all those first impressions have had a chance to settle in. A parental response either positive *or* negative can produce an oppositional response simply because of adolescence and not because of a school."

Single-Sex Colleges

"I can't emphasize enough how important it is that women consider all-women's colleges—or at least higher education institutions with high percentages of tenured women faculty," asserts Barbara Kerr, professor at Arizona State University and author of *Smart Girls, Gifted Women*. "I believe that these institutions are the ones which take women seriously. If a young woman finds that, at her college, she is ignored in class, forgotten when fellowships and mentorships are awarded, and surrounded by a 'culture of romance' which discourages females' achievement—it's time to transfer to an all-women's college!"

Sports

"Our son, Peter, was initially looking at colleges more than 1,000 miles from home," says Gerald. "However, his older brother had picked a college just a two-hour car drive from us, and so we were able to continue to attend most of his basketball games. Peter thought that having his parents around for collegiate competitions would be a pretty nice perk, so he narrowed his radius and just considered places closer to home."

Maxine remembers that "a friend's child received a golf scholarship at the University of Mississippi. The parent pushed the child to go to Vanderbilt, instead. He went and skipped classes to play golf !"

Test Scores

Yes, there is life after college entrance exams. Said one Philadelphia father on the day of his son's Ivy League law school graduation, "When we saw David's SAT results, we took a detour on the road to Harvard and made tracks to Franklin and Marshall. In retrospect, I can't imagine a better college experience for my son, and he's ended up right about where he was headed back in high school, anyway. I wonder now whether he was better off without those super SAT scores."

That "Special" Something

"While our primary focus in the selection process is to identify top students who will challenge our professors and be challenged by our professors in the classroom, we're also seeking interesting people," maintains John L. Mahoney, director of undergraduate admission at Boston College. "Those who have excelled in atypical pursuits intrigue us because they will enrich the learning culture for all members of the community. So, the 'top chess player in the state of Indiana' caught our attention several years ago, as did a student who expressed a predilection for 'reading anarchist essays' in his spare time. The admission process is about creating a community of scholars and personalities."

215

APPENDIX

Checklist/Calendar for Parents

Keeping on top of college-related deadlines, dates, and things to do is one of the toughest parts of the admission process. The list below can help you see the "big picture," but (as you've probably learned the hard way, at least once) calendars work best when you check them in advance to see what's ahead, not after the fact, to realize what you've missed!

However, before you begin, consider some of these general points:

- Encourage independent reading and writing throughout your child's school career.

- If your child has a special passion or talent (e.g., music, math, fly-fishing, hula dancing), try to arrange enrichment opportunities via classes, camps, or private "mentoring."

- "Keyboarding" (what we used to call "typing" in our day) could be one of the most useful classes your child takes. If it isn't available at school, look for a summer or evening course.

- Don't become obsessed with the college admission process, and don't forget your life—spouse, other children, job, friends, etc.—beyond it.

- You may fret too much about decisions and nag too much about deadlines, but it's not possible to tell your child "I love you" too often.

9th Grade

This is the first year that admission officials will see on your child's transcript and, thus, a good time to take stock. What strong academic interests should be encouraged? What areas should be strengthened? If your child has any inkling of career goals, consider what prerequisites may exist. This is especially true in scientific and technical fields. Use your school's course listings to sketch out a Comprehensive Academic Program that includes all classes your child will take throughout high school. Think about which extracurricular activities your child plans to continue. Have past passions been outgrown?

September/October:

_____ Be aware of your child's academic adjustment. Are course levels appropriate?

_____ Urge your child to engage in meaningful activity, in and out of school. Consider community service. Begin an Activities Record which records all participation, along with a brief mention of accomplishments, awards, and leadership positions.

January:

_____ Evaluate academic progress so far. Are grades up to par? Are course levels on target? Do study habits need improvement?

_____ Is your child enjoying extracurricular involvement? If not, assess what changes might be made.

_____ Begin thinking about worthwhile summer plans (study, camp, job, volunteer work, travel, etc.).

May/June:

_____ Evaluate and update Comprehensive Academic Program and Activities Record.

_____ Finalize summer plans.

_____ Develop a summer reading list.

217

10th Grade

Classes chosen in grade 10 often determine which courses (and course levels) your child will be qualified to take in the important junior and senior years.

September:

_____ Contact the guidance counselor about "warm-up" PSAT/NMSQT for sophomores in October (or ask about PLAN schedule in ACT regions).

_____ Ask the guidance department about college fairs in your area and college admission-representative visits to the school. Encourage your child to start investigating by attending one fair and a session or two with reps at school.

October:

_____ Save the date for the PSAT/NMSQT.

_____ Are first-semester classes going well? Extracurriculars?

December:

_____ Questions about PSAT scores? Contact the guidance counselor. If necessary, discuss strategies for improving weak areas.

January:

_____ Evaluate academic progress so far. Are grades up to par? Are course levels on target? Do study habits need improvement?

_____ Is your child enjoying extracurricular involvement? If not, re-evaluate.

_____ Begin thinking about worthwhile summer plans (job, study, camp, volunteer work, travel, etc.).

March:

_____ Consider whether your child should be taking any SAT II tests in May or June. Will he or she be completing any subjects this year? (The test most commonly taken by sophomores is biology.)

_____ Register for May SAT II tests, if appropriate.

April:
_____ Register for June SAT II tests, if appropriate.

May/June:
_____ Save dates for SAT II tests, as needed.

_____ Oversee registration for next fall's classes and activities. Urge your child to select (or continue) the most challenging classes possible and at least one community-service activity.

_____ Finalize summer plans.

_____ Develop a summer reading list.

Summer:
_____ Make sure your child has a job or constructive activities *throughout* the summer. Summer study, jobs, and volunteer work always rate high with admission officials.

_____ If your child has a career goal in mind, help organize a "shadow day" where he or she spends time with someone at work in that field.

_____ If you have a home computer but are not connected to the Internet, consider investing in an online service. The World Wide Web provides some good (albeit excessive) college entrance information, as well as online applications to many institutions. Summer is a good time for students to experiment with the Internet without jeopardizing homework time.

11th Grade

This year the college search process begins in earnest. Exploration and testing should help you and your child to start developing a list of target schools by spring. Poor grades will not be as easily forgiven as those from previous years, and colleges will look for commitment and accomplishment outside of the classroom.

September:
_____ Make sure that PSAT/NMSQT registration is handled by guidance staff (except in regions where ACT test is prevalent). Ascertain and save the date.

219

_____ Ask the guidance department about college fairs in your area and college admission-representative visits to the school. Encourage your child to attend fairs and sessions with reps at school.

_____ You and your child should begin to familiarize yourself with guidance-office resources.

October:

_____ Make sure PSAT/NMSQT date is on the family calendar. Diplomatically remind your child, if necessary, to read the Student Bulletin and to try the practice questions. Try not to grill your child about probable performance as soon as the test is over. (Instead, plan a non–test-related treat.)

_____ Schedule a day trip to visit nearby colleges. Don't worry if these are places where your child won't apply. The goal is to explore different types of schools. Aim for variety. Discuss which characteristics are attractive and which aren't.

December:

_____ Questions about PSAT scores? Contact the guidance counselor. If necessary, discuss strategies for improving weak areas. Evaluate different SAT prep options, as needed. (See the end of Chapter 3.)

_____ Begin informal brainstorming about possible target colleges, with test results in mind.

_____ Take advantage of college students home for vacation. Ask them questions. Ask their parents questions. Ask your child to ask even more questions!

_____ Take an introductory look at financial-aid forms (see Chapter 5), just to see what you'll need by this time next year.

_____ Buy a copy of this book as a holiday gift for every parent on your shopping list.

January:

_____ Evaluate academic progress so far. Are grades up to par? Are course levels on target? Do study habits need improvement?

_____ Begin thinking about worthwhile summer plans (job, study, camp, volunteer work, travel, etc.).

_____ Mark projected SAT I & II or ACT test dates on family calendar. Also mark registration deadlines.

February:

_____ Look ahead to SAT or ACT registration deadlines for the tests your child plans to take. Are you about to miss one? Mark appropriate dates on your calendar. (A few juniors have reason to take the SAT I in March. If your child will do so, heed February registration deadline.)

_____ Buy a general guidebook to U.S. colleges and universities.

March:

_____ Consider and plan spring-vacation college visits.

_____ Begin listing target colleges in a notebook ("The College Bible").

_____ Begin calling, writing, or e-mailing target colleges to request publications.

_____ Set aside an area for college propaganda. Invest in folders for materials from front-runner schools.

_____ Look ahead to SAT or ACT registration deadlines for the tests your child plans to take. Are you about to miss one? Mark appropriate test and registration dates on your calendar.

_____ Make sure your child discusses plans to take Advanced Placement exams with teachers and/or guidance counselor, as needed.

April:

_____ Look ahead to SAT or ACT registration deadlines for the tests your child plans to take. Are you about to miss one? Mark appropriate test and registration dates on your calendar.

_____ Discuss senior-year classes. Urge your child to include at least one math course or lab science, as well as the most challenging courses possible. Recognize that colleges weigh senior classes and grades as heavily as the junior record.

_____ Update Activities Record.

May:

_____ Look ahead to SAT or ACT registration deadlines for the tests your child plans to take. Are you about to miss one? Mark appropriate test and registration dates on your calendar.

_____ Assess the need for and affordability of special services such as standardized test-prep courses, independent college counselors (see Chapter 2), and private group-tour programs (see Chapter 4).

_____ Does your child need to take the TOEFL (Test of English as a Foreign Language)? Select date and oversee registration.

June:

_____ Look ahead to SAT or ACT registration deadlines for the tests your child plans to take. Are you about to miss one? Mark appropriate test and registration dates on your calendar.

Summer:

_____ Make sure your child has a job or constructive activities throughout most of the summer. Study, jobs, and volunteer work always rate high with admission officials.

_____ Consider and plan summer and fall college visits.

_____ Oversee standardized test preparation, as needed.

_____ Request publications from additional target colleges.

_____ Plan and execute supplemental submissions such as audition tapes and art slides/portfolios, if required and/or appropriate.

_____ Review and update target college list. Include pros and cons. Make tentative plans for fall visits.

12th Grade

This is the year when the college search can feel like a full-time job—with all of the toil, tedium, and triumphs that that implies.

September

_____ Plan a special evening out (e.g., dinner at a favorite restaurant) with just the college-bound child. Discuss plans and goals for the months ahead; pros and cons of target schools.

_____ Look ahead to SAT or ACT registration deadlines for the tests your child plans to take. Are you about to miss one? Mark appropriate test and registration dates on your calendar.

_____ Ask the guidance department about college fairs in your area and college admission-representative visits to the school. Make certain that your child attends fairs and sessions with reps at school.

_____ Ask about "Parents' Night" or other high school-sponsored parents' events.

_____ Finalize fall college-visit plans. Include campus overnights, where possible. Visit!

_____ Request additional publications and *applications* from target colleges.

October:

_____ Look ahead to SAT or ACT registration deadlines for the tests your child plans to take. Are you about to miss one? Mark appropriate test and registration dates on your calendar.

_____ Help your child draw up a master schedule of application and financial-aid due dates, and put them on the family calendar.

_____ Oversee the start of applications. Your child should be considering essay topics and requesting teacher recommendations.

_____ Visit colleges. Include interviews on campus (or with local alumni representatives).

_____ Attend college fairs with your child.

_____ For another look at college life, rent a movie like *Animal House* or *School Daze.*

_____ Discuss "Early Decision" and "Early Action" options.

_____ Plan an "adults only" night out—no college talk, no kids!

November:

_____ Look ahead to SAT or ACT registration deadlines for the tests your child plans to take. Are you about to miss one? Mark appropriate test and registration dates on your calendar.

_____ Nag about early application deadlines, as needed.

_____ Reduce target college "long list" to a "short list," where applications will be made.

_____ Plan a Thanksgiving break that includes college visits (to almost-empty campuses) OR plan a Thanksgiving break where *no one* mentions the word "college."

_____ Check up on application completion. Volunteer to proofread, and steel yourself for a wide range of reactions.

December

_____ Look ahead to SAT or ACT registration deadlines for the tests your child plans to take. Are you about to miss one? Mark appropriate test and registration dates on your calendar.

_____ Pick up financial-aid material from guidance office and attend planning workshops, if available.

_____ Nag about completion of all applications due in January or February.

_____ Make sure that teachers and guidance staff are up to date with reference forms and that transcripts are being sent to all short-list colleges.

_____ Usher in the New Year with a family toast to the future—*whatever* it may bring.

January

_____ File income taxes if you can, and then begin filling out financial-aid forms. Finish and mail these forms as soon as possible—and *never LATE*.

_____ Encourage completion of *all* applications, including those with later deadlines. Don't forget to photocopy everything and save in accordion files.

_____ Celebrate with the whole family when the last application hits the mailbox.

_____ If SATs are being taken this month, are "Rush" scores required? Ask target colleges, if you're not certain.

February:

_____ Unless confirmations have been received, call colleges to check on completion of applications. Record the name of the person you spoke with. Track down missing records.

March:

_____ WAIT!

April:

_____ Take a cold shower and resist the urge to open letters addressed to your child. (Holding them up to the light *is* permissible.) Keep in mind that "thin" letters aren't always rejections. Some schools send out enrollment forms later.

_____ Applaud acceptances; help put rejections in perspective. For example, try saying "It's an extremely competitive college, and your math test scores must have hurt." (But not "Those admission folks at that school seemed like a bunch of Bozos from the get-go.")

_____ Plan "crunch-time" visits to campuses, as needed, to help prompt final decisions.

_____ Compare financial-aid decisions, where applicable. Contact financial-aid offices with questions.

_____ Make sure your child returns "Wait-List" cards, as needed. Contact admission offices to check on Wait-List status. Send updated records and other information, if available. Encourage your child to write an upbeat "Please take me, and this is why you should" letter.

_____ Is the verdict final? Send the required deposit. Don't dawdle and miss the May 1 deadline or colleges can give away your child's place. Also notify those schools your child *won't* attend, especially if an aid offer was made.

May:

_____ Make sure your child takes AP exams, if appropriate.

_____ Write (or urge your child to write) a thank-you note to anyone who may have been especially helpful. Guidance counselors are often unsung heroes. Don't forget teachers who wrote recommendations, admission counselors or secretaries, tour guides, or other students.

(Of course this isn't obligatory, but recipients are sure to be pleased and surprised.)

_____ Stay abreast of housing choices, etc. When will forms be mailed? Should your child be investigating living-situation options? When is freshman orientation? (Some schools have spring and summer programs.) When is course registration?

June:

_____ Consider summer school for those who want to accelerate or place out of requirements. ALWAYS check with colleges first to make sure credits will count. Get permission in writing when it's questionable.

_____ Make sure that a final high-school transcript is sent to the college your child will attend. (Most schools should do this automatically.)

_____ Dig out some of those masterpieces you've saved since your child's grade-school days. Where did the time go?

_____ Otherwise, help your child land a summer job that pays at least $20,000. (That's after taxes.) Call Brooke Shields for details. (She went to Princeton, after all.)

INDEX

**Achievement Tests
(See "SAT II")**
ACT Assessment Test,
49, 68-71, 81,
172-173
Average scores, 70
Comparison to SAT,
70-71
Conversion to SAT,
70
Preparation for (See
"SAT Program")
Registration for,
68
Use of scores,
60-62
When to take, 68
Advanced Placement
Program, 168-169,
195-198
Advanced Standing,
195-199
Alumni
Connections, 160,
176-177
Interviews, 92, 102
Applications (See also
"Common Applica-
tion," College Link,"
and "Universal
Application),
133-163
Confirmation of
arrival, 142
Deadlines, 134,
140-141
Fee, 162
Number of, 25-26,
104-105
Athletes
Admission advan-
tages, 176-178

Campus visits,
89-90
Scholarships, 118,
178

**Books, cost of, 108,
110**
Bribes, 212

**Candidates' Reply
Date, 122,
184-185**
Catalogs, College
Course, 35-36
Checklist/Calendar,
221-231
Class Rank, 28-29,
169, 171
CLEP, 199
"College Bible,"
26, 43, 92
College Board
(CEEB), 50-51,
81, 168
College Cost Explorer
Fund Finder,
114-115, 131
College Impressions
Tour Service, 88
College Link,
137, 155
College Scholarship
Service (CSS),
113-115, 118
Common Application,
136-138, 155
Community Colleges
(See "Two-Year
Colleges")
Competitiveness/
Selectivity Ratings,
28-29, 36

Computers
Application by,
136-140
College search and,
37-40
Financial aid and,
114-115, 122, 126,
129, 131-132
Conditional Accep-
tance, 182
Conflicts (within
family), 3, 15-19,
30, 32-33
Course Selection
Importance of
(high school),
166-171
CSS (See "College
Scholarship
Service")

**DANTES
(See "DSST")**
Deadlines
Application, 134,
140-141
Financial Aid,
119-121, 134,
140, 162
Decisions
Application Plans,
134-136
Explanation of,
165-182, 188
Deferred Admission,
199-201
Demonstrated Need,
114, 116, 125
Dependent Status,
124
Deposits,
184-185

Direct Educational
  Costs, 110
Disabilities, students
  with, 158, 160-161,
  207-210
Divorced Parents,
  17-18, 46
  Finances and,
  113, 116
DSST (DANTES
  Subject Standard-
  ized Tests), 199

Early Action, 134
Early Admission/
  Entrance,
  201-203
Early Decision,
  134-136
Early Enrollment,
  201-203
E-mail, 37-41
Essays, Application,
  137, 147-155,
  173, 212
  Supplemental,
  158-159
Expected Family
  Contribution,
  114-116, 124-125
Extracurricular
  Activities
  Importance of,
  146, 174-176
  Résumé of,
  144-145

**FAFSA (Free Applica-
tion for Federal
Student Aid),
115-116, 119-120,
127**
Family Contribution
  (See "Expected
  Family Contribu-
  tion")
Fee Waiver, Applica-
  tion, 138, 162
Federal Loans, 122,
  125-126
FSEOG, 125

Pell Grants, 125
Perkins Loans,
  126
PLUS Loans, 124
Stafford Loans,
  124-126
Supplemental Loans
  for Students,
  126
Federal Methodology,
  114
Federal Student Aid
  Information Center,
  122, 126
Federal Work-Study,
  121-122, 126, 131
Financial Aid,
  107-132, 200-201
Financial Need,
  114-118
Front Loading,
  117
Full-Pay Students,
  129-131, 176

GED, 202
Gift Aid, 122
Gimmicks, 143-144,
  159-160, 187
Guidance Counselors
  (See also "Indepen-
  dent Counselors"),
  43-46, 173-174

**Handicapped Stu-
dents (See "Dis-
abilities")**
HEATH (Higher
  Education & Adult
  Training for people
  with Handicaps),
  210
Home-schooling,
  166
"Hooks," 129,
  176-180
Honors
  College programs,
  42
  High school courses,
  168-169

**Independent Counse-
lors, 46-48**
Independent Student
  Status, 124-125
International Bacca-
  laureate (IB), 169,
  197-198
International Students,
  71-72, 143, 203-204
Interviews
  Alumni, 92, 102
  Campus, 90-100
  Preparing for,
  93-98
  Scheduling of,
  86-90
Ivy League Colleges,
  17, 28-29, 46, 64,
  134

**Junior Colleges
(See "Two-Year
Colleges")**

**Kaplan Educational
Centers, 78-79**

**Learning Disabilities
(See "Disabilities")**
Letting Go, 15
Liberal Arts Colleges,
  23-24
Loans (See also
  "Federal Loans"),
  113, 122, 124-128

**Majors (college),
30-31, 143**
Matchmaking
  (students/colleges),
  21-48, 104-105
Merit Aid,
  118, 130
Minority Students
  (See "Students of
  Color")
Most Competitive
  Colleges, 17,
  28-29, 52, 60,
  64, 105, 167-168,
  171, 180-181

National Merit
 Scholarship
 Program, 50, 52
Need-Based Financial
 Aid, 117-118, 129
Need Blind Admission,
 117-118
Need, Financial (See
 "Financial Need")
Need-Gapping,
 117-118, 128
Noncompetitive
 Admission, 22

Open Admission,
 22, 134
Overnight Visits
 (See "Visits")

Parent Letters
 (See "Supple-
 mental Letters")
Payment Plans,
 129-130
Pell Grants (See
 "Federal Loans")
PEP (Proficiency
 Exam Program),
 199
Perkins Loans (See
 "Federal Loans")
Personal Statements
 (See "Essays")
PLAN Test,
 51, 68
PLUS Loans (See
 "Federal Loans")
Post-Graduate (PG)
 Year, 190,
 205-207
Preferential Pack-
 aging, 117
Pressure (of admis-
 sion process),
 2-3, 15-19
Prestige, importance
 of, 3, 17, 24
Princeton Review,
 39, 78-79
PROFILE, 115-116,
 119-120

PSAT/NMSQT, 50-54
 Average Scores, 52
 Preparation for,
 53
 Sophomores and,
 53-54

Recommendations
 Guidance Counselor,
 46, 156,
 173-174
 Supplemental,
 157, 160
 Teacher, 156-157,
 173-174
Religious Affiliations,
 32-33, 130
Requirements,
 Admission,
 166-167
Rolling Admission,
 25, 134, 141
Room and Board,
 111

Safety (See "Security")
 "Safety" Schools,
 25-26, 98, 105,
 130, 162
SAR (Student Aid
 Report),
 116, 120
SAT Program,
 49-81
 SAT I, 54-65
 Average scores,
 59-61
 Poor scores, 60,
 63-64, 158,
 172-173
 Preparation for,
 72-80
 Recentering, 52,
 59-61
 Registration,
 55-57, 81
 Use of Scores,
 61-62, 172-173
 When to take,
 54-55
 SAT II, 65-68

Scholarships
 Athletic, 118,
 177-178
 College-sponsored,
 127
 Merit, 50, 52, 118,
 130
 Need-based,
 117-118, 129
 Private, 127, 130
 Search (See "Student
 Search")
 Search Services
 (Financial Aid),
 121-122, 128-129
Security (on campus),
 192-193
Self-Assessment
 Survey
 for parents, 2-9
 for students,
 2-4, 10-14
Self-Help, 122
Siblings, 17-18, 110
Single Sex Colleges, 15,
 18, 65, 215
Size (of colleges),
 27-28
Special Needs (See
 "Disabilities")
Stafford Loans (See
 "Federal Loans")
Standardized Tests
 (See "ACT," "SAT,"
 and "TOEFL")
Student Aid Report
 (See "SAR")
Student Search,
 34-35, 53
Students of Color,
 33-34, 52-53,
 142-143, 176,
 178-179
 Advantages for,
 178-179
 Recruitment of,
 33-34
 Scholarships for,
 52-53
 Standardized tests
 and, 65

Subject Tests (See
  "SAT II")
Supplemental Letters,
  160
  from parents,
    160-162

TOEFL, 71-72, 143,
  204
Tours, campus
  (See "Visits")
Transcripts
  Evaluation of, 166-172
  Submission of,
    141, 168
Transferring, 22-23,
  189, 193-194

Tuition, 24-25,
  107-110, 112-113
Two-Year Colleges,
  22-23
  "Trading up" from,
    23, 189, 194

Universal Application,
  137-138, 155
Universities
  Definition of, 24
  Departments in,
    30-31, 36, 141

Viewbooks, 35-36
Visits (to campus),
  83-101

Overnight, 87
Tours, 83-88

Wait List, 181,
  185-187
Weighted Rank (See
  "Class Rank")
Women's Colleges (See
  "Single Sex Col-
  leges")
Work-Study (See
  "Federal Work-
  Study")
World Wide Web (See
  "Computers")
Writing Samples (See
  "Essays")